THE ATOMIC ENERGY COMMISSION UNDER NIXON

Also by Glenn T. Seaborg with Benjamin S. Loeb

Kennedy, Khrushchev, and the Test Ban

Stemming the Tide: Arms Control in the Johnson Years

THE ATOMIC ENERGY COMMISSION UNDER NIXON

Adjusting to Troubled Times

Glenn T. Seaborg
with
Benjamin S. Loeb

St. Martin's Press
New York

First published in the United States of America in 1993

Printed in the United States of America

ISBN 0-312-07899-4

Library of Congress Cataloging-in-Publication Data

Seaborg, Glenn Theodore, 1912–
The Atomic Energy Commission under Nixon : adjusting to troubled
times / Glenn T. Seaborg with Benjamin S. Loeb.
        p. cm.
  Includes bibliographical references and index.
  ISBN 0-312-07899-4
    1. U.S. Atomic Energy Commission—History. 2. Nixon, Richard M.
(Richard Milhous), 1913– . 3. Nuclear energy—Government policy-
-United States—History. I. Loeb, Benjamin S., 1914– .
II. Title.
HD9698.U52S43 1993
353.0085'6—dc20   92-30137
                                               CIP

*To the spirit of
international cooperation in science, wherein
may lie mankind's best hopes
for the future.*

TABLE OF CONTENTS

FOREWORD

My resignation as chairman of the Atomic Energy Commission (AEC) became effective on August 16, 1971. I had served in that capacity for ten and a half years, longer than any other chairman and extending over the administrations of three presidents. I have written elsewhere about my service under presidents John F. Kennedy and Lyndon B. Johnson, confining those accounts, however, to important arms control initiatives in which the Atomic Energy Commission played a significant and constructive role.[1] This volume, relating to the first two and a half years of the administration of Richard M. Nixon, will cover a wider front. For one thing, I cannot give as complete an account of arms control developments as in the earlier volumes because the Nixon administration, for reasons I will seek to explain later, chose to exclude the Atomic Energy Commission from much of its former participation in this arena.

But then I also want to tell a broader story. It is the story of what it is like to preside over a once proud and privileged government agency that is declining in reputation and influence; how one establishes goals when choices are limited by an impoverishment of means; of the maneuvers that are employed to sustain what seem to be worthwhile endeavors; and of how one sorts out policy and politics, chooses between adherence to principle and compromise, and in the end must sometimes fight rearguard actions for survival.

Let it be clear that this book does not purport to be a complete history of the Atomic Energy Commission during this troubled period. The multifaceted nature of the agency's activities, extending across a wide spectrum of military and civilian endeavors, would make that too daunting a task. I have chosen instead to use a case study approach and to concentrate on just a few stories. These include the effort to maintain standards limiting the release of radioactivity from nuclear power plants to levels that would both protect public health and permit the industry to survive; the efforts, probably unrealistic and largely frustrated, to move forward with a new generation of reactors (breeders) that would produce more fissionable material than they consumed; the attempt, against technical and political obstacles, to keep alive a program to use nuclear explosions for peaceful purposes; the difficulties encountered in carrying out the AEC's obligation to test a warhead for an antiballistic missile program already approved by Congress; a brief look at how the Nixon administration approached its arms control challenges; a confrontation with the Department of Justice in which the AEC sought to defend the rights of an individual who we believed was being falsely accused of disloyal behavior; and, finally, the struggle, ultimately partly successful, to maintain the integrity of the AEC's basic structure against the consequences of drastic reorganization proposals that would have splintered it.

All in all, it is far from being a triumphant story. The Nixon years were difficult ones for the AEC. In part this may have been due to the special foibles of this president and his administration. More significantly, however, our difficulties can be attributed to the spirit of the times, particularly the opposition to the Vietnam War and a rising environmental consciousness. Such factors produced an atmosphere that was not friendly to large-scale science and technology initiatives, particularly those that involved some government participation. In this uncongenial atmosphere the AEC sustained some frustrations and defeats. Not all of these were due to circumstance. The AEC made its share of mistakes, some of which I freely acknowledge herein. On the other hand, we did some things right, and for this the agency deserves some credit.

As in my previous historical writings, a main source for this book has been the journal that I maintained on every day of my government service. The entire journal has been published in 28 volumes.[2] A principal component of the journal was a daily diary, from which I quote frequently herein. Using such a source has the advantage that it records how things appeared at the time, not in retrospect over a time gap of many years. Excerpts from the diary are not always so labeled, but they can be recognized because *they are set in this typeface.* I should note that the diary entries included herein, while substantively the same, may occasionally not be the same in every word or phrase as the original diary entries included in the published journal. The original entries, usually dictated in haste during or at the end of a busy day, may not have been couched in the clearest language, especially for a lay audience, and may also have lacked context needed, or may have contained detail not needed, for this narrative. In making these changes, I bear in mind what John Kenneth Galbraith noted to justify similar changes in his book, *Ambassador's Journal*: "No historical merit attaches to bad English."[3]

The journal also contains copies of important documents (correspondence, reports, press releases, minutes of meetings, newspaper articles, and so on) relating to each day's events. If no other documentation is offered in footnotes or endnotes for a document referenced in the text, the reader can infer that it is available in my daily journal.

DRAMATIS PERSONAE

One of the things to remember about the Atomic Energy Commission is implicit in its name: it was headed by a *commission* consisting of five persons. In enacting the Atomic Energy Act of 1946 that established the AEC, Congress apparently believed that matters coming before the agency would be of such moment that the collective wisdom of a number of people of different backgrounds would be needed in order to make correct decisions. As the years passed, many who served on the Commission felt that an agency headed by a single executive would be more agile and responsive to the myriad of problems that confronted us, and on several occasions the Commission as a whole voted to recommend its own abolition in favor of a single executive form of organization. But that proposal never got very far. Nor did the Atomic Energy Act endow the chairman of the Commission with any special powers not accorded to the other commissioners. When the 1954 revision of the act was being debated, Chairman Lewis Strauss sought to have the chairman legally designated as the Commission's "principal officer." This was successfully resisted by Commissioner Thomas E. Murray, however, with the result that the 1954 legislation merely designated the chairman as "official spokesman" and stipulated that each member of the Commission "have equal responsibility and authority" in all actions. As has been pointed out, this resolution of the problem "underscored the ambiguities defining the role of the chairman and the commissioners, [and], in effect, allowed the chairman's position to be based on the personality and operating style of a particular incumbent."[4] Some chairmen, notably Strauss and my successor, James Schlesinger, used the office to place a strong personal imprint on the work of the AEC. My own style was to seek consensus among the commissioners by talking things out, formally or informally. Some who have written about the AEC have concluded that the Strauss-Schlesinger style made them "strong" chairmen and that my style made me "not strong." I do not quarrel with these assessments other than to say that I did it the way I did it because that is what seemed best to me and, I imagine, because that is how I am.

Obviously, my style of chairmanship depended crucially on the contributions of the other commissioners who served with me. I was most fortunate in having a most remarkable group of colleagues. They came from diverse backgrounds. They often had strong points of view and were not reluctant to state those views with considerable emphasis. For the most part, however, they were amenable to reasonable argument from those who differed with them, with the result that the great majority of actions the Commission took were decided upon unanimously.

The thirteen commissioners who served with me during my ten years as chairman are listed, with their dates of service, in the appendix. But I would like to pause here to take special note of those who were on board during the 31-month period covered in this book.

Dr. Gerald F. Tape was appointed to the Commission by President Kennedy in July 1963 to fill the unexpired term of Leland J. Haworth, who had resigned. In 1966, he was reappointed by President Johnson for a full five-year term. I first crossed paths with Tape in the 1930s when he was pursuing his graduate research at the University of Michigan in isotope identification, the same field in which I was working. After being on the physics faculty of Cornell University and the University of Illinois, he held executive posts at Brookhaven National Laboratory, becoming president of Associated Universities, Inc. (AUI), the organization that ran Brookhaven, the year before he was appointed to the Commission. Cooperative and pleasant at all times, dependable and responsible in carrying out his duties, solid and balanced in his knowledge and his views, Tape was a tremendous source of help and support. His special fields of interest while on the Commission were basic research and weapons development, but he was also constructively attentive to the civilian power reactor development program and to cooperative relations with other nations and with the International Atomic Energy Agency. When he chose to resign in April 1969 to return to his post as head of AUI, it was a grievous loss to the Commission and to me personally.

Wilfred E. Johnson was first appointed to the AEC by President Johnson in the summer of 1966 to fill the unexpired term of John G. Palfrey, who had resigned. He was reappointed by President Johnson a year later for a full five-year term. Holding bachelor's and master's degrees in mechanical engineering from Oregon State College, Johnson worked for the General Electric Company in Schenectady, New York, from 1930 to 1951, becoming manager of several departments. In 1951 he became assistant general manager, and a year later general manager, of GE's Hanford Atomic Products Operations at AEC's facility in Richland, Washington. As an AEC commissioner, Johnson paid special attention to the civilian nuclear power program. I appreciated particularly the sense of responsibility he demonstrated when he took his turn as acting chairman while I was away on my not infrequent travels; on those occasions he prepared superb records of everything significant that transpired in my absence.

James T. Ramey was first appointed to the AEC by President Kennedy in August 1962. He was reappointed by President Johnson to a full five-year term in June 1964 and to a second five-year term in July 1968. A graduate of Columbia University Law School, Ramey was associated with the Tennessee Valley Authority from 1941 to 1947. He worked in AEC's Chicago Operations

Office from 1947 to 1956, first as assistant general counsel and then as principal administrative officer. From 1956 until 1962 Ramey was executive director of the Joint Committee on Atomic Energy, and his views after he became an AEC commissioner were generally, although not invariably, consonant with those of the committee.* Ramey strongly supported the civilian power program, taking a special interest in industry's role as regulated by the AEC. He was also vigorous and effective in pushing various applications of nuclear technology, such as in space and medicine. I found Ramey the most difficult of the commissioners to get along with on a personal level. The ill will seemed to be chiefly on his side. He seemed to think I was too cautious and also sometimes to suspect me of devious motives when I took positions contrary to his own. Ramey tended to state his views in a contentious manner that contravened the collegial atmosphere I and other commissioners tried to maintain. When the Commission was not unanimous in a decision, it was often Ramey who was in the minority position and who insisted on stating his objections publicly. Yet he was very able and intelligent, and although our personal relations were never easy, he and I were able to achieve a working relationship, often cooperating effectively in pushing agreed-upon objectives. By the time his term expired in June 1973, Ramey had served longer than any other commissioner.

Theos J. Thompson was sworn in on June 12, 1969, having been appointed by President Nixon to fill the unexpired term of Gerald F. Tape. I first saw him on January 1, 1941, when he quarterbacked the University of Nebraska football team in a losing Rose Bowl effort against Stanford. He went on to gain a Ph. D. in nuclear physics from the University of California, Berkeley, and to become a professor of nuclear engineering at the Massachusetts Institute of Technology and director of MIT's nuclear reactor facility. He served as a member (1959–65) and chairman (1960) of AEC's Advisory Committee on Reactor Safeguards. In 1964 he was awarded the AEC's prestigious Ernest O. Lawrence Memorial Award, being cited for leadership in developing safe, useful, and economic nuclear reactors and for inspired teaching of nuclear engineers. Under the AEC's system of assigning commissioners lead roles in certain fields, Thompson was a "lead commissioner" in weapons and civilian nuclear power matters. Authoritative in his knowledge of reactors, strong-willed, and persistent, Thompson frequently took a vigorous position defending civilian nuclear power against

* President Kennedy had been reluctant initially to appoint Ramey because of his ties to the Joint Committee. Also, during that service, Ramey had antagonized members of the Commission during some sharp clashes. In fact, Commissioner Robert E. Wilson announced an intention to resign when he heard of Ramey's appointment, but was dissuaded from doing so.

critics who challenged it on environmental or safety grounds. On November 25, 1970, we received the tragic news that Thompson, along with his assistant, Jack Rosen, had been killed while on AEC business in the crash of a small plane into Lake Mead in Nevada.

Clarence E. Larson became an AEC commissioner in September 1969. Holder of a Ph. D. in biochemistry from the University of California, he had served in the Manhattan Project under Ernest Lawrence during World War II, specializing in the electromagnetic process for separating uranium-235. After the war he became superintendent of a large production plant (Y-12) at AEC's Oak Ridge reservation in Tennessee. There he developed the solvent extraction method for refining and purifying uranium. From 1950 to 1955 he was director of the Oak Ridge National Laboratory (ORNL). In 1955 he became associate director of research for Union Carbide, ORNL's operator, in New York. In 1961 he returned to Oak Ridge as general manager and president of Union Carbide's nuclear plant, charged with administering the firm's operations for the AEC. By virtue of his strong scientific background, Larson became a lead AEC commissioner in the weapons and research fields. He alternated with me in representing the AEC on the Federal Council for Science and Technology. Larson always struck me as the consummate science executive. While pleasant and easy to work with, he could be very firm in upholding the views that grew out of his great knowledge and very strong experience.

Francesco Castagliola was appointed by President Johnson in October 1968 to fill out the short remainder of an unexpired term. A retired Navy captain and a resident of Rhode Island, Castagliola's appointment had been recommended by Rhode Island senator John Pastore, then chairman of the Joint Committee on Atomic Energy. Castagliola's most prominent role came when he strongly advocated withdrawing all AEC research contracts from universities that, under the pressures of the student and faculty unrest of 1969, had refused to carry on secret government research. On his own, he publicly warned the presidents of MIT and Stanford that such an action was impending and threatened to write warning letters to additional universities. He won no support for this proposal from the other commissioners.

This, then, was the cast of characters who led the AEC during the difficult Nixon years. When the account herein speaks from time to time of statements that "I" made or letters that "I" wrote, the reader should remember what was stated earlier: the AEC chairman was "chief spokesman" for a collective body.

It must also be pointed out, with emphasis, that the vast majority of the AEC's employees and their day-to-day activities were under the direct supervision, not of the five members of the Commission, but of two co-equal operating heads: the general manager and the director of regulation. Each of them reported to the Commission and had the responsibility of determining, for the most part, which matters under their supervision were of sufficient moment to bring before the Commission.

Robert E. Hollingsworth was general manager for seven of my ten years as chairman, including the period covered by this book. He was a veteran AEC employee who knew the organization and its personnel intimately. Well-organized, popular both with commissioners and staff, absolutely dependable, he kept things moving in a very effective manner. I relied on him heavily.

Harold L. Price was AEC's first director of regulation after the function was split out from under the general manager in 1961. He remained in that post during my ten years as chairman, handling with composure and creativity the rapid increase in workload, constantly changing conditions, and storm of controversy that surrounded the AEC's regulatory activities during this period, particularly the later years. Unassuming and businesslike, he was able to balance competing pressures and retain the confidence of the Commission, Congress, industry, and the public with considerable intellectual adroitness and political finesse.

NOTES

1. *Kennedy, Khrushchev and the Test Ban* (1981) and *Stemming the Tide: Arms Control in the Johnson Years* (1987).
2. *The Journals of Glenn T. Seaborg.* As of the end of 1992 copies were available in the the Library of Congress (Manuscript Division); the National Archives; the Nuclear Regulatory Commission; the presidential libraries of John F. Kennedy (Boston, Massachusetts), Lyndon B. Johnson (Austin, Texas), and Richard M. Nixon (Newport Beach, California); the Bancroft Library of the University of California, Berkeley; the main libraries of the University of California at Los Angeles and Santa Barbara; the Lawrence Berkeley (California) Laboratory; and the Los Alamos (New Mexico) National Laboratory.
3. John Kenneth Galbraith, *Ambassador's Journal: A Personal Account of the Kennedy Years* (London: Hamilton Publishers, 1969), p. xvi.
4. Mazuzan and Walker, *Controlling the Atom*, p. 28.

ACKNOWLEDGMENTS

I am deeply grateful for the generous assistance rendered by former colleagues and associates Gerald F. Tape, Justin Bloom, Myron Kratzer, John Conway, Edward Giller, and Fred Albaugh, each of whom read all or parts of the manuscript and provided insightful comments and suggestions. Tape's review of the entire manuscript helped set things right on some important matters of accuracy and balance. Kratzer's review of the chapter on the Nonproliferation Treaty was especially thorough and painstaking, making available the benefit of his experience and authoritative knowledge in this field. J. Samuel Walker, the Nuclear Regulatory Commission's chief historian, shared freely the product of his researches into regulatory history and provided guidance to useful sources. Spurgeon Keeny furnished insights based on his own experience working in the Nixon White House. His associates at the Arms Control Association, Jon B. Wolfsthal and Dunbar Lockwood, provided essential guidance in their areas of special expertise: nonproliferation and nuclear testing, respectively. Valuable suggestions, editorial and otherwise, were offered by Helen Seaborg, Paul Green, Ellen Loeb, and Frank Duncan. Jeanne Loeb collaborated on the index and performed much essential research as well as other useful tasks too numerous to mention. And finally, at St. Martin's Press, senior editor Simon Winder and his assistant, Laura Heymann, were unfailingly supportive and constructive in guiding this project to completion, Ms. Heymann contributing an outstanding job of copyediting in addition to her other efforts on our behalf.

GLOSSARY OF ACRONYMS AND ABBREVIATIONS

AAAS	American Association for the Advancement of Science
ABM	antiballistic missile
ACDA	U.S. Arms Control and Disarmament Agency
ACRS	Advisory Committee on Reactor Safeguards (AEC)
ALWR	advanced light water reactor
ASLB	Atomic Safety and Licensing Board (AEC)
AUI	Associated Universities, Inc.
BEIR	Committee on the Biological Effects of Ionizing Radiation
BWR	boiling water reactor
CCD	Conference of the Committee on Disarmament (UN)
CRBR	Clinch River Breeder Reactor
CSC	Atlantic-Pacific Interoceanic Canal Study Commission
CTBT	Comprehensive Test Ban Treaty
DDRE	Director of Defense Research and Engineering
DNR	Department of Natural Resources (proposed new agency)
DOD	U.S. Department of Defense
DOE	U.S. Department of Energy
ENDC	Eighteen Nation Disarmament Committee
EBR-1	Experimental Breeder Reactor No.1
EBR-2	Experimental Breeder Reactor No. 2
EPA	U.S. Environmental Protection Agency
ERDA	U.S. Energy Research and Development Administration
EURATOM	European Atomic Energy Community
FFTF	Fast Flux Test Facility
FRC	Federal Radiation Council
GAC	General Advisory Committee (AEC)
GAO	General Accounting Office
GCBR	gas-cooled fast breeder reactor

HEW	U.S. Department of Health, Education, and Welfare
IAEA	International Atomic Energy Agency
ICBM	intercontinental ballistic missile
ICRP	International Commission on Radiological Protection
JCAE	Joint Committee on Atomic Energy (U.S. Congress)
KBI	Kawecki Berylco Industries, Inc.
LMFBR	liquid metal fast breeder reactor
LTBT	Limited Test Ban Treaty
LWBR	light water breeder reactor
LWR	light water reactor
MECCA	Minnesota Environmental Control Citizen's Association
MIRV	multiple independently-targetable reentry vehicle
MPCA	Minnesota Pollution Control Agency
MRV	multiple reentry vehicle (not independently-targetable)
MSBR	molten salt breeder reactor
MWe	electrical megawatts
NCRP	National Committee on Radiation Protection and Measurements
NEPA	National Environmental Policy Act of 1969
NRC	U.S. Nuclear Regulatory Commission
NSC	National Security Council
NSP	Northern States Power Company
NUMEC	Nuclear Materials and Equipment Corporation
ORNL	Oak Ridge National Laboratory
PNE	peaceful nuclear explosive or explosion
PNL	Pacific Northwest Laboratory
PSAC	President's Science Advisory Committee
PWR	pressurized water reactor
SALT	Strategic Arms Limitation Talks
SFRC	Senate Foreign Relations Committee
SIPI	Scientists' Institute for Public Information
SNM	special nuclear material (enriched uranium, plutonium, and uranium-233)
SST	supersonic transport
ZPPR	zero power plutonium reactor

Prologue:
Brief Encounters

I first met Richard Nixon, a fellow Californian, in Chattanooga, Tennessee. It was January 21, 1948, and we were both there to attend ceremonies recognizing our selection by the United States Junior Chamber of Commerce, the Jaycees, as two of the ten outstanding young men of 1947. (The eight other selectees are identified in the photo on page 2.) At the time, Nixon, 34, was a member of the House of Representatives and already well known for his work on the Alger Hiss case while a member of the House Un-American Activities Committee. I, a year older, was director of the nuclear chemistry division of the Radiation Laboratory, now the Lawrence Berkeley Laboratory, at the University of California, Berkeley. The Jaycees cited me for my work in the discovery of several transuranium elements.*

The ceremonies began with a late afternoon reception. Then came an appearance on ABC's "Vox Pop" radio program (they did interviews with average Americans, if I recall), which originated that day as a nationwide broadcast from Chattanooga High School. My diary records:

> *Highlighting the Vox Pop program for me was the appearance of Barbara Jo Walker, Miss America for 1947.*

---

* Transuranium elements are elements above uranium in the periodic table, that is, their atomic numbers (numbers of protons in the nucleus) are greater than that of uranium. All transuranium elements are produced artificially, and all are radioactive.

Barbara Jo Walker, Miss America for 1947, poses with eight of those designated by the United States Junior Chamber of Commerce as the "Ten Outstanding Young Men of 1947." This was at ceremonies on January 21, 1948, in Chattanooga, Tennessee, recognizing the selections. It was on this occasion that I met Richard Nixon, then a member of the House of Representatives, for the first time. From left, Adrian S. Fischer, general counsel of the Atomic Energy Commission; Cord Meyer, Jr., head of United World Federalists; James Quigg Newton, Jr., mayor of Denver; Lavon P. Peterson, himself blind, who founded an engineering school for the blind; Seaborg; Dr. Robert A. Hingson, a surgeon and a developer of caudal anesthesia to eliminate childbirth pain; Nixon; and Glenn Davis, congressman from Wisconsin. The two selectees who did not attend the ceremonies were Thomas R. Reid, vice president of McCormick Co. and a human relations expert; and De Lessups S. Morrison, mayor of New Orleans.

Next came a banquet at which the speaker was Harold Stassen, who had just launched the first of his several tries for the presidency. Finally, at about 10:30 P.M., we honorees were each presented with a ruby-studded distinguished service key in a ceremony filmed by Paramount News. During the course of the evening Nixon suggested to me that we should remain in touch with each other and "stick together." In coming years, both he and I were to refer several times to this start of our acquaintance.

My next contact with Congressman Nixon occurred in May 1950 when he was running for the Senate against Helen Gahagan Douglas in the notorious campaign in which he used anticommunist smear tactics. At the Radiation Laboratory we learned on the morning of May 22 that candidate Nixon was planning to visit us that afternoon. During our usual "brown-bag" lunch meeting the senior staff discussed how we should react to the visit. In protest against Nixon's campaign tactics, noted scientist Al Ghiorso threatened not to show him his equipment. My diary recorded the actual visit as follows:

> As scheduled, I gave Richard Nixon and his entourage a tour through our chemistry research labs. Even Al Ghiorso was polite (though cool). But when one of Nixon's aides proposed that the candidate and I go to the Claremont Hotel for a photo session, I realized that such photographs would be interpreted as an endorsement of Nixon's candidacy, which I opposed. I therefore promptly, and ineptly, refused. Nixon graciously accepted my lame excuse.

My next meeting with Nixon was also an awkward one. It was at the Rose Bowl, January 1, 1951. Before taking our seats, I and a friend visited the men's room. There we encountered now Senator-elect Nixon, whom I introduced to my friend wrongly, giving him the first name "James." (I was undoubtedly thinking of Dr. James Nickson, an associate during my war work at the University of Chicago's Met Lab.) It was a bad day all around; final score: Michigan 14, California 6.

I crossed paths again with Nixon, now vice president, on February 25, 1958, when we both attended a foreign aid conference in Washington that had been arranged at President Eisenhower's request. The conference boasted a stellar guest list and a bipartisan slate of speakers that included ex-President Harry Truman, who delivered the main address, ex-Secretary of State Dean Acheson, Adlai Stevenson, Thomas E. Dewey, John Foster Dulles, Allen Dulles, Secretary of Defense Neil McElroy, and Bishop Fulton Sheen.

Nixon presided over a question-and-answer forum after the speeches. At the end of the meeting I went up on stage and spoke with him. He invited me to drop in and see him on one of my future trips to Washington, and I promised to do so.

I took Nixon up on his invitation in April 1959. By that time I had become chancellor of the University of California's Berkeley campus, and I wanted to discuss with the vice president some U. C. problems that seemed to have national implications. Among them was a loyalty oath required of student loan recipients under the National Defense Education Act.* I told him that there was widespread dissatisfaction in the academic community over this. He seemed sympathetic and, I believed, sincerely so.† At this same meeting I briefed Nixon on scientific matters in the Soviet Union before his departure on the trip that was to feature his famous "kitchen debate" with Khrushchev. I expressed concern that the Russians were getting ahead of us in research on the transuranium elements. I also told him, in case he might be able to use it to advantage on his trip, the story of how our group at Berkeley had given the name Mendelevium to a newly discovered synthetic transuranium element (the one with atomic number 101), honoring Dimitri Mendeleev, the great Russian chemist and the originator of the periodic table of the elements.

Nixon made good use of the Mendeleev story during his Soviet trip. I learned this in a most gratifying way. In August 1959 I received a package from the American embassy in Moscow. It contained a book and the following message:

> During his visit to the USSR, Vice President R. Nixon, U.S.A., informed us that before his departure for the Soviet Union, he was visited by his friend, professor of chemistry, Mr. Seaborg, who

---

* The act required recipients to execute two oaths: (i) an affidavit that he or she "does not believe in, is not a member of, and does not support any organization that believes in or teaches the overthrow of the United States Government by force or violence or by any illegal or unconstitutional methods"; and (ii) the oath of allegiance to support the Constitution. Objections focused principally on the first requirement, some institutions refusing to accept educational aid funds as long as it was in effect. Among those who spoke out most vigorously against this provision of the act was Senator John Kennedy of Massachusetts. My recollection is that the objectionable provision was deleted within a year or two.

† During his vice presidential years, Nixon appeared to be a moderate on social issues, occupying a centrist position within the Republican party between the Rockefeller wing and the Goldwater-Reagan wing. After he became president, Nixon seemed to move somewhat to the right on such matters, possibly to solidify his political base and to make inroads among southern Democrats.

named the 101st element, discovered by him, of D. I. Mendeleev Periodic Table after this great Russian chemist. In this friendly act of the American scientist each Soviet citizen discerns a great respect toward our people and its culture, as well as one of the steps toward the liquidation of the absurd, according to Nikita Sergeevitch Khrushchev, tense state of "cold war" between two great nations.

May I present to you, in commemoration of your remarkable discovery and your noble act, the book by Dimitri Ivanovitch Mendeleev "Fundamentals of Chemistry" with his autograph.

The autograph reads: "To my deeply appreciated colleague, Dr. N. I. Bistrov, in commemoration of saving my son. D. Mendeleev, 1889." The book remains one of my most treasured possessions.

On December 14, 1959, when I was in Washington for a meeting of the President's Science Advisory Committee, I met with Vice President Nixon again, this time for a wide-ranging discussion about education. He asked me whether there had been improvements in American education since the Sputniks (the two 1957 Soviet space launches that had called into question America's presumed scientific superiority). I said that there had been some, but not enough, that we still needed improvement in fundamentals such as English composition and arithmetic, better salaries for teachers, and better textbooks.

We ended up talking about the upcoming 1960 presidential race. He thought the Republican nomination would go either to Nelson Rockefeller or to himself and that the Democrats would nominate either Stuart Symington or Adlai Stevenson. He expressed a low opinion of Symington, a higher one of Stevenson. Less than three weeks later, on January 2, 1960, John F. Kennedy, to the surprise of no one, announced his candidacy for the presidency, giving formal status to planning that had been going on for over three years. Almost immediately, Kennedy became the front-runner among Democratic aspirants, and it seemed surprising that Nixon, in his talk with me, gave Kennedy's chances so little credence.

I met again with Vice President Nixon on the morning of May 16, 1960, when I went to his office to discuss the future of the President's Science Advisory Committee, which was meeting that day. He said that if elected he intended to keep the same members. To replace chairman George Kistiakowsky, who intended to retire the following autumn, he said that he preferred a scientist-scholar to an "operator" if a choice had to be made. He asked that Kistiakowsky and I give him recommendations. (It is interesting to note that when Nixon replaced his own disaffected first science adviser, Lee

DuBridge, in September 1970, it was not with a scientist-scholar but with an engineer, Edward E. David, Jr.*)

On June 24, 1960, I took two of my children, Lynne and Peter, and two of fellow scientist Paul Aebersold's children, around to Nixon's office for a very friendly social visit (see photo).

My next association with Nixon was one concocted by the press. In the *U.S. News and World Report* for August 29, 1960, during the Nixon-Kennedy presidential campaign, I was shocked and dismayed to see my name and picture prominently featured in an article entitled "Nixon's Idea Men—Who They Are, What They Stand For." The article contained photos and brief profiles of ten men and said: "You can now see the kind of men . . . Nixon looks to for ideas . . . They are an older group, more conservative than the men who are advising Kennedy." Included with me were nuclear scientist Edward Teller, President Eisenhower's chief economist Arthur Burns, two bankers, and several academicians. As I wrote in my diary:

> As a lifelong Democrat, it is uncomfortable, to say the least, to be described as a "Nixon man." My wife, who is always a shade more liberal than I, will probably be outraged. [She was.]

The unwelcome publicity in August 1960 briefly threatened my appointment as AEC chairman in January 1961. I had been questioned about my availability for the job on January 9 in a phone call from President-elect Kennedy. But the next day McGeorge Bundy phoned with some disquieting news. Congressman Chet Holifield (D-CA), who was to be chairman of the Joint Committee on Atomic Energy in the upcoming Congress and whom at this time I scarcely knew, had told Kennedy that I was an "ardent Nixon supporter." I suspected that Holifield had based this "information" on the article in *U.S. News and World Report.* I therefore described to Bundy the limited nature of my prior contacts with Nixon and my consistent Democratic voting record. In due course this information was passed along to Kennedy and also to Holifield, who then said he would not oppose me. A firm offer from Kennedy followed soon after and I quickly accepted.

In December 1963 I had a friendly chat with Nixon, who was then in private law practice, when we both attended the annual pre-Christmas luncheon in New York given by William E. Knox, chairman of the Westinghouse Electric International Company. I did not meet him again until January 28, 1969, a week after his inauguration as president.

---

* I do not wish to disparage the appointment. David performed very creditably in the position.

With two of my children, Lynne and Peter, on a social visit to Vice President Nixon in June 1960.

PART I

EXPLOSIONS

1

The Demise of Plowshare

I have long favored a drastic escalation of our testing program
for the peaceful use of atomic explosives . . . I think we
should be very aggressive in going forward.

—President Richard M. Nixon, January 25,1969[1]

PLOWSHARE AND THE TEST BAN

The occasion for my first meeting with Richard Nixon after he became
president was an aide-mémoire that the Soviet chargé d'affaires had handed
the State Department on the first day of the new administration. The note
alleged that there had been a possible violation of the 1963 Limited Test Ban
Treaty (LTBT) in connection with the December 8, 1968, explosion in Nevada
of an excavation experiment named Schooner in AEC's program for the peaceful
uses of atomic explosions.

The program, called Plowshare (after the passage from Isaiah 2:4: "They
shall beat their swords into plowshares . . ."), had been initiated following the
Suez crisis of 1957. The suggestion was made then that nuclear explosives be
used to excavate a second and less vulnerable canal to replace the Suez Canal.
Although this suggestion was not implemented, the idea of nuclear excavation

continued to be studied. Among the ambitious projects that were studied in some detail, primarily at AEC's Livermore, California, weapons laboratory,* were: a project to shorten the distance and remove some of the vertical curves of the Santa Fe Railroad's route in the Mojave desert; a canal to connect the Mediterranean Sea with the Qattara Depression in Egypt in order to produce electricity; removing rapids on the Madeira and Paraná rivers in South America; a sea-level canal across Thailand's Isthmus of Kra; increasing the amount of water for irrigation from the Niger River in Africa; and several dams for conserving and managing flood waters in various locations.

The excavation proposal that was the focus of attention at the beginning of the Nixon administration was the construction by nuclear means of a sea-level canal across the Isthmus of Panama. Early in 1962 President Kennedy, following talks with President Roberto Chiari of Panama, directed that studies be undertaken as to the need for and means of construction, location, and cost of such a canal. It was thought that a sea-level canal would be militarily less vulnerable than the existing lock canal and that it could transit large aircraft carriers, something the existing canal could not do. It was also thought that the existing canal would reach capacity by the end of the century and that it soon would not be able to handle the increasing numbers of huge tankers and bulk carriers.

In 1964, bloody anti-American riots erupted in Panama, underscoring the security threat to the existing canal. In consequence, the Atlantic-Pacific Interoceanic Canal Study Commission (CSC) was established by Congress in September 1964 with a mandate to determine "the feasibility of, and the most suitable site for, the construction of a sea-level canal . . . ; the best means of constructing such a canal, whether by conventional or nuclear excavation; and the estimated cost thereof."† Plowshare's excavation program thereupon became focused on providing evidence that the nuclear option for building the canal was technically feasible. Schooner, the explosion that occasioned the Soviet protest, was one of a series of tests conducted at AEC's Nevada test site to develop peaceful nuclear explosives. Considerable progress had already been made in the development of low-cost,

---

* Formally, the Livermore facility was part of the E. O. Lawrence Radiation Laboratory, operated for the AEC by the University of California, with branches at Berkeley and Livermore. The two facilities are today titled the Lawrence Berkeley Laboratory and the Lawrence Livermore National Laboratory, respectively.

† Ex-Treasury Secretary Robert Anderson was made chairman of the five-man commission. Other members were Milton Eisenhower, president of Johns Hopkins University; ex-AEC general manager Kenneth E. Fields; Robert Storey, a lawyer; and Raymond Hill, a civil engineer.

very "clean" (free from radioactive fallout) devices and in achieving a capability for accurately predicting the size and other characteristics of craters resulting from nuclear explosions in varying media.

The Soviet note stated that Schooner had caused a "two- to fivefold increase in fallout in the regions along the Baltic, Volga, Northern Caucasus, and Crimea." In the Soviet view, this constituted a violation of Article I of the LTBT, which, besides banning nuclear explosions in the atmosphere, in space, and under water, also prohibited an explosion "in any other environment [meaning underground] if such explosion causes radioactive debris to be present outside the territorial limits" of the nation conducting the test. The Soviets told the State Department that they had no intention of making the aide-mémoire public. However, there was a danger that it might leak from our side, in which case both they and we might be forced to take a public stance with respect to this incident and as to the treaty as a whole. I thought the administration should therefore be ready with a plan of action, and this is what led up to the meeting with the president on January 28, 1969.

A week earlier, the day after the Soviet aide-mémoire was filed, I had discussed this subject with Assistant to the President Robert F. Ellsworth and two other members of the White House staff. As I told Ellsworth and the others, whether the Soviet accusation was valid hinged on a long-standing controversy about how the key clause in Article I of the LTBT was to be interpreted, particularly the words "causes radioactive debris to be present." Did this mean a minute trace of radioactivity that could barely be measured? The Arms Control and Disarmament Agency (ACDA), with some support from the State Department, had been arguing very seriously for such a strict, literal interpretation. ACDA contended that to adopt any other standard would impugn the good faith of the United States in seeking arms control agreements and injure our reputation as a country that took its treaty obligations seriously.

The AEC argued that the strict interpretation supported by ACDA was unrealistic and, to be frank, absurd. For one thing, it caused the treaty to amend itself constantly as more sensitive detection instruments were developed. I pointed out that the "two- to fivefold increase" in radioactivity alluded to by the Soviets in their aide-mémoire amounted to a very tiny amount of radioactivity. Ellsworth asked what the Soviets might be referring to as their point of reference. I said that if their technique was similar to ours, it involved the passage of large amounts of air through filter paper, followed by a chemical identification of the products obtained. In that case, the background radiation used as a basis for the calculation probably corresponded to something like 0.1 picocurie per cubic meter of air. By contrast, the room in which we were meeting, as well as the air anywhere else in the world, was likely to contain concentrations of naturally occurring radioactivity (such as gaseous radon) hundreds of times greater. I contended that this illustrated the absurdity of interpreting the test ban treaty on the basis of such sensitive methods of detection; yet this was what State and ACDA seemed to be advocating. The AEC favored an interpretation of the treaty under which the concentration of radioactivity crossing a national border would need to have some practical significance, such as a relationship to human health, before it could be considered "present" under the terms of the treaty.*

Even more serious than the potential effect on the Plowshare program was the high risk that an ultra-strict interpretation of the LTBT might outlaw many underground weapons tests. In the meeting with Ellsworth I expressed strong doubt that the SFRC would have recommended the treaty to the Senate had the committee members understood there was such a risk. I added that, despite their current protest, it was evident that the Soviets had themselves adopted a liberal interpretation of the treaty since they had conducted at least ten tests from which we had detected radioactivity outside Soviet territory.

I noted that the controversy about the treaty had already proved a severe handicap to the AEC in the conduct of its underground weapons testing and Plowshare programs. It had resulted, for example, in the imposition of elaborate administration reviews before each explosion in order to assure that there would be no treaty violation. These reviews sometimes delayed shots for months. In addition, to minimize the likelihood of venting (emitting radioactive debris into the atmosphere), we were burying underground weapons tests to great depths. The Soviets were not burying theirs nearly so deeply and were therefore escaping some of the difficulties and costs we encountered.

Another relative U.S. disadvantage I cited was that we announced all our cratering Plowshare experiments days ahead of time, and we also announced all

---

* It was with such an interpretation in mind that I had told the Senate Foreign Relations Committee (SFRC) during its ratification hearings in 1963 that the LTBT would allow Plowshare cratering experiments to go forward if they had a "downwind distance of several hundred miles from the project site to a territorial limit." Based principally on my testimony, I believed, the SFRC had reported to the Senate its understanding that "the Plowshare program . . . will not be seriously inhibited by the treaty." I believed further that this conclusion had exerted a strong influence in moving Senators Clinton Anderson (D-NM), Henry Jackson (D-WA), and perhaps others, from a doubtful to a favorable position on the LTBT's ratification. Now, as the strict interpretation of the treaty threatened seriously to inhibit Plowshare, I was disturbed that there might be an appearance that I had willfully deceived the senators in my testimony.

ventings from our weapons tests. It was impossible under our open system to follow any other course. The Soviets then took advantage of our venting announcements to send us protests. We occasionally responded with protests of our own, and so a game of diplomatic one-upmanship was going on that had no positive result whatever.

I pointed out further that the AEC had been attempting for several years to arrange discussions with the Soviets on the interpretation of the LTBT. My counterparts in the Soviet Union seemed to want to proceed with such discussions, but arrangements always seemed to stall when they got to higher levels. In the summer of 1968 it had looked as though talks might soon begin, but this was prevented by the ill feeling that followed the East bloc's invasion of Czechoslovakia. There had been recent overtures by the Soviets to revive the idea of talks but our State Department, still wanting to punish the Soviets for Czechoslovakia, was not ready to do so. I conjectured that one of the reasons the Soviets were protesting Schooner might be to enhance the prospect of getting talks started.

Ellsworth and his associates seemed very interested in all this; they took copious notes. It was therefore no surprise to me that a meeting with President Nixon was soon scheduled.

PRESIDENTIAL PREJUDICE

Also present at my meeting with President Nixon on January 28 were National Security Adviser Henry Kissinger, White House Chief of Staff H. R. Haldeman, White House Science Adviser Lee DuBridge, and Ellsworth. The president began by saying that, like all people, he had his quirks and that one of these was a special prejudice in favor of the Plowshare program. He wanted it to have a high priority in his administration.

President Nixon asked me first of all to describe a Plowshare project we had going with Australia. I said that at Keraudren Bay in the northwestern part of Western Australia it was proposed to detonate five nuclear explosives buried below the ocean bottom in order to excavate a narrow harbor for the shipment of iron ore mined nearby. It was to be the first practically useful nuclear excavation experiment. The Australians wanted it accomplished before the end of 1970.

The president asked what was required to get on with the Australian project. I said two things were required: first, we would need additional funding for this and related aspects of Plowshare; and second, we would need a more realistic

Before a meeting at the White House, January 28, 1969. From left, Henry A. Kissinger; White House assistant Robert F. Ellsworth; Patrick E. Haggerty, chairman, Texas Instruments Co. (he did not participate in the meeting); the president; Seaborg; and Science Adviser Lee A. DuBridge. We met to discuss a Soviet note alleging that an experimental explosion in AEC's Plowshare program had violated the Limited Test Ban Treaty. White House chief of staff H. R. Haldeman (not shown) also took part.

interpretation of the test ban treaty than the one that was being adopted by the ACDA and the State Department. The occasion of this meeting was neither the time nor the place to expand on the first item, but I did go into the second at some length, repeating much of what I had told Ellsworth a week earlier.

The president then asked what the prospects were for excavating a second Panama Canal using nuclear explosives. I answered that the prospects were good, and went on to describe the situation as noted above. The meeting ended with a brief discussion of other topics: peaceful uses of atomic energy in general, testing of high-yield weapons, and the proposed shutdown of two reactors at AEC's plutonium production complex in Hanford, Washington.

It was then suggested that I meet with the press as part of Press Secretary Ron Ziegler's regular 4 P.M. briefing. The president said he was making such meetings a part of his mode of operation. He proceeded to tell me in some detail exactly what I should say to the press. (This apparent need to orchestrate his administration's press relations was to become a recognizable hallmark of Nixon's presidency.)

After Ziegler introduced me, I summarized my meeting with the president, saying: "The president expressed a great interest—and he asked me particularly to tell you this—in the peaceful uses of atomic energy. He particularly identified the peaceful uses of nuclear explosives as an area in which he had a special interest." There were then several questions about the Australian project. I was also asked by the reporters whether the president had asked me to stay on as AEC chairman, and I answered that he had. (This had indeed transpired during the meeting, Nixon remarking, I hoped jokingly, that it had been a close decision in the administration but that he had prevailed.)

FIZZLE DOWN UNDER

On January 31, 1969, I helped draft an affirmative reply to an Australian request for a joint U.S.-Australian feasibility study of the Cape Keraudren project. The State Department, never enthusiastic about the Plowshare program, had been dragging its feet on a reply until a query from Australia sent directly to the president shook the matter loose.

The Australian project drew an inquiry from Soviet Ambassador Anatoly Dobrynin in early March. He asked whether it would not violate the LTBT, since "under water" was one of the treaty's prohibited environments. My assistant, Justin Bloom, and I drafted some language that the State Department could use in reply. We pointed out that the explosion was to take place *in earth* several hundred feet below the earth-water interface. We stated our understanding that "under water," as used in the treaty, meant *in* water.*

President Nixon, embracing the Australian project with vigor, decided to establish an ad hoc National Security Council study group to report on the project's relationship to the test ban and nonproliferation treaties. He also asked the Bureau of the Budget to coordinate a study on the project's "economic and technological benefits." At this point, the Cape Keraudren project was rapidly becoming a centerpiece of administration activity in science and technology.

What was our dismay, then, when we learned on March 25, 1969, that the Sentinel Mining Company, the American firm that had proposed to ship iron ore from the excavated harbor, had reached the conclusion that economic developments made the ore no longer worth exporting. Our embarrassment was increased by the fact that President Nixon was scheduled to hold talks with Prime Minister John Gorton of Australia the following week. Hastily, the American and Australian atomic energy commissions cobbled together a different project in Australia that could utilize the $500,000 that had been made available on the U.S. side for the feasibility study. When I wrote President Nixon that Cape Keraudren had fallen through, I mentioned that there was this other possibility. But in the end nothing came of the substitute proposal.

RULISON

In the same letter in which I broke the news to President Nixon about the collapse of one project, Cape Keraudren, I was able to announce the beginning of another. Project Rulison proposed the detonation of a nuclear explosive deep underground in Colorado to stimulate the release of natural gas that was too tightly imbedded in formations of hard rock to be economically recoverable by conventional means. I participated in the contract-signing ceremony on March 26, 1969, in the office of Secretary of the Interior Walter J. Hickel. The cost of the project was estimated at $6.5 million, 90 percent of which was to be borne by the Austral Oil Company (an American company, despite the name), the remaining 10 percent by the AEC. The CER Geonuclear Corporation was

---

* This question, and the one about export of "radioactive debris" referred to earlier, point up the difficulties involved in drafting treaties dealing with technical matters. They help explain why it has taken so long to negotiate most arms control treaties.

to act as program manager. The Los Alamos Scientific Laboratory was to provide technical direction for the AEC. The explosion was scheduled for May 22, 1969.

Rulison was part of a program intended to demonstrate that nuclear explosions could help overcome what appeared to be a looming shortage of natural gas.* The concept was that the nuclear explosions would fracture imprisoning rock formations, thereby freeing the gas so that it would flow into accessible wells in greater quantities than could be made available by conventional drilling methods. The Bureau of Mines had estimated that more than 300 trillion cubic feet of gas were potentially recoverable from the Rocky Mountain area alone if the program proved successful. A smaller experiment in the program, Project Gasbuggy, had been conducted in 1968 in New Mexico and had achieved a rate of production several times greater than that of neighboring wells. Because the gas was slightly radioactive, however, none of it had been sold commercially. Rulison was to be carried out at a greater depth than Gasbuggy (8,400 versus 4,240 feet), and with a more powerful device (50 versus 29 kilotons).

Several additional experimental blasts were planned after Rulison to develop improved explosives and methods for gas production. On the horizon was the prospect that the AEC might provide a commercial nuclear explosion service to domestic gas producers. Legislation authorizing such a service (the Hosmer Bill—named for its sponsor, Congressman Craig Hosmer [R-CA]) had been introduced in Congress by the Joint Committee on Atomic Energy, on which Hosmer was the most influential Republican. All in all, nuclear gas stimulation seemed to promise what all of us in the AEC wanted: an additional peaceful use of atomic energy that might provide substantial economic benefit to large numbers of people. There were also plans to extend the nuclear explosion technique to the recovery of oil shale and other underground resources.

It soon became evident that detonation of Rulison would have to be postponed from its scheduled date of May 22, 1969, because there was need to assess further whether the explosion would threaten the safety of a nearby dam. The new date was to be September 4.

Throughout the summer an environmentalist attack was mounted against Rulison. This was something that the Plowshare program had not previously encountered and something that had probably not entered sufficiently into our planning. A feature of the attack was a mail campaign conducted by a student group at the University of Colorado. One claim the opponents made was that

---

* The *Oil and Gas Journal* had predicted that, with existing production methods, U.S. gas reserves would be insufficient to meet demands after 1974 (AEC Annual Report to the Congress of the Atomic Energy Commission for 1969, p. 200). We know now that this estimate was unduly pessimistic.

radiation from the explosion might contaminate underground water resources, fouling wells and springs. The AEC was kept busy helping members of Congress respond to the numerous letters. We provided the legislators with fairly detailed accounts of the extensive precautions the AEC was taking to prevent any adverse consequences from Rulison. We confidently predicted that there would be none. Governor John A. Love of Colorado, after an extensive briefing by project officials, also expressed confidence that the detonation would be carried out safely but said he wanted to look closely into whether the gas production that followed would be equally safe.

As September 4, the scheduled explosion date, drew near, a number of public interest groups, including the American Civil Liberties Union, attempted to have Rulison stopped by court injunction. The Federal District Court in Colorado, and then the Circuit Court of Appeals, ruled against them. Finally, the plaintiffs appealed to the Supreme Court for a restraining order, a request denied by Justice Thurgood Marshall on September 3.

There was to be one more delay, this time because of adverse weather. Then, on September 10, as we announced to the White House with ostentatious precision, "at one-tenth of a second past 3 P.M.," Rulison was detonated. No abnormal radiation levels were detected. The 36 families living within a five-mile radius from the site were evacuated from their homes before the explosion and returned to their homes after it, each family accompanied by a Public Health Service representative. Six minor gas leaks and six cases of minor structural damage were reported. There were no reports of injury to people or to livestock. Railroad and vehicular traffic resumed normally within hours. Subsequently, 100 claims for property damage (cracked walls and chimneys, broken windows, etc.), totaling $18,871.10, were honored by the AEC.

Following the detonation, a standby period of several months ensued to allow liberated gas to flow into the reservoir created by the explosion. More than 400 million cubic feet of gas were liberated in the first 70 days, more than had been produced in the first five years from nearby wells using conventional methods. The next steps were to be flaring (burning) of some of the gas to determine its chemical composition, particularly as to radioactivity, and then production testing to determine the extent to which nuclear fracturing of the rock might have increased gas production. Before any of this could take place, however, there was another legal hurdle to cross.

The same plaintiffs who had been defeated in their attempt to stop the explosion now sought to prevent the planned flaring and testing of the gas on the grounds that it would create a radiation hazard endangering public health and safety. The trial, which took place in Federal District Court in Colorado, quickly focused on two issues: (1) the adequacy of the specific measures being taken by the AEC to protect public health and safety during flaring operations and (2) the adequacy of the Federal Radiation Council (FRC) standards that the AEC was applying in implementing the project.* Witnesses for the plaintiffs contended that the FRC standards were too lenient and should be lowered by a factor of ten. The court's decision, announced on March 16, 1970, was to deny the petitions. In a lengthy opinion, Judge Alfred A. Arraj found, in essence, (1) that the AEC had planned its activities and was carrying them out with all due regard for health and safety considerations; and (2) that the plaintiffs had failed to establish that the FRC standards adopted by AEC were not reasonably adequate to protect health, life, and safety. The latter finding was considered a shot in the arm not only for Plowshare projects but also for the nuclear power program, which, as will be developed in later pages, was at that time facing a similar challenge.

Following the court's ruling, the production aspects of Rulison continued. Drilling began in mid-April 1970. It reached the area of broken rock in July. Flaring and testing of the gas then began and continued intermittently until mid-October. The amount of radioactivity found was significantly lower than in Gasbuggy. As we cautiously expressed it in reports to the White House, "average concentrations of tritium and krypton- 85 are well within limits to assure public health." Tests then began to determine the effects of nuclear stimulation on gas quantity and production rates. Results from these tests, which continued well into 1971, also were "encouraging."

A certain amount of self-delusion was going on, however. Radioactivity from Rulison, while lower than that from Gasbuggy and within guidelines, was not zero. We were made aware of this fact in August 1970 in a draft report emanating from the Bio-Medical Division of the Livermore Laboratory entitled "Assessment of Potential Biological Hazards from Project Rulison." My diary comment was: *This will surely lead to adverse public reaction when it is issued.* By this time, we had become aware that, stimulated by the environmental movement that had erupted in full flower in 1969 (see chapter 7), the public was

---

* The FRC was established by presidential order in 1959. It advised the president and all federal agencies on the formulation of radiation standards. Its formal membership consisted of the secretaries of health, education, and welfare; defense; agriculture; interior; commerce; labor; and the chairman of the AEC, although its actual work was done by lesser officials of these agencies. In formulating its standards, the FRC tended to rely on the recommendations of other expert bodies, principally the National Committee on Radiation Protection and Measurements (NCRP) and the International Commission on Radiological Protection (ICRP).

becoming increasingly intolerant of any radioactivity whatsoever. As had been the case with Gasbuggy, therefore, no attempt was made to sell Rulison's gas commercially, and the future of nuclear gas stimulation was again placed in doubt.

In December 1970, Governor Love of Colorado wrote to me requesting that from that time forward, "no experiment involving the detonation of a nuclear device in the State of Colorado be conducted . . . without official sanction by the state." Having won several battles, it appeared now that the AEC had lost the war.

A SECOND PANAMA CANAL?

As I told President Nixon during our meeting in January 1969, an important reason for AEC's interest in the Cape Keraudren project was that it could serve as one of the experiments needed to obtain information required by the Canal Study Commission. I also told him that it had been only within the past year that we had succeeded in obtaining permission from the Johnson White House for three other important excavation experiments and that we still did not have funding to complete them. I was clearly hoping through these comments to loosen the budgetary purse strings by stimulating the president's personal interest.

The prospects for nuclear excavation of a trans-Isthmian canal were among the subjects discussed on October 14, 1969, by the National Security Council's Under Secretaries Committee chaired by Under Secretary of State Elliot Richardson. Among the many others in attendance were Joint Chiefs of Staff Chairman Earle Wheeler, Deputy Secretary of Defense David Packard, ACDA Director Gerard C. Smith, Acting Deputy Director James R. Schlesinger of the Bureau of the Budget, and high ranking staff members of State, CIA, USIA, and the Office of Science and Technology. Representing the AEC, besides myself, were Commissioner Theos J. Thompson; John Kelly, director of our division of peaceful nuclear explosives; and my disarmament assistant, Allan Labowitz.

To start the meeting, Richardson asked me to state what additional excavation shots were required before a decision could be made about whether nuclear methods could be used for digging the Panama Canal. I said only two shots would be required, Sturtevant, which would be ready for execution within a month, and Yawl, which could be executed the following spring. If the decision about the canal favored the nuclear option, we would then contemplate additional experiments later in 1970 and in 1971.

A two-hour, generally confused discussion then ensued. One question was: Would Sturtevant violate the test ban treaty? I offered my usual defense of AEC's "rule-of-reason" approach buttressed by the notion that, in the Russian text, the term used where the English text says "radioactive debris" could be translated to mean "radioactive fallout," implying more than an insignificant amount. Packard and Wheeler then pushed strongly for approval of Sturtevant on the grounds that we shouldn't give in to public clamor against testing. (They were, of course, more concerned about weapons testing than about Plowshare.) But ACDA's Smith, who doubted that it was a good idea to go ahead with Sturtevant (or any Plowshare experiment, for that matter), suggested that its approval or disapproval was not the agenda item for the meeting and should be decided separately. I agreed with Smith on that point. I said that whether the American public would accept Sturtevant on environmental grounds was a more important issue than whether the Soviets would raise a fuss about it as a treaty violation.

Later, in private conversation, I told Richardson that I thought a smaller group should discuss the public acceptance question and that it should then be taken up with the president, acquainting him fully with the potential opposition so that he would not be surprised by it as the firing date for Sturtevant drew near. I pictured as the worst possible outcome having to cancel the shot at the last minute because of public opposition—such a step would damage the president as well as Plowshare. I told Richardson that the AEC was prepared to change Sturtevant from an excavation experiment to a completely contained device-development test in which there would be no danger of venting, to be followed by an excavation explosion later if the public climate permitted.

A week later I met with former AEC commissioner John Palfrey, who was now a professor of law and history at Columbia University. He urged us to go ahead with the cratering version of Sturtevant. He thought AEC's recent success with the Milrow weapons test (see chapter 2) and with Rulison was sufficient to establish our credibility with the public. I didn't see it that way. I pointed out that deliberately planning an explosion that would vent radioactivity when that explosion bore no direct relation to national defense brought us into uncharted territory with respect to public acceptance. By this time, I told Palfrey, the AEC was inclined to go with the fully contained version of Sturtevant.

Late in January 1970 a "Symposium on Nuclear Explosives" was held in Las Vegas. There, General R. H. Groves of the Army Corps of Engineers (a son of General Leslie Groves of Manhattan Project fame) made very clear which way the wind was blowing. As engineering agent for the Canal Study Commission, Groves said that he could not support the use of nuclear explosives for the canal project. He gave two reasons. The first was that tribal populations along the canal's path would have to be uprooted from their homes and deprived of their means of livelihood. One estimate was that as many as 25,000 people might have to be evacuated, and for some years.[2] The second was that the inability to conduct sufficient tests had left large gaps in knowledge that made it impossible to state unequivocally that nuclear explosive techniques were feasible. Alarm was also being expressed by biologists about undertaking a sea-level canal unless there was extensive preliminary ecological research. Their concern was that linking the two oceans in this way might seriously upset the balance of marine life. In addition, as I had readily acknowledged in my 1968 testimony to the Senate Foreign Relations Committee, the canal project itself, as distinct from excavation experiments leading up to it, could not be carried out without amending the Limited Test Ban Treaty.[3] There was a strong likelihood that such an amendment would be agreed to by the needed majority of parties to the treaty, but this was far from a certainty.

In May I formally asked Under Secretary Richardson to withdraw Sturtevant from further consideration by the Under Secretaries Committee. It was never conducted, nor was any other Plowshare cratering experiment. By the time the Canal Study Commission made its report to Congress on November 30,1970, the nuclear excavation issue was no longer in doubt. The report recommended that a sea-level canal go forward because of its military and economic advantages. It did not mince words, however, in stating the conclusion that "no current decision on U.S. canal policy should be made in the expectation that nuclear explosive technology will be available for the construction."

CURTAINS FOR PLOWSHARE

The long-delayed technical talks with the Soviets about peaceful nuclear explosions (PNEs) finally got under way in April 1969 in Vienna. The focus at the start was on implementing Article V of the Nonproliferation Treaty, under which both our countries undertook to provide a PNE service to other countries on a commercial basis. The AEC hoped the meeting would also include some discussion about interpretation of the "debris outside the territorial limits" clause of the test ban treaty.

The meeting was not successful. As I learned later,[4] the Soviets felt that the United States had downgraded the proceedings by having its delegation headed by an AEC commissioner, Gerald F. Tape, who had already resigned effective two weeks hence. They also were miffed that the U.S. delegation planned to have the meeting last only two days. They thought two or three weeks should have been allowed so that the explosions carried out by the two sides could be discussed in detail. These factors gave the Soviets the impression that the United States was more interested in world politics and in getting publicity than it was in actually making peaceful explosives available to mankind. Thus antagonized, the Russians decided not to bring full data to the table. This, in turn, antagonized the American side. There was agreement, however, to try again, and in February 1970 a second series of technical talks about Plowshare was held in Moscow. This time the Soviets were more forthcoming, revealing details of what appeared to be a very active and advanced program. For example, they presented reports describing projects for stimulating oil production, extinguishing gas-well fires, and creating water reservoirs. They also reported on experiments leading to projects for canal excavation, underground mining, and creation of storage cavities. At the conclusion of the meeting, there was a joint communiqué stating that a further meeting, to be held in Washington, would be desirable.

In March 1971, Ambassador Dobrynin approached Secretary of State William P. Rogers about getting the Washington talks started. John Irwin, who had succeeded Elliot Richardson as Under Secretary of State, called me about this on April 20. He said there was some feeling at State that further talks on Plowshare were pointless, since no further peaceful explosions were provided for in the AEC's budget for the next two years. Or, Irwin asked, should we have one more meeting "and then get out"? I argued strongly that the talks should go ahead, nor did I believe we should enter into them with the feeling they would be the last. I added that the Soviets had been very helpful and constructive in all areas in which we had agreements for cooperation with them and that we should think twice before rejecting their strong interest in these talks.

My arguments prevailed, and the third get-together took place in Washington, July 12-23, 1971. There was further exchange of technical data, and certain favorable technical conclusions were stated in a final communiqué. They were prefaced, however, by a disclaimer: the technical conclusions of the meeting, it said, "did not represent in any sense an agreement by either government on what would constitute permissible applications of peaceful nuclear explosions." It was clear that the diplomats intended to hold the enthusiasm of the technical people under a tight rein.

Despite President Nixon's averred prejudice in its favor, Plowshare was rapidly disappearing from the AEC's budget. In 1957 the amount budgeted for the program had been over $150 million. By 1970 this had shrunk to $13.7 million (less than half the amount requested by AEC), by 1973 to $7 million. I would not want to convey the impression that a lean budget was solely responsible for the demise of the program. The story really went the other way around—the budget was lean because the program lacked support. Even in its most vigorous days, it had never enjoyed a wide base of support. The Joint Committee in general, and its frequent chairman, Congressman Chet Holifield (D-CA) in particular, were far less supportive of Plowshare than of other AEC programs, such as the fast breeder reactor.* State Department and ACDA types clearly regarded Plowshare as a diplomatic hazard. Public opinion increasingly discouraged taking risks with radioactivity, especially when national security was not involved. Even in the White House, where President Nixon's favorable sentiments might have been expected to have some influence, there was little enthusiasm. Thus, explaining the complete elimination of funds for excavation projects from the 1971 budget, a "White House aide" told the *New York Times* on July 16, 1970: "On the basis of priorities, it just didn't seem to be something that was really urgent."

One more natural gas stimulation experiment, Rio Blanco, was conducted in May 1973 in western Colorado. It involved the simultaneous detonation of three vertically stacked explosives. The experiment was regarded as a failure because the fracture zones from the three explosives failed to link up as expected.

By this time, after three gas stimulation experiments, the people of Colorado had had enough. The state's constitution was amended in 1974 to require a referendum on each further nuclear explosion proposed to take place within the state. Since Rio Blanco, the United States has conducted no peaceful nuclear explosions.

POST MORTEM

Plowshare got its start at a time when AEC activities enjoyed great public prestige and when the agency's budgets were still relatively immune from review in the Congress, even in the executive branch. (See the Epilogue for a fuller discussion of this point.) By the time of the Nixon years these conditions had greatly changed. Opposition to the Vietnam War had stimulated a loss of faith in government endeavors. This was correlated with the flowering of the environmental movement and some loss of confidence in science and technology generally. Questions raised about the fallout from nuclear tests and about the safety and environmental effects of reactors had given rise to antinuclear

---

* Under the terms of the Atomic Energy Act the JCAE chairmanship rotated with each Congress between Senate and House. Holifield, who had been a member of the committee since it was established in 1947, was either chairman or vice chairman in all the Congresses between 1961 and 1971.

sentiments and then to organized antinuclear movements. The harmful effects of radiation had become a focus of public fear. In the changed circumstances much more intense scrutiny was given to AEC programs, particularly to their possible deleterious effects. Plowshare could not survive the increased scrutiny; the benefits thought to be obtainable from peaceful nuclear explosions did not appear to be of sufficient magnitude or certainty to overmatch the potential hazards.

The Soviet Union's PNE program, probably also favored by a lack of critical scrutiny, continued quite vigorously for a number of years. But the Soviet program also shut down after President Mikhail Gorbachev announced a unilateral moratorium on nuclear tests in August 1985. It is highly doubtful that the peaceful use of nuclear explosives, once considered so promising, will be revived.

NOTES

1. Letter to Science Adviser Lee DuBridge, in Bruce Oudes, ed., *From: The President: Richard Nixon's Secret Files,* pp. 12-13.
2. David R. Inglis and Carl L. Sandler, "The Nonmilitary Use of Nuclear Explosives," *Bulletin of the Atomic Scientists,* December 1967, p. 48.
3. Senate Committee on Foreign Relations, Nonproliferation Treaty Hearings, 1968, 116.
4. I received a verbal report from Dr. Henry F. Coffer (vice president of CER Geonuclear Corporation) of his meeting in June 1969 with three members of the Soviet delegation.

2

Testing the
ABM Warhead

SENTINEL

For a while after the first Soviet nuclear test in 1949, the United States relied for defense against nuclear attack on a combination of interceptor aircraft, antiaircraft missiles, and civil defense measures such as shelters. Once the Soviets acquired an arsenal of intercontinental ballistic missiles (ICBMs), however, these measures no longer seemed sufficient. Beginning in the late 1950s, therefore, the Army repeatedly sought authorization to begin producing and deploying on a nationwide basis a nuclear-tipped antiballistic missile (ABM) system called Nike-Zeus. Although the Army won substantial support in Congress, both the Eisenhower and Kennedy administrations resisted on three grounds: first, Nike-Zeus, which had a relatively slow rocket booster, was considered technically inadequate to deal with the growing number of Soviet ICBMs and their accompanying decoys and other penetration aids; second, the proposed nationwide deployment of Nike-Zeus was inordinately expensive— analysis indicated that the Soviets could multiply offensive missiles at far less cost than we could provide defensive missiles to counter them; and third, there was growing concern that an ABM deployment by the United States would provoke a Soviet reaction, leading to further U.S. actions, and that the action-reaction sequence thus initiated would greatly accelerate the arms race.

To overcome the objection about Nike-Zeus's technical inadequacy, research began in 1963 on a new ABM system called Nike-X. It was to employ a much faster interceptor, called Sprint, and more effective radars. Sprint was to be used to intercept incoming Soviet missiles just after they reentered the atmosphere, making it easier to sort out decoys. In 1965, the Army also began to develop the Spartan missile. It was intended to detonate a warhead above the atmosphere where it would generate intense X rays that might be expected to knock out several Soviet reentry vehicles at a time.

By 1966, evidence that the Soviets were deploying an ABM system of their own ("Galosh") around Moscow became unmistakable. They were also deploying around Leningrad an enhanced antiaircraft system ("Tallinn") that some analysts thought had ABM potential. These developments led to "worst-case" estimates that the Soviets intended to negate the U.S. offensive missile deterrent by erecting a nationwide ABM curtain. One U.S. reaction was the decision to equip our Minuteman ICBMs and some of our submarine-launched missiles with up to ten MIRVs (multiple independently-targetable reentry vehicles) per missile, the better to penetrate and overwhelm the Soviet ABMs.* In addition, the Joint Chiefs of Staff, supported by growing sentiment in Congress, attempted to obtain production and deployment authority for a U.S. ABM system. What the chiefs had in mind was a deployment in which Spartan missiles would furnish an area defense of the United States and Sprint missiles would provide a local defense of 25 cities, with provision for later expansion to 52 cities. Over administration objections, Congress actually voted money for procurement of some of the necessary ABM hardware.

Secretary of Defense Robert S. McNamara attempted to persuade Congress that the proposed system would be ineffective against a Soviet attack. He was unable to still the clamor for deployment, however. Beating a strategic retreat, he suggested a compromise whereby funds to meet the Chiefs' request would be appropriated but would not be spent pending attempts to explore limitation of strategic arms with the Soviets. President Johnson agreed at first to McNamara's suggestion, but when the Soviets, reluctant to give up their own ABM, dragged their feet over engaging in arms limitation talks, Johnson felt it politically necessary to make some concession to the Joint Chiefs and the powerful pro-ABM forces in Congress. Consequently, on September 18, 1967, at the conclusion of a long speech in which he argued the futility of a "thick" system to defend American cities against a *Soviet* attack, McNamara announced

---

* When it was later determined that the Soviets' ABM threat had been vastly exaggerated, both as to capability and intent, the decision on MIRVs was nevertheless not rescinded.

an administration decision to deploy a "thin" system to defend some cities against such an attack as the *Chinese* might be able to launch in the 1970s.* The system was to be called Sentinel, and was to consist of twelve sites and something like a thousand launchers, using both Spartan and Sprint missiles. Development work then began on the missiles, with the AEC performing its accustomed role of developing and testing the nuclear warheads.

Pursuant to the Limited Test Ban Treaty's prohibition of nuclear tests in the atmosphere, in space, and under water, tests of the warheads had to be conducted underground. This presented no special problems with regard to Sprint, whose warhead was to yield only a few kilotons. Spartan, however, was quite another matter. In order to accomplish its formidable mission, its warhead had to yield about five megatons and would therefore require by far the largest underground tests yet performed anywhere.

The first of these high-yield tests was to be Boxcar, scheduled for April 1968 at the Nevada Test Site. Eccentric billionaire Howard Hughes attempted to persuade the Johnson administration not to conduct this test because of the alleged dangers of earthquakes and other harmful consequences to his extensive holdings in Las Vegas, about 100 miles to the south. He was joined in this effort by several environmental and scientific groups. Their intervention, including a direct personal appeal by Hughes to President Johnson, was unsuccessful, and Boxcar went forward on schedule without the feared consequences.[1] It yielded 1.3 megatons, making it the largest underground test up to that time.

While much exaggerated, Hughes's indictment of AEC tests had a measure of validity. We had indeed experienced follow-on seismic events on the order of 4.0 to 4.5 on the Richter scale when we had conducted high-yield underground tests in the past. In view of this problem and of the publicity given to the Hughes campaign against Boxcar, Science Adviser Donald F. Hornig decided, with AEC's concurrence, to assemble a panel of specialists headed by Dr. Kenneth S. Pitzer, president of Stanford University, to look into the safety of underground nuclear tests. To AEC's discomfiture, the Pitzer panel submitted to Hornig a rather alarming report. The gist of it was that they could not rule out the possibility of serious aftershocks following a high-yield underground test.

The Pitzer report, completed early in December 1968, immediately became a "hot potato." The first question was whether to release it publicly and, if so, when. President Johnson didn't want to release it immediately because of his concern that public reaction might jeopardize a further Spartan-related test

---

* Both in this country and in the Soviet Union, many regarded the anti-China system as but the first step toward a thick anti-Soviet system.

called Benham, which did in fact take place on December 19, 1968. (Benham yielded 1.15 megatons, as against Boxcar's 1.3 megatons.)*

The problem of what to do about high-yield underground tests and about the Pitzer panel's report then passed to the Nixon administration.

SAFEGUARD

During the course of my meeting with President Nixon on January 28, 1969, referred to in the last chapter, he asked me what I thought should be done about testing in view of all the opposition that had developed. As noted in my diary:

> *I replied that I thought we should continue our forthright public posture and also continue to carry out the tests that were needed and not lose our nerve. I said these tests were necessary to develop the ABM warhead. It was as simple as that. I told him that we were developing a new test site suitable for high-yield testing on Amchitka, a remote, barren island in the Aleutian chain. The president indicated by a gesture that Amchitka didn't seem to him to be the best place in the world for testing, but I said we had made a real search for sites; that this was the best we could find; and that if anyone in the room could come up with a better suggestion I would be very surprised.*

The choice of Amchitka for ABM-related high-yield tests had, in fact, been made in 1967. Three alternative sites were given serious consideration at that time: a new site in central Nevada, the Brooks Range in central Alaska, and Amchitka.† Central Nevada was eliminated because it was thought that tests in excess of about 2.5 megatons might cause structural damage in communities

---

* Ten claims were submitted for alleged minor damage from Benham. Investigators found three to have merit, and these, involving cracks in walls and a shifted roof line, were settled for a total of $575.

† In a recent conversation, ex-AEC Commissioner Gerald F. Tape recalled that while he, I, and others were on a brief (ten days) round-the-world tour in January 1967, he approached an Australian government official about the possibility of our conducting high-yield underground tests in that country. The idea was not pursued because, upon reflection, it was concluded that conducting U.S. tests in another country was politically infeasible. Tape mentioned that an island site in the Pacific was also given early consideration.

near the test site. The logistics problems with developing a test site at Brooks Range were severe, with costs estimated to be twice those at Amchitka. The decision was therefore made to accept Amchitka as the least undesirable of the alternatives, and work commenced to develop a test site there. The preparations included the transplantation of more than 350 sea otters from Amchitka to other areas; the otters were moved by plane during 1968.

On February 25, 1969, I had a meeting at the Pentagon with the new secretary of defense, Melvin Laird, and Deputy Secretary David Packard. Among the items we discussed was the matter of high-yield tests.

> *I mentioned the complaints we had been receiving from the Hughes organization and from scientific and public interest groups regarding high-yield tests at the Nevada Test Site. I noted that one of the alleged dangers—that of delayed seismic effect— was likely to be given added respectability soon through release of the Pitzer panel report. I conjectured that the political problems caused by the criticisms were in total so severe that they might force the curtailment of high-yield tests. The immediate importance of this was that a minimum of four, preferably as many as fifteen, high-yield tests were needed to prove out the Spartan warhead required for the ABM system soon to be announced by President Nixon.*

The president's announcement came on March 14. It followed a one-month review of the Sentinel ABM system that had been initiated by the Johnson administration. (Sentinel had been running into strong resistance from communities where the Sprint missiles were to be deployed. This popular revolt had changed the position of quite a few members of Congress from pro- to anti-ABM.) What Nixon announced on March 14 was a modified ABM system called Safeguard. Its primary purpose was to protect the American deterrent against any Soviet first strike. Thus, Sprint missiles, which under Sentinel would have been deployed in and around a few cities, were instead to be deployed at missile sites in North Dakota and Montana. It was contemplated that the system might later be expanded to protect the whole country against any attack the Chinese might be able to launch in the 1970s and to protect against an accidental launch from any source.

In his statement, Nixon said that deployment of Safeguard by 1973 was essential to meet intelligence estimates of the 1973 threat. He estimated the total cost of the system at between five and seven billion dollars. Asked what kind of reception he expected in Congress, the president was prophetic indeed. He expected "a very spirited debate and a very close vote." Recalling a measure for extending the military draft that passed in 1941 by only one vote, he said, "This might be that close."

Before Nixon's noon press conference on March 14, I was called out of a Commission meeting by a phone call from White House assistant Robert F. Ellsworth. He noted that I might be a likely contact for members of Congress, reporters, and others after the announcement was made and said that whatever help and support I could give to the president on this highly controversial subject would be deeply appreciated. Perhaps to encourage my support, he emphasized that the system would be the least provocative thing that could be done under the circumstances and that it was designed to damp down the arms race, not to exacerbate it.

Ellsworth's suggestion that I might help to sell Safeguard was later made more specific when word reached me through John Harris, AEC's director of public information, that the White House wished me to make some speeches in behalf of the program. These requests placed me in a very difficult position. Like very many in the scientific community, I was personally opposed to deployment of an ABM system by the United States. My position was similar to that adopted by preceding administrations, as discussed above. In brief, I believed that such deployment would be (1) ineffective, (2) excessively expensive, and (3) dangerously provocative. I regarded it as my duty as chairman of the Atomic Energy Commission to do all within my power to see to it that weapons adopted as part of any approved national program were tested fully and promptly. Indeed, I could not have remained as AEC chairman had I adopted any other approach toward this duty. I did *not* consider it part of my official duties, however, to make public pronouncements in favor of a policy being debated by Congress. I therefore ignored the White House requests that I do so. While nothing was ever said to me about the matter, this episode probably did not enhance my standing in an administration that had a rather low tolerance for dissent.

A CLOSE VOTE

On March 29, 1969, Science Adviser Lee DuBridge made known his decision not to release to the public the Pitzer panel's report about the possible dangers of nuclear testing, although he encouraged the group's members to make their views known in scientific journals and other professional discourse. This appeared to clear the way for the AEC to release a report it had itself been preparing that described the precautions taken in underground testing and that evaluated the hazards from high-yield tests in less alarming fashion than did the Pitzer report.

But on April 14 Pitzer found his own way of going public with some of his panel's views. That evening, in Minneapolis, the American Chemical Society awarded him its annual Priestley Medal. In what I considered a contrived addition to his acceptance speech, Pitzer took the AEC to task for being too secretive about the potential seismic effects of underground nuclear explosions. (I surmised at the time that he had done this to placate students at Stanford who were protesting the university's involvement in defense research.) I wrote to Pitzer on April 19 expressing the AEC's surprise and dismay that he had chosen to attack our testing program in this manner.

On April 24, I met with National Security Adviser Henry Kissinger to consider whether it might not be advisable to postpone a high-yield test (Jorum) scheduled to take place in Nevada in late May in view of the fierce congressional debate then raging about Safeguard. Kissinger next discussed this with the president, and it was decided to put off Jorum until after Congress had voted on the ABM.

On August 6, 1969, the Senate approved authorization of funds for Safeguard by a margin of only one vote, this being a tie-breaking vote cast by Vice President Spiro T. Agnew. Although Nixon had predicted the vote might be close, he must have been surprised that it was that close. After this vote, the administration began to think of Safeguard more for its value as a bargaining tool in SALT and less in terms of its becoming a formidable military reality. For even this more limited role to be credible, however, it was necessary that AEC proceed with its testing of the Sprint and Spartan warheads.

MILROW

Jorum was detonated on September 16, 1969, yielding about a megaton. A further high-yield test, Milrow, was scheduled for October. It was to be the first test at the new Amchitka site. Involving a Los Alamos device of known yield—about one megaton—Milrow's purpose was to calibrate instruments on Amchitka in preparation for a later, more powerful test of the Spartan warhead. Announcements of the forthcoming test evoked an extremely strong public reaction. It was so intense as to cause some wavering in the government about the yield of Milrow. At an executive meeting of the Joint Committee on April 22, Chairman Chet Holifield and other members suggested that it might be more judicious to seek to achieve the purposes of Milrow with a smaller test in order to still the clamor and to be more certain that there would not actually be a follow-on earthquake and/or tidal wave. (Amchitka was known to be a seismically active area.) In a letter to me dated May 17, Holifield suggested a yield of 570 kilotons. We in the AEC continued to argue that Milrow should remain at its planned magnitude in order to give meaningful information. But Deputy Defense Secretary Packard wrote to me on July 22 saying, to my surprise, that he now found the technical arguments for one yield or another weak in comparison with the political considerations. He urged that we keep open the possibility of using a lower-yield device.

The controversy over Milrow was considered on August 29 by the Under Secretaries Committee. Among those present were Under Secretary of State Elliot Richardson, chairing the committee as usual; Joint Chiefs Chairman Earle G. Wheeler; CIA Director Richard Helms; Under Secretary of Interior Russell Train; Deputy Secretary of Defense David Packard; and Acting Deputy Director of the Bureau of the Budget James Schlesinger.

> *Richardson asked me to summarize the issues. I described the risks involved, such as the possibility of triggering a large earthquake or tidal wave, and the ecological risks to bald eagles, sea otters, and peregrine falcons. I said that the likelihood of adverse consequences was minimal but that they could not be ruled out entirely. Train said that the Interior Department was satisfied with the precautions AEC had taken. Packard said that Defense supported the test and its planned yield unless a serious public relations problem developed, in which case he thought we might consider lowering the yield. Richardson raised a question about the date, which AEC had proposed be between October 3 and 15. I explained that October 1 was the earliest date we could be ready, but that I would be in Bucharest, Romania, on that date opening an AEC Atoms-in-Action exhibit. The reason for wanting to have the test before October 15 was that the Canadian Parliament was scheduled to reconvene on October 22 and it was thought best to present that body with a fait accompli.* * *It was decided to recommend widening the time range to October 1–20 in order to be*

---

* Canadian public opinion was adamantly hostile to U.S. testing on Amchitka. The Canadian government, while quite temperate in expressing its attitude to us, pointed out that while the test site was located "on an island extremity of the United States . . . such risk as there is might be particularly likely to affect Canada."

more sure of finding a day with the right weather and wind. There was a brief discussion of alternative sites, all of which seemed inferior to Amchitka. The question of public relations was raised and I described AEC's plans for bringing news people into Amchitka before and after the test, as well as for establishing an information center in Anchorage. The committee decided to recommend that the president approve the test as planned.

But controversy persisted about whether Milrow was safe. Washington senator Warren Magnuson wrote me on September 2 asking that the AEC consider postponing the test for a month or two while information as to its likely effects was more fully examined. He pointed out, correctly, that there were many unknowns about the Amchitka area. On September 10, Alaska senator Ted Stevens asked me whether we were granting Magnuson's request for a delay. He said that if we were granting it, he and Washington's other senator, Henry Jackson, wished to join in the request, but that otherwise they wouldn't do so. I told him that it was not possible to grant the request.

Another strong letter requesting deferral of Milrow came from Hawaii senator Daniel Inouye on September 11. He complained that the dates, size, and purpose of projected Amchitka tests were shrouded in secrecy. (Our inability for security reasons to reveal more about the purpose of the tests was a constant embarrassment.) He recounted the history of tsunamis (tidal waves) originating from earthquakes in the Aleutians, several of which had caused large losses of life and property damage in Hawaii. He contended, with some validity, that it was impossible to predict the exact effects of large tests and complained that the judgments about risk on which the AEC seemed to be relying were made by people involved with the test program. This was a point made also by Pitzer—that the risks were being examined in "closed circles with the effective judgment rendered by officials committed to the test program." Inouye pleaded that any upcoming "multi-megaton tests" on Amchitka be deferred pending an "independent" study to weigh more carefully "the possibility of devastation and death to the citizens of Hawaii."

On September 12 I discussed Milrow with Peter Flanigan of the White House staff. I said we needed a presidential approval within a day or two so that the device could go downhole in time to meet an October 1 readiness date. (Approval came four days later, while I was in Europe.) Flanigan and I agreed that the Pitzer panel report, along with an AEC explanatory statement, should be released before Milrow was fired.

Late in September, the Senate Foreign Relations Committee held a hearing on a resolution introduced by Senator Mike Gravel of Alaska calling for the establishment of a committee to review the "international implications of underground nuclear weapons testing." The list of witnesses, heavily weighted against nuclear tests, included Pitzer. Gravel himself was the most outspoken witness.* The entire Hawaiian congressional was present to express concern about tsunamis. There was large press attendance. Milrow went on October 2, despite a last-minute appeal by the foreign minister of Canada for a delay.† The decision to proceed was made at the White House. The test performed almost exactly as expected, yielding about a megaton and registering a seismic reading a little below 6.5, without follow-on earthquakes or tidal waves. Joint Committee chairman Holifield was on the island for the test and later broadcast a complimentary message over the Armed Forces Radio Network.

Proceeding with Milrow over objections such as had been raised by Senator Inouye and others was not an easy call for the AEC. We relied heavily on advice from eminent geologists and other scientists, most of whom, despite accusations to the contrary, seemed to us to be objective. Even so, there could be no certainty. There was indeed a limited risk that there would be follow-on seismic events. It was a degree of risk we would in all probability not have accepted for a civilian project.

DOUBTS ABOUT CANNIKIN

Handley, another test in the program to develop the Spartan warhead, was planned for late March 1970 at the Nevada Test Site. In preparation, steps were taken in February to strengthen the Bank of Nevada building in Las Vegas at government expense. This is another indication of how close to the edge we

---

* Gravel had begun in 1968 to seek a place on the Joint Committee, arguing that the committee should have at least one nuclear opponent. He continued this quest for eight years, but was consistently blocked by the leadership (*Congressional Quarterly Almanac*, 1976, p. 160). The issue became moot in 1977 when the Joint Committee was abolished.

† The Canadians noted that there had been an earthquake in California earlier in the day. Such quakes were generally followed within a day by tremors off the coast of British Columbia. They thought it almost inevitable that the Canadian public would blame the tremors on Milrow. The foreign minister therefore thought that holding off the test for a few days might be a wise political/public relations step.

were skating in developing this warhead. Handley, yielding more than a megaton, went off without major damage on March 26.

The AEC, already sorely beset in its public relations by the environmental opposition to nuclear power plants described in chapter 7, was becoming increasingly nervous about the clamor that was arising about weapons tests. In February 1970 I suggested to Deputy Defense Secretary Packard that we study again the possibility of developing a smaller warhead for the ABM in order to obviate the international and public relations problems attendant to testing the planned one. I thought these problems might escalate to the point where the president might feel he had to call off the additional tests needed. (A half-yield test of the Spartan warhead, Adagio, was scheduled for Nevada in October 1970, and the full-yield event, Cannikin, was slated for October 1971 on Amchitka.) Packard said he had raised this question with the president before Milrow and that the president had firmly directed we go ahead with the shot.

I raised the same question with Packard again a month later at a meeting also attended by Joint Chiefs chairman Wheeler. I suggested that congressional opposition might mount to the point where it was irresistible. For example, Senator Gravel was reported to be making plans to haul the AEC before a Public Works Subcommittee he headed to answer charges that the thirteen shots that had vented radioactivity into the atmosphere over the last six years might have violated the National Environmental Policy Act of 1969 (NEPA). Packard then offered to brief a number of senators on the need for high-yield testing in connection with the ABM, and I offered to furnish him with a list of key senators for that purpose.

Cannikin was considered by the Under Secretaries Committee on December 15. I was able to tell the committee that progress in development of the Spartan warhead had been so satisfactory that we had been able to cancel the two-megaton Adagio test. I then introduced to the committee three experts who, in turn, rated as negligible the risks that Cannikin would cause a damaging earthquake, a tsunami, or groundwater contamination. Russell Train, now chairman of the newly established Council on Environmental Quality, nevertheless expressed his continuing concern about these hazards and questioned us closely about the possibility of getting by with a smaller warhead or delaying the test. Dr. John Foster, director of defense research and engineering, expressing a harder Pentagon line than we had heard heretofore, said that it would not be possible to get by with a smaller warhead and that a delay was unacceptable. Unlike the situation when the Under Secretaries had considered Milrow, however, there was this time no favorable consensus. Under Secretary of State John Irwin,*

---

* Irwin had replaced Elliot Richardson, who became secretary of health, education, and welfare in June 1970.

presiding, merely concluded that Cannikin presented a very serious problem that the committee would have to consider again.

THE VENTING OF BANEBERRY

A complicating event occurred on December 18. As recorded in my diary:

> *A nuclear test of low yield (Baneberry), which was conducted at the Nevada Test Site today, vented and apparently released relatively large amounts of radioactivity in a large cloud. We received hour-by-hour reports on this cloud as it left the test site and traveled to neighboring states. Some 600 Test Site employees had to be evacuated and decontaminated. The event was reported in a sensational manner on the evening national TV news programs. This will clearly be a very troublesome matter.*

The venting of Baneberry continued to be featured the next day in large newspaper stories across the country. On December 21 we learned that the radiation count at Salt Lake City was substantially higher than usual. It appeared, however, that no member of the public had received a radiation exposure above the permitted standards. Investigation at the site revealed a large surface fissure (300 feet long and 20 feet wide) through which the radioactive products had been released. In order to reduce the probability of a recurrence, we decided to authorize no further tests in Nevada while investigation of Baneberry proceeded.

On February 1, 1971, the AEC commissioners were briefed by staff of the weapons laboratories on the results of the Baneberry review. The conclusion was that the venting had been caused by an abnormal geological condition that included an excess of water in the terrain surrounding the explosion site. Following the briefing session, the Commission met in executive session. I made the point that a situation had developed where the AEC took all the heat whenever anything went wrong in the testing program. I said I thought we should make it clear to the White House, State, Defense, the Environmental Protection Administration, and others involved that we could not guarantee that there would be no future venting. Armed with this information, those agencies should then share responsibility with the AEC in determining the necessity for further underground tests. We decided that we would proceed slowly, making a very careful evaluation involving geologists and interested people from other agencies before we made a decision to resume testing.

I reemphasized the need for caution in a conversation with Michael May, director of the Livermore laboratory, on February 22. I told him that even small on-site venting was likely now to cause a great deal of consternation, extending to the White House, and that I would have to prepare the White House for the probability of more venting.

Consideration now turned again to Cannikin. On February 23, 1971, some eight months in advance of the scheduled date for the test, the Canadian ambassador handed the United States a strong note requesting that the project be reconsidered. The note observed that "it would be imprudent to discount and impossible to eliminate completely an element of risk for Canadian territory." It concluded: "The anxieties stimulated by the testing on Amchitka reinforce the long-felt need for urgent measures to curtail underground testing by international agreement." The ambassador indicated that his government intended to make the note public.

THE NEED FOR CANDOR

The Canadian demarche, added to other public expressions of apprehension, moved me to write to Secretary of Defense Laird on March 2. I warned him that Cannikin might fail to receive final presidential approval unless problems of public reaction were resolved. To save the test, I said, it was "absolutely necessary to provide the public with some meaningful evidence of candor." Specifically, I recommended that two previously secret items of information be made public: the approximate yield of the device and its purpose. I appended some extracts to show that Soviet analysts could easily piece together the essential facts from unclassified information already available. Releasing the information would therefore not harm national security. It would, however, help enormously toward gaining public support. I concluded by suggesting that a public statement by the Department of Defense (DOD) in support of the weapons testing program as a whole would be valuable at that moment since we were planning soon to resume testing in Nevada, suspended after the Baneberry venting on December 18, 1970.

On March 4, 1971, Carl Walske, assistant for atomic energy to the secretary of defense, called me regarding my letter to Laird. He said that DOD people concerned with Cannikin wanted to preserve "an area of confusion" about the yield of the test to keep the Soviets guessing and suggested we state it as a "maximum credible" yield, somewhat larger than the expected yield. Also, there was still a reluctance to state Cannikin's purpose because of a fear that it might revive the domestic ABM debate. All that would do, he said, would be to transfer an AEC problem to DOD. I noted that the AEC was the only agency in government stating that testing was necessary. I asked again that DOD make a statement that continuation of the testing program was absolutely necessary for the security of the country and that this statement be issued at the time we resumed testing in Nevada.

The commissioners decided the next day to resume testing in Nevada but, to preclude another venting episode such as Baneberry, with changed procedures that closely and publicly involved the U.S. Geological Survey. I wrote Chairman Irwin of the Under Secretaries Committee, informing him of the decision to resume testing, explaining the Baneberry venting, and offering to meet with the committee if that was his wish. Irwin did so wish, and the meeting occurred on March 16. Major General Edward B. Giller, director of AEC's Division of Military Affairs, went over the Baneberry matter, including the reviews by three different committees, all of which agreed that the venting had been due to an unrecognized amount of water in the geologic environment. He also described AEC's new, more thorough evaluation procedures. I made the point, however, that no matter what we did, perhaps one in every seven to ten underground shots would vent and that when this occurred it would be highly publicized. Again I suggested that members of the administration be alerted to this and that they try not to be unduly alarmed when it happened.

I conveyed quite a different message to the directors of AEC's two weapons laboratories (Livermore and Los Alamos) when we met on March 25 preparatory to Joint Committee hearings on the AEC's 1972 budget. The message was that another venting like Baneberry would have an almost devastating effect on the future of the weapons testing program. Also, I called their attention to the increasing international pressure for a comprehensive or threshold test ban treaty and urged that in planning their programs they take into account the possibility of some such treaty within a year or two.*

On March 31, 1971, DOD's Walske called me again regarding declassification of the yield and purpose of Cannikin. He said there was no problem

---

* In one of his final acts as president, Nixon joined Soviet chairman Brezhnev on July 3, 1974, in signing the Threshold Test Ban Treaty limiting the yield of underground tests by the superpowers to 150 kilotons, far below the yield of tests that supported the Spartan missile. The treaty was not ratified until 1989, although both sides claimed to have observed its terms after its specified effective date of March 31, 1976.

about declassifying the yield but that there had been disagreement within the Pentagon about declassifying the purpose. He said that he and Director of Defense Research and Engineering John Foster wanted to go along with the AEC and disclose the purpose but that DOD legislative and public affairs people had demurred. Thereupon, two alternative letters to me had been laid before Packard and he had signed the one reflecting the views of the legislative and public affairs people. It said, in part:

> I feel that officially linking this shot with the Safeguard program could generate sufficient adverse Congressional and public reaction to jeopardize the entire Safeguard program. There could also be public affairs problems for the entire AEC underground testing program. In addition, there is the possibility of a public debate concerning the need for such a large yield for the SPARTAN . . . [I]t would be very difficult to make our position understood in an unclassified discussion. Therefore, I feel we should not elaborate on the purpose of CANNIKIN, saying that it is essential to national security.

But on March 16 the *Washington Post* (Thomas O'Toole) all but disclosed what DOD wanted concealed. Predicting that the yield would be five megatons, the article said: "While the AEC will not comment on the purpose of Cannikin, it is understood that it will be a test of an enlarged warhead for the Spartan ABM missile." It also quoted AEC studies as indicating that weapons yielding as much as 20 to 25 megatons could safely be tested on Amchitka.

The *Post*'s article led AEC to issue a clarifying public statement. We said that the Cannikin device would yield "less than five megatons." We disclosed that a group of AEC and weapons lab officials had visited Alaska the preceding week to meet with the governor, other state officials, newspaper publishers, and heads of civic organizations in principal Alaskan cities. There was also the softening information that the sea otter program would continue. The year's plans were to fly 60 or more otters to Oregon, adding to the more than 600 already transplanted to coastal areas.

A CASE OF JITTERS

The *Washington Post*'s article also elicited a reaction on the Senate floor on April 26 from Hubert Humphrey, the 1968 Democratic nominee for president. Humphrey stated that it was difficult to say with assurance what effects such a large test as Cannikin might have. He went on to challenge the necessity for the ABM and to urge instead that the United States be more responsive to Soviet and other international proposals for a comprehensive test ban and other steps to call a halt to the nuclear arms race. Such statements evoked a familiar ambivalent reaction in me. In my official capacity I wanted Cannikin to go forward. Privately, I agreed with what Humphrey was saying.

On April 30 I received a letter signed by eighteen senators, including Humphrey, stating that the National Environmental Policy Act required the AEC to file an environmental impact statement on Cannikin and calling also for public hearings in Alaska on the test. The signatories included the senators from Alaska, Hawaii, and Washington. The senators appeared not to have done their homework. I was able to point out in reply that we had issued a draft environmental statement a year before, had received comments on it, and had just completed a revised statement, which I enclosed. Further, in response to a request from Alaska's Governor William A. Egan, we had already scheduled hearings in Alaska.

The fact is that the AEC was doing a pretty good job in the public relations aspects of Cannikin. That, at least, was the conclusion of our General Advisory Committee (GAC) when it met in May. They added the following qualification, however:

> We note that there is a significant possibility that an earthquake might occur naturally following Cannikin. In this event, public reaction could seriously jeopardize future underground testing even though the earthquake was not related to the test. Such jeopardy might even extend to other AEC programs. While the AEC is aware of this situation, we feel it is very important that all concerned carefully weigh the gains of doing the test against this possibility.

I think this cautionary approach by the GAC reflects how jittery we all had become by this time about the overhanging threat to all AEC activities from an increasingly hostile public. This was not a concern we would have had ten, or even five, years earlier—before the environmental movement burst onto the scene in full vigor in 1969. In spite of the confident words we might utter in public, how some of us felt in private was mirrored by a conversation I had on June 9.

> *Commissioner Larson dropped in about 5:45, and we discussed the complicated question of whether there was any way of avoiding carrying out the Cannikin shot.*

The report of the Under Secretaries Committee on Cannikin came down on June 16. Whereas they had unequivocally recommended going ahead with

Milrow two years earlier, they were more cautious this time. (The greater strength gained by the environmental movement in the interim may well have explained the difference.) The committee began by listing a number of alternatives from which the president could choose. These ranged from canceling the test to going ahead as planned, with the concepts of reduced yield, an entirely different lower-yield warhead, and delay of the test for a year or two as intermediate possibilities. Pending the president's decision, the committee recommended that the Cannikin device be held in a readiness posture, possibly even downhole, but with the possibility of its being retrieved should the president decide to postpone or cancel the test. The report also recommended that the purpose of Cannikin be declassified, despite DOD's objections.

On July 19 I learned that Packard had relented and agreed to reveal Cannikin's purpose. By that time, of course, it was pretty much an open secret.

SEQUELS

On Sunday, August 1, 1971, after I had resigned from the AEC but before the resignation became effective, I was the guest on NBC's "Meet the Press" television program. To read the transcript of that interview today is extraordinarily revealing as to the number and depth of suspicions harbored about the AEC and its programs. I was on the defensive for virtually the entire broadcast. There was hardly a question that was not couched in the form of an accusation, often followed by a query such as "How do you justify that?" ("When did you stop beating your wife?") The first question about Cannikin reflected the lonely position the AEC had long occupied as apparently the only agency that favored the test.

> MR. [Howard] SIMONS [*Washington Post*] : The environmentalists aren't only worried about the civilian nuclear power program. They are also worried about the proposed five-megaton underground test on Amchitka Island and the AEC has been one of the agencies, we are told, that favors that test against advice from environmentalists in the government and the State Department and the President's own science advisers. What is your own feeling about it?
> DR. SEABORG: Well, the conduct of the Cannikin test is a matter of national policy. The AEC feels that this test can be carried out entirely safely and I personally feel, on the basis of all the studies that have been made, including the precursor Milrow test, in which the environmental effects came out almost precisely in the way that

Appearance on "Meet the Press," August 1, 1971. Interviewers, from left: John Finney (*New York Times*), Burt Schorr (*Wall Street Journal*), Howard Simons (*Washington Post*), and Irving R. Levine (NBC). On the right: host Lawrence E. Spivak and Seaborg.

had been predicted by the AEC, that the Cannikin test can be conducted safely and that there will not be any earthquake or tsunamis or release of radioactivity. I feel that so strongly that I would be willing to go up to Amchitka myself, my family, my friends—I just don't think there is any appreciable chance at all that anything untoward will happen.

Cannikin was detonated on November 6, 1971, with a yield reported by the AEC as "less than 5 megatons." Just as I had said I would be willing to be, my successor, James Schlesinger, was on the island, along with a member of his family. There was no detectable release of radioactivity. While there were seismic aftershocks, no large earthquake was triggered. Rockfalls occurred that were more numerous and severe than expected. Cracks in the tundra drained two small lakes. A few bald eagle and falcon nesting sites were destroyed. A year later it appeared that there had been no long-term bioenvironmental damage.

Cannikin was the last test conducted on Amchitka. Work to close down the testing facility began on July 1, 1972. It had been used for only two tests, Milrow and Cannikin. These were obviously enormously expensive tests. It was thought necessary to go to such extravagant lengths in order to have an ABM missile that would protect our offensive missiles against the possibility of a first-strike attack by the presumed antagonist with whom we were locked in such a deadly and wasteful embrace.

The 1974 ABM Treaty, as subsequently modified, permits each side to deploy up to 100 launchers and 100 interceptor missiles to protect one site, either the national capital or an ICBM launch area. The Soviet Union elected to continue its deployment around Moscow. The United States elected to continue a deployment that was under way at Grand Forks, North Dakota, to protect ICBM missiles located nearby. The deployment was completed in 1974 at an estimated cost for the one site that exceeded the $7 billion predicted by President Nixon for deployment at two sites. The system was deactivated in 1976, largely because it was considered ineffective. Subsequently, the Spartan missiles were placed in storage in Army depots and, still later, dismantled. The huge effort that went into their development and testing can stand as a monument to the futility and wastefulness of the nuclear arms race.

NOTE

1. For an account of this episode, see my book *Stemming the Tide: Arms Control in the Johnson Years*, pp. 238–43.

PART II

ARMS CONTROL

3

The Nonproliferation
Treaty

This treaty . . . is a triumph of sanity
and of man's will to survive.

—President Lyndon B. Johnson[1]

NEGOTIATION UNDER JOHNSON

The successful negotiation of the multilateral Nonproliferation Treaty
(NPT) was the crowning achievement of the Johnson administration in
arms control. The negotiation was a very arduous and complex process, made
so largely by the fact that while the superpowers were the treaty's principal
architects, its main objects were the nonnuclear weapon countries of the world.
The chief purpose of the treaty, from the superpowers' point of view, was to
make sure that the nonnuclears stayed that way. Added to the familiar task of
reconciling their own different approaches, therefore, the United States and the
Soviet Union in this case had the problem of overcoming the reservations,
anxieties, and suspicions of a large number of other countries. To accomplish
this, the superpowers had to accept some compromise treaty provisions that
were not entirely to their liking.[2]

The NPT's principal purposes are achieved by Article I, in which nuclear weapon states undertake not to transfer nuclear explosive devices, and by Article II, in which nonnuclear weapons states undertake not to acquire such devices. In Article III nonnuclear weapons states agree to assure, through safeguards agreements with the International Atomic Energy Agency (IAEA), that they will not divert nuclear materials from peaceful to military activities.* Nations with advanced nuclear programs agree in Article IV to assist the peaceful nuclear programs of other countries. In Article V nuclear weapons countries agree to provide a peaceful nuclear explosions service to non-weapons countries on a commercial basis.† In Article VI the nuclear powers undertake to pursue negotiations leading to an early termination of the nuclear arms race.

The two superpowers wanted the NPT to be of indefinite duration. The nonnuclears balked at this, hesitating to sentence themselves to inferior status in perpetuity and wishing to have some protection against the contingency that the nuclear powers might fail to live up to their obligations. Consequently, at the insistence of the nonnuclears, the duration of the treaty was limited to 25 years, after which the length of its extension must be approved by majority vote of a conference of the parties to the treaty. Since the treaty entered into force in 1970, that vote must be taken in 1995.

To hold an additional club over the nuclear powers, the nonnuclears obtained a provision for a review conference to be held after five years "with a view to assuring that the purposes of the Preamble and the provisions of the Treaty are being realized" and for further review conferences at five-year intervals if so voted by a majority of the parties.‡ Review conferences were indeed held in 1975, 1980, 1985, and 1990. A prominent feature of the conferences was a running disagreement between the superpowers and the nonnuclears

---

* The safeguards agreements involve a system of accounts, reporting requirements, audits, and on-site inspections applied to nuclear facilities by the IAEA to assure that the facilities are not being used to support nuclear explosive activities.

† Although this provision was crucial to acceptance of the treaty by a number of nations interested at the time in peaceful nuclear explosions, it is now generally agreed to be obsolete and inoperative.

‡ The particular clause of the preamble that the nonnuclears had mostly in mind was the one that read: "Recalling the determination expressed by the Parties to the 1963 [Limited Test Ban] Treaty in its preamble to seek to achieve the discontinuance of all test explosions of nuclear weapons for all time and to continue negotiations to this end."

about whether the former's lack of progress toward a comprehensive test ban agreement did not constitute a failure to comply with Article VI.

CONSENT TO U.S. RATIFICATION

The Nonproliferation Treaty was opened for signature in Washington, London, and Moscow on July 1, 1968, by the United States, the United Kingdom, and the Soviet Union, the three "depositary governments." Sixty-five other countries signed on that first day, including, incidentally, Iraq. Instruments of ratification were deposited by only three, however: Ireland, Nigeria, and the United Kingdom. The Senate Foreign Relations Committee (SFRC) held hearings on the NPT later that same month. I testified for the treaty, along with Secretary of State Dean Rusk, Deputy Secretary of Defense Paul Nitze, ACDA Director William C. Foster, Congressman Chet Holifield (D-CA), Congressman Craig Hosmer (R-CA), Edward Teller, and others. Holifield and Hosmer represented the views of the Joint Committee on Atomic Energy, of which Holifield was at that time vice-chairman. On September 17, 1968, the SFRC, by a vote of 13 to 3, with three abstentions, recommended that the Senate consent to ratification. The full Senate, however, bearing in mind the recent invasion of Czechoslovakia by the Soviet Union and the fact that it was a presidential election year, voted on October 11 to postpone action. Presidential candidate Richard Nixon was among those who opposed action on the treaty as long as Soviet troops were on Czechoslovak soil. President Johnson briefly considered calling Congress back into special session in December to vote on the treaty but gave up on the idea when then President-elect Nixon refused to concur.

On February 5, 1969, President Nixon resubmitted the NPT to the Senate in a statement that again condemned the Soviet action in Czechoslovakia but said that it was "time to move forward" in accord with his administration's policy of "negotiation rather than confrontation."[3] But Nixon's support of nonproliferation seemed to be mingled with some doubts. During the election campaign in 1968, he had deplored the failure of the NPT to permit transfer of "defensive nuclear weapons."[4] On the same day that now-President Nixon resubmitted the treaty to the Senate, Henry Kissinger circulated within the administration a National Security Decision Memorandum that stated:

> The president directed that, associated with the decision to proceed with the United States' ratification of the Nonproliferation Treaty, there should be no efforts by the United States government to

pressure other nations, particularly the Federal Republic of Germany, to follow suit. The government, in its public posture, should reflect a tone of optimism that other countries will sign or ratify, while clearly disassociating itself from any plan to bring pressure on these countries to sign or ratify.[5]

Morton Halperin, who worked on Henry Kissinger's staff, has said that "Nixon and Kissinger didn't believe in the treaty. Henry believed it was good to spread nuclear weapons around the world." Kissinger's thinking was reported to be that "most of the major powers would eventually obtain nuclear weapons and the United States could benefit more by helping them in such efforts than by participating in an exercise of morality."*

As the second set of Senate Foreign Relations Committee hearings on the NPT drew near, a problem arose involving Senator George Aiken (R-VT). He was concerned about Article V, which stipulated that in providing a peaceful nuclear explosions service, the providing country's charge to the recipient country must be "as low as possible and exclude any charge for research and development." Aiken's fear was that in order to provide the explosive devices more cheaply, virtually all costs would be classified as R and D and the United States would end up with very heavy expenditures. The senator had expressed a similar concern during the 1968 SFRC hearings. At that time he complained that Article V could be construed in such a manner that American taxpayers would end up subsidizing the use of nuclear explosives by international oil and mining companies to search for new mineral deposits. In response, ACDA director William Foster had written to Aiken assuring him that Article V would not commit the United States to support any such ventures.[6] This appeared to assuage the senator's concerns temporarily, and he voted for the treaty in committee in 1968. But now, in 1969, his suspicions seemed to have resurfaced.

At a dinner that Aiken and I attended on February 5, 1969, he told me there would not be an NPT unless his renewed concerns were satisfied. On February 10, Under Secretary of State Elliot Richardson called me from Brookline, Massachusetts, where he was snowed in.

---

* Hersh, *The Price of Power*, p. 148. Another who at one time doubted that a nonproliferation treaty was all that great an idea was Dean Rusk. At a Committee of Principals meeting in June 1964 I heard him say he "wasn't sure we might not want to give India and Japan nuclear weapons after China attained them" (Seaborg, *Stemming the Tide*, p. 132). Later, however, after President Johnson made a strong personal commitment to the treaty, Rusk worked strenuously and effectively on its behalf.

Richardson said that Gerard Smith and Adrian Fisher [the top two in ACDA] were concerned that, unless Aiken's worries were met, ratification of the treaty could indeed be jeopardized. It was thought that Aiken, by virtue of his memberships in both the Senate Foreign Relations and Joint Atomic Energy committees, could influence as many as ten senators. Richardson read me two paragraphs from a communication they were sending me, hoping I could use this language to reassure Aiken, perhaps by letter. I warned Richardson that if we reassured Senator Aiken publicly we had to be careful that we did not in the process sound so negative about helping other countries with peaceful nuclear explosions as to scare off countries like Brazil and India, who were interested in benefitting from the technology and were on the fence about ratifying the treaty.

I called Senator Aiken at his home in Vermont the following day.

I told the senator that I thought we could work things out to his satisfaction. He said he wanted a ceiling on the costs the U.S. would have to bear under Article V. I said that the transactions would be on a strictly commercial basis, with full-cost recovery except for research and development, and that we would not be obligated by the treaty to carry out any additional R and D. He said that sounded good.

I sent Aiken a letter conveying these assurances, and learned from State and ACDA sources that it satisfied him. I'm not sure that the threat of his displeasure was as great as had been represented, but it certainly didn't hurt to have him favorably disposed toward the treaty.

The Foreign Relations Committee's second hearings on the NPT took place on February 18 and 20, 1969. I appeared jointly with Secretary of State William P. Rogers and the ACDA team of Gerard C. Smith and Adrian S. Fisher.* As had been true in the 1968 hearings, most of the questions the senators asked seemed to focus on whether implementation of the treaty would adversely affect U.S. security or finances. Thus, the day I testified there was repeated need for witnesses to reassure senators about what the treaty would *not* do, for example:

---

* I also testified on February 28, 1969, before the Senate Military Affairs Committee in closed hearings on the treaty's military implications. That testimony focused on the safeguards and inspection procedures under Article III.

- that it would not adversely affect existing defense alliances
- that it did not create any new security commitment
- that it would not require the United States, under its offer to place certain peaceful nuclear facilities under IAEA safeguards, to accept an IAEA inspector of Soviet origin
- that it would not require U.S. military facilities to be inspected
- that it carried with it no pledge by the nuclear powers not to use nuclear weapons
- that it did not prohibit the United States from deploying its nuclear weapons on the soil of another country
- that it did not prohibit the United States from stockpiling nuclear weapons in its own territory
- that the fact that the Soviets seemed eager to enter into the treaty did not mean it was to their advantage and our disadvantage

Despite the various misgivings, there never seemed to be any doubt that the treaty would be recommended by the Foreign Relations Committee and approved by the required two-thirds vote of the full Senate. Its prior recommendation by a president of each party seemed to assure that. The committee's vote was 14 to 0, an improvement over the previous year's 15 to 3 vote. The full Senate gave its consent to ratification on March 13, 1969, by a vote of 83 to 15. Voting in opposition were eight Republicans, all from the South and West, and seven southern Democrats.

CHICKEN AND EGG

For many another treaty, approval by the U.S. Senate would have meant that the treaty was ready to enter into force, requiring only a pro-forma signature of ratification by the president. That was far from being the case with the NPT, whose Article IX stipulated that the treaty would enter into force only when the 3 depositary governments and 40 others had deposited instruments of ratification. As of the date the Senate acted, 86 nations had signed the treaty, but only 8 had ratified it. Many countries seemed to be waiting to take their cues on ratification from the actions of the superpowers, neither of whom had ratified. For their part, the Soviets had indicated an intent not to ratify the treaty until the United States did so.

The issue of when the United States should ratify the treaty was discussed at a meeting of the National Security Council Subcommittee (later known as the Under Secretaries Committee) on May 1, 1969. Under Secretary of State Elliot Richardson presided. The attendance, unusually stellar for this group, included, among others, National Security Adviser Henry Kissinger, CIA director Richard Helms, Joint Chiefs of Staff chairman Earle G. Wheeler, Deputy Defense Secretary David Packard, and ACDA director Gerard C. Smith.

> *Richardson indicated that the U.S. faces a dilemma as to whether it should ratify before the Soviet Union does. Germany believes strongly that we should not go first, fearing that the Soviets might then challenge U.S. interpretations of the treaty to Germany's disadvantage. Apparently the Germans themselves do not intend to ratify until after their elections in September. Thus, the issue we face is whether we should continue to tie our actions to those of the Soviets, considering that the Soviets may decide to delay until Germany signs.*
>
> *Smith said that, since the Germans may wait until September, we should perhaps make another effort with the Soviets for a simultaneous superpower ratification before then. He added, however, that the Soviets think the U.S. made a commitment to deliver the German ratification before the Soviets ratify. Richardson observed aptly that we are thus faced with a chicken-and-egg situation.*
>
> *Another factor in the mix is the prospective beginning of SALT talks. Richardson said that Leonard Meeker (State's general counsel) had made the legal interpretation that signing the NPT ratification papers and depositing them could be separate actions. Thus, it might be possible to sign the papers simultaneously with the Soviets, perhaps tying the action to the announcement of SALT talks, and then not deposit the papers until such talks actually began. But Kissinger said he didn't think that ratification should be tied in with SALT because the president wasn't ready yet to commit himself to such talks. He said we might have another look at this possible tie-in when the president definitely decides to go ahead with SALT.*
>
> *As the meeting was breaking up, I suggested that the treaty could be jeopardized if many months went by without U.S., Soviet, or German ratification, and that we might consider unilateral signing of the ratification papers, withholding deposit until there was some action by the Soviets.*

The best characterization of this jumbled and frustrating situation was one made by ACDA's Adrian Fisher. He likened it to "an old Tennessee law that was once passed. It says if two trains meet at a grade crossing both must stop and neither shall proceed until the other has passed."[7]

BREAKING THE LOGJAM

The subject of Soviet intentions came up in a discussion between ACDA director Gerard Smith and Rolf Pauls, German ambassador to the United States, on July 8. Pauls said that some outstanding issues needed clarification before Germany would sign the NPT. They were trying, for example, to obtain from the Soviets an exchange of renunciation-of-force declarations. He also reported that Soviet ambassador Dobrynin had told him that German signature was not a precondition to Soviet action, although it would be a consideration. Smith said that the Soviets were "employing their usual double-talk" as to their NPT intentions, obviously believing they could exert more pressure on Germany and other non-signatories by this means. Smith added that we thought this was a short-sighted policy and had told the Soviets so.[8]

A breakthrough of sorts occurred early in November 1969 when Willy Brandt, newly installed after the elections as chancellor of West Germany, pledged to sign the NPT. That apparently removed the Soviet Union's last hesitation and started the wheels moving for a simultaneous signing of ratification instruments by the superpowers. This occurred on November 24. There was still a distance to travel at that point before the treaty could enter into force, however, since only 23 of the required additional 40 nations had deposited their ratifications. Nevertheless, as Secretary of State Rogers announced after the signing ceremony, the plan was to deposit the U.S. and Soviet ratifications "in a couple of weeks."

It didn't happen that way. It was decided instead to wait until the requisite 40 nations had ratified, at which point—the United Kingdom having already deposited its ratification—ratification by the two superpowers would usher the treaty into force. This occurred on March 5, 1970. The White House ceremony was attended by legislative leaders and by officials of both the Johnson and Nixon administrations. (The Johnson administration was represented by former Secretary of State Dean Rusk and by former ACDA head William C. Foster. Johnson himself was invited but had to decline because of illness.)

THE NUCLEAR POWERS ACCEPT SAFEGUARDS

Even though technically "in force" after March 5, 1970, the NPT was not being fully implemented in the absence of the safeguards agreements prescribed by Article III. As of that date there were no such agreements in effect, nor had the IAEA adopted a safeguards system that it could recommend to a nation that wished to conclude an agreement. To understand the safeguards impasse one must go back to the negotiations on the treaty during the Johnson administration. To begin with, a number of industrialized countries had then expressed serious concern about the prospect of IAEA safeguards. They feared commercial disadvantage if the inspection procedures interfered with operations or if the inspectors were nationals of a commercial rival. There was also a concern about security disadvantage if the inspectors were nationals of a potential adversary. It was noted further that three powerful competitors for peaceful nuclear business, the United States, Great Britain and France, seemed likely to gain a competitive advantage over other industrial countries because, being nuclear weapons states, they would not be subject to safeguards under the treaty. It was to assuage these latter concerns that the United States in December 1967 offered voluntarily to place its own peaceful atomic energy activities under IAEA safeguards, President Johnson stating: "I want to make it very clear to all the world that we in the United States are not asking any country to accept safeguards that we are unwilling to accept ourselves." The British followed with a matching offer two days after the president's announcement.

While in Vienna for the IAEA General Conference in September 1969, Myron Kratzer, AEC's assistant general manager for international affairs, and I raised with chief Soviet delegate Igor Morokhov the question of the Soviet Union following American and British example and offering to place some of its peaceful nuclear facilities under IAEA safeguards. The apparent unwillingness of the Soviets to do this had been a source of criticism in the United States. Joint Committee chairman Chet Holifield, for example, had stated the issue quite bluntly in a letter to me:

> It seems to me that it is time to let other nuclear powers increase their share of the burden of supporting the IAEA safeguards program. In this connection would you advise the Committee if the United States or the IAEA is pursuing the issue of getting the USSR to open its facilities to IAEA inspection in the same manner as the U.S. has done.

During a visit to the United States by a Soviet scientific delegation in April 1971, the Seaborgs hosted a reception for the visitors at our home in Washington. A number of gifts were exchanged in a very relaxed atmosphere. From left, V. F. Menshikov; Andronik M. Petrosyants (chairman of the State Committee for the Utilization of Atomic Energy); the author; R. Lavroff; Helen, Lynne, and Eric Seaborg. Through a number of such visits and many other exchanges, very cordial relations were achieved between Soviet and American scientists. I am persuaded that this bond acted as a moderating influence amid the Cold War tensions.

Morokhov's answer was that the Soviet Union was against following the U.S. example as a matter of principle; they thought it would contribute nothing to the prevention of proliferation and would merely waste the time of IAEA personnel. But when Kratzer pointed out that IAEA personnel could gain very useful training by actual practice at a nuclear plant, Morokhov said that offering such training at a Soviet plant might be a possibility; he wouldn't rule it out. In time, the Soviets followed through on this semi-commitment; an agreement placing one research reactor and one power reactor in the Soviet Union under IAEA safeguards entered into force in February 1985.

SAFEGUARDS FOR EURATOM

The safeguards problem was particularly acute with respect to the six member countries of the European Atomic Energy Community (Euratom): Belgium, France, Italy, Luxembourg, the Netherlands, and West Germany. They preferred to retain an inspection system of their own that had been in force for some years and contended during the NPT negotiations that the existence of the Euratom safeguards system obviated the need for IAEA controls on their territories. In this they had some support from the U.S. State Department. But the idea was a red flag to the Soviet Union, one of whose primary motives in seeking an NPT was to prevent the acquisition of nuclear weapons by West Germany. The Soviets refused to accept Euratom safeguards, which they termed "self-inspection," as a substitute for IAEA safeguards. Eventually, compromise language was adopted for Article III stipulating that all nonnuclear nations signing the treaty had to negotiate safeguards agreements with IAEA, but that this could be done "either individually or together with other States." This was interpreted to mean that data developed by Euratom safeguards could be used so long as the IAEA satisfied itself independently, through an agreement with Euratom, that the information was valid. Each of the Euratom countries made it clear upon signing the treaty that it would not deposit its ratification until after the successful negotiation of such a Euratom-IAEA agreement. Here we encountered another chicken-egg relationship. Euratom countries were in no hurry to conclude a safeguards agreement, waiting to see what commercial rivals would do. On the other hand, Sweden and Japan were hanging back from accepting IAEA safeguards until it was clear what the Euratom countries would do. At the meeting of the NSC Under Secretaries Committee on May 1, 1969:

I suggested that the United States take the initiative to resolve the difficult IAEA-Euratom safeguards relationship since otherwise no progress would be made. Richardson suggested this was a matter of our encouraging the Euratom countries but not leaning on them, and Kissinger agreed this was the way it must be done.

IMPLEMENTATION OF SAFEGUARDS

There was in fact no need to lean on the Euratom countries just yet because the IAEA still did not have ready a safeguards system on which to begin negotiations with the community. The IAEA did have a safeguards system that it applied to a country's entire peaceful nuclear program when specifically requested to do so by parties to a bilateral or multilateral agreement. The United States, for example, used that IAEA system to police most of the bilateral agreements under which it had provided assistance in the peaceful uses of atomic energy to other countries since President Eisenhower started the Atoms for Peace program in 1954. It was recognized, however, that the safeguards system used to police bilateral agreements did not accord in all respects with the criteria set forth in Article III of the NPT. Accordingly, on the very date, March 5, 1970, when the NPT entered into force, the IAEA established a Safeguards Committee for the purpose of producing a new guide to be followed in negotiating agreements under the treaty. The AEC's Myron Kratzer represented the United States on the committee and took a leading part, perhaps *the* leading part, in its deliberations.

It took a full year and 82 meetings before the committee completed its assignment. Some 50 IAEA members sent representatives to one or more of the meetings. A key issue discussed at a meeting in February 1971 was whether the agreements should permit IAEA to make unannounced inspections. There was some opposition to this idea, but the U.S. delegation took the lead in arguing for it, and it was approved. In March 1971 the committee produced a document entitled "The Structure and Content of Agreements between the Agency and States Required in Connection with the Treaty on the Nonproliferation of Nuclear Weapons." This guide has been followed in all IAEA safeguards agreements with NPT parties, including that with Euratom.

The full year's delay between the NPT's entry into force and the conclusion of an IAEA safeguards guide set back the timetable for implementing the treaty. In fact, the first IAEA safeguards agreement under the NPT, with Finland, did not officially enter into force until February 9, 1972.[9] Negotiations on an IAEA-Euratom safeguards agreement did not begin until November 1971, and one was not signed until April 1973. The Euratom countries, France excepted, deposited their NPT ratifications on May 2, 1975. Japan followed suit thirteen months later. At that point, the conditions laid down by President Johnson for implementation of the U.S. offer—that it would only be implemented "when safeguards are applied under the treaty"—appeared to be satisfied. Accordingly, negotiations began on a U.S.-IAEA agreement. It was signed in Vienna on November 18, 1977, ratified by the Senate on July 2, 1980, and entered into force on December 9, 1980. In order not to overwhelm the IAEA staff, safeguards under the agreement are applied at any one time only to a small number of facilities, selected by the IAEA from a list submitted by the United States.

TRAVELING SALESMAN

As a militant supporter of the NPT, the AEC sought to facilitate the treaty's acceptance within the world community whenever an opportunity presented itself. Several times during my travels I tried to overcome the resistance of leaders of other governments. In so doing I was exposed to a variety of views that helped to explain why the NPT has been from the first a treaty in some degree of trouble.

In September 1969 I was asked by Sigvard Eklund, IAEA's director general, to contact Sweden's prime minister, Tage Erlander, in an effort to speed that country's ratification of the treaty. (Sweden had signed in August 1968.) Eklund knew that I would be in Stockholm attending a Nobel symposium and that I had had several prior contacts with Erlander. In my conversation with the prime minister I explained to him the hope of the United States that Sweden would ratify the NPT promptly because in view of Sweden's traditional leadership in disarmament matters, this might help in getting others to follow suit. Erlander, commenting that Sweden had perhaps an exaggerated idea of its own importance, said that they had held back hoping that they could thereby "blackmail" West Germany into ratifying. He also commented somewhat pointedly that neither the United States nor the Soviet Union had yet ratified. I noted that the U.S. Senate had at that point approved ratification but explained that we also wished to encourage the Germans and believed much might be achieved along that line if we and the Soviets ratified together. So we were, in essence, waiting for the Soviets. Erlander next said that Alva

Myrdal, Sweden's disarmament representative, now believed Sweden's delay was not likely to influence the West Germans into acceding and that she regretted the delay.* He said that Sweden would ratify the NPT "in the same moment" that it became known that the superpowers were going to ratify. I then told the prime minister that it would be helpful for Sweden to ratify *before* the United States and the Soviet Union did. Erlander, with apparent interest, then asked, "Do you think so?" and when I assured him that prompt Swedish ratification would help, asked his staff to check further into this. Sweden ultimately deposited its ratification on January 9, 1970, more than a month after the superpowers signed the instruments of ratification, but some two months before they deposited them.

On October 2, 1969, while still on my European trip, I met in Lisbon with members and officials of Portugal's Nuclear Energy Board. One official (Nogueira da Costa) indicated that Portugal would feel a lack of security in renouncing the use of nuclear weapons while there were hostile neighbors (Zambia and Tanzania) on the borders of its territories in Africa. He felt that the growing influence of China in these neighboring countries was particularly menacing. He suggested the need for a quid pro quo, namely, an informal assurance that the United States would protect the African territories if, after Portugal joined the NPT, they were attacked with nuclear weapons by a non-signatory country (meaning China). I responded that there was undoubtedly a risk in signing the treaty due to world circumstances. I argued, however, that the risks of nuclear attack would be greater for a nation that did not sign the treaty than for one that did. I thought that if every nation would sign the treaty this would itself provide a quid pro quo: greater security for all. Portugal, ruled at the time by a repressive, military-dominated government, delayed its accession to the treaty until December 1977.

On a trip to Japan in March 1970 I urged in separate meetings with government and industry officials that Japan follow up its signing of the NPT, which had occurred the previous month, with speedy ratification. Foreign Minister Kiichi Aichi and others made it clear that Japan's ratification hinged on the development of safeguards arrangements that would be satisfactory to Japanese industry. They were concerned that the IAEA safeguards system would be too complex and intrusive, hampering industrial operations and

---

* The issue here may well have had to do with the fact that once a nation became a party to the treaty it could no longer export nuclear items to countries not under IAEA safeguards. Countries like Sweden and Switzerland were therefore eager to see Germany and other Euratom countries ratify the treaty so that nuclear commerce with them could continue.

imposing a financial burden. In addition, they were concerned that safeguards applied to Japan might place it at an economic disadvantage relative to the Euratom member states. I said that the United States shared Japan's interest in having a simple system, since we also would have facilities under safeguards. Japan delayed depositing its ratification until June 1976, more than a year after the Euratom countries deposited theirs.

On September 20, 1971, after I had left the AEC, I held a wide-ranging conversation with President Nicolae Ceauşescu of Romania.* After he spoke in favor of greater cooperation between the United States and Romania, I described the just completed Fourth Geneva Conference on Peaceful Uses of Atomic Energy and the related cooperation among many nations in this field. He observed that this was all very well but that the important problems of the world had more to do with nuclear weapons and the lack of progress in controlling and reducing them. I then emphasized the importance of the NPT and expressed satisfaction that Romania had already signed (July 1, 1968) and ratified (February 4, 1970) the treaty. He acknowledged that this had some value but went on to say that Romania's decision to refrain from developing nuclear weapons applied only as a "current posture." When I questioned his meaning on this he said that it would be necessary for the nuclear weapons states to make some progress in limitation or cutback of nuclear weapons, because otherwise countries like Romania would themselves have to adopt the option of producing nuclear weapons. Ceauşescu also pointed out that certain critical countries had not yet ratified the NPT and named India, Brazil, Japan, South Africa, Germany, and Israel. I agreed with his list as including most of the critical absentees and said it was important somehow to convince these countries to change their stands. He said that, as is usually the case when it comes to breaking a monopoly, it would be necessary for more countries first to acquire nuclear weapons. I denied there was any analogy to breaking economic monopolies and argued that the prevention of more proliferation had to come first in order to make a cutback by the superpowers manageable. Ceauşescu disagreed; he said it should be the other way around: the cutbacks by the superpowers should come first in order to make manageable the renunciation of nuclear weapons by others. Chicken and egg again!

---

* This conversation looms larger in memory in light of the December 1989 revolution in which Ceauşescu was overthrown and subsequently executed along with his wife.

On September 20, 1971, I held a wide-ranging conversation with the ill-fated president of Romania, Nicolae Ceausescu, shown at right. The man at center was an interpreter. Having shown a modicum of independence from the Soviet Union, Ceausescu was being courted by the United States at the time. President Nixon had paid him a visit the preceding month.

At a reception during the 1970 General Conference of the International Atomic Energy Agency given by IAEA Director General Sigvard Eklund, far left, and V. A. Sarabhai of India, president of the Conference, far right. Also shown are the Seaborgs, Austrian Chancellor Bruno Kreisky, and Mrs. Eklund. The AEC was a strong supporter of the IAEA. I led the U.S. delegations to all the General Conferences from 1961 to 1971, the last one occurring after I had left the AEC.

SEQUELS

With the end of the Cold War, nonproliferation has increasingly been recognized as the foremost arms control challenge of the 1990s. As of late 1992 the NPT had over 150 parties, the most for any arms control agreement. Changing political realities have recently induced some important holdouts to change their position. South Africa deposited its ratification on July 10, 1991. China followed suit on March 9, 1992. France, which had pledged from the first that it would behave as if it were a party, became one on August 3, 1992. As of late 1992 Brazil and Argentina had not joined the NPT, contending that it was discriminatory.* They did, however, on December 13, 1991, sign a joint agreement with the IAEA under which safeguards equivalent to those in NPT agreements are to be applied to all their nuclear activities. They have also agreed to ratify the Treaty of Tlatelolco, which designates Latin America as a nuclear weapon-free zone.

There are still significant holdouts, technically advanced countries that are thought to be moving toward at least a primitive nuclear weapons capability. As of this writing (late 1992) concern is focused on India, Pakistan, and Israel, none of whom has signed the NPT. The India-Pakistan rivalry continues to be an ominous one, with both parties seeming quite clearly to have the components with which to assemble a number of nuclear weapons. Israel is a case apart in that it is believed already to have a modest arsenal of fairly sophisticated weapons and the means of delivering them.† Concern has also been felt about North Korea and Iran. North Korea, which signed the NPT in 1986, dragged its feet about completing and ratifying a safeguards agreement, thus being in default on its treaty obligations. It signed an agreement in January 1992 after months of intense international pressure; the agreement entered into force on April 10, 1992.[10] Iran, an NPT party with a safeguards agreement, is nevertheless suspected by some of having clandestine, undeclared programs. There is also still lingering uncertainty about the disposition of some of the former Soviet Union's weapons that were deployed outside Russia and about the future

---

* Their principal complaints were (1) that the failure of the major powers to disarm embodies a double standard with respect to nuclear weapons, and (2) that the major powers (principally the United States) have used the NPT to block the aspirations of nations like themselves to achieve equality in nuclear technology.

† Estimates of the size of Israel's arsenal range from 100 to 300 weapons (Center for Defense Information, *Defense Monitor* 21, no. 3 [1992], p. 3).

activities of the many former Soviet scientists and technicians, some of whom may be subject to tempting offers from nuclear aspirants.

The fact that proliferation threats continue has stirred some misgivings about the adequacy of the NPT. A singular case of apparent NPT failure involved Iraq, which was revealed after the Gulf War to have been conducting an ambitious program to develop a nuclear weapons capability despite having been subject to a number of IAEA inspections under the NPT. As to this, I would offer the following:

1. It is true that IAEA safeguards, *as administered,* failed to disclose Iraq's undeclared activities. As noted earlier, IAEA had the power under the NPT to inspect undeclared facilities, but hung back from doing so. Largely, in consequence of the Iraq experience, IAEA has already moved aggressively to correct this deficiency.
2. The failure in Iraq was a failure of intelligence, not simply, or primarily, of safeguards. One cannot inspect something if one doesn't know it exists.
3. Being a party to the NPT made it necessary for Iraq to conduct its clandestine activities underground, greatly increasing their cost and time scale. Also, the fact that Iraq was in violation of its NPT obligations made it much easier following the Gulf War to obtain an international consensus for physically dismantling Iraq's program.

Largely in consequence of the Iraq experience, steps have been or are being taken to strengthen the nonproliferation regime, such as by:

- tightening up on nuclear commerce (keeping tabs, for example, on dual-use items that have been sold)
- carrying out safeguards agreements to the letter, even if this means that IAEA's resources must be increased
- restricting the use of weapons-grade nuclear materials in civilian facilities such as research reactors
- establishing international controls over the nuclear material in dismantled warheads
- broadening the coverage of the nonproliferation regime to cover not only "nuclear explosive devices," the currency of the NPT, but all weapons of mass destruction and their means of delivery

The nonproliferation regime would also benefit significantly from corollary arms control measures, such as a permanent ban on nuclear testing (see below), further deep cuts in nuclear arsenals, and the cessation of all further production of weapons-grade materials.

THE TEST BAN FACTOR

For some years there has been doubt about the fate of the Nonproliferation Treaty when it comes up for renewal in 1995. This has been based primarily on the claim by nonnuclear signatories that the nuclear powers failed to live up to their Article VI commitment to make progress in bringing the nuclear arms race to an end. What the nonnuclears have emphasized as a touchstone of compliance with Article VI is the achievement of, or at least the undertaking of serious negotiations toward, a comprehensive test ban treaty (CTBT). When both the Reagan and Bush administrations backed away from such negotiations, there was a tide of resentment among the nonnuclears that made an unfavorable vote on the NPT in 1995 a distinct possibility.

As of late 1992, however, the situation had changed considerably. Both France and Russia had declared temporary moratoria on testing while making clear that whether the moratoria would be extended depended on the U.S. response. In September 1992 Congress attached a rider to an energy-water appropriations bill suspending all U.S. tests through June 1993, allowing only fifteen tests through September 1996 (almost all for safety purposes), and then banning all further U.S. tests unless a foreign country resumed testing. President Bush signed the legislation on October 2, 1992, stating, however, that, if reelected, he would seek a reversal of its test ban provisions. Following the president's action, the Russian moratorium, which was to have expired in October 1992, was extended for another eight months.

The election of Bill Clinton, who has announced that he favors a CTBT,[12] greatly enhances the prospects for such a treaty. A possible mechanism for achieving a CTBT is through a provision in the Limited Test Ban Treaty (LTBT) that states that a conference to consider amendments to the treaty must be convened if requested by one-third or more of the parties. A proposed amendment would then enter into force if ratified by a majority of the parties, including all three of the "original parties" (the United States, the United Kingdom, and Russia as successor to the Soviet Union). Such a conference was convened in January 1991 to consider an amendment converting the LTBT into a CTBT. Primarily because of opposition by the United States, however, the conference took no action other than to agree to reconvene at some later date. The Parliamentarians for Global Action, an international organization of national legislators, has taken the lead in late 1992 in urging Ali Alatas, foreign minister of Indonesia and president of the amendment conference, to reconvene the conference in 1993, the 30th anniversary of the LTBT. Should that take place, there would be every prospect (because of the changed position of the United States) that the proposed amendment would be approved.

Even should the movement for a comprehensive test ban treaty fail, nonnuclear NPT parties can no longer justifiably complain that Russia and the United States are failing to live up to their commitments under Article VI (disarmament) in view of the sweeping cuts agreed to in the Strategic Arms Reduction Treaties signed in July 1991 (START I) and January 1993 (START II). Accordingly, it is highly likely that the NPT will receive a very favorable vote at its 1995 renewal conference.

NOTES

1. Letter transmitting Nonproliferation Treaty to the Senate, July 9, 1968.
2. I have described these negotiations in some detail in my book, *Stemming the Tide.*
3. U.S. Arms Control and Disarmament Agency, *Documents on Disarmament,* 1969 , pp. 33-34.
4. Hersh, *The Samson Option,* p. 209.
5. Quoted in Hersh, *The Price of Power,* p. 148.
6. *Congressional Quarterly 1969,* p. 166.
7. Senate Foreign Relations Committee, *NPT Hearings,* 1969, p. 353.
8. ACDA Memorandum of Conversation, July 8, 1969.
9. Stockholm International Peace Research Institute, *SIPRI Yearbook—1979,* cited in Congressional Research Service, *Nuclear Proliferation Factbook,* 1980 p. 398.
10. *Arms Control Today,* May 1992, p.18.
11. *New York Times,* September 26, 1992, p. 1; *Washington Post,* September 26, 1992, p. 1.
12. *Arms Control Today,* March 1992, p. 6.

4

SALT

In cases of defense 'tis best to weigh
The enemy more mighty than he seems.

—William Shakespeare, *Henry V* (III, 4)

BEGINNINGS UNDER JOHNSON

In December 1966, when President Johnson was beset by powerful political
pressure to deploy an antiballistic missile (ABM) system, he convened a
meeting of distinguished defense experts to advise him on the essential questions: Would the existing U.S. technology (NIKE-X) work, and should it be
deployed?* Assured that both answers were "No," the president wrote to Soviet
Premier Aleksey N. Kosygin in January 1967 setting forth the imperative need
to "curb the strategic arms race" lest both sides incur "colossal costs without
substantially enhancing the security of our own peoples or contributing to the
prospects for a stable peace in the world." The president suggested that the two
sides meet for bilateral arms limitation talks.[1]

---

* Present at this meeting, held in Austin, Texas, were Secretary of Defense
McNamara; Science Adviser Donald F. Hornig; past science advisers James R.
Killian, George B. Kistiakowsky, and Jerome Wiesner; Director of Defense
Research and Engineering (DDRE) John S. Foster; and past DDREs Harold
Brown and Herbert F. York.

The Soviets hesitated, and there were signs of disarray within their leadership on how to respond to Johnson's initiative. On February 27, 1967, they agreed to hold talks "in the future." President Johnson pressed them to name a date. They continued to hesitate, but Kosygin announced that he would welcome a chance to meet with the president when he attended a UN General Assembly meeting in June 1967. Johnson leaped at this opportunity and the Glassboro (New Jersey) summit of June 23 and 25 was hastily arranged. A feature of the meeting was an impassioned plea by Secretary of Defense McNamara over lunch on June 23 that the two sides "together . . . begin to put a lid on weapons."

While Kosygin was reported to have been impressed with the force and logic of the American presentation at Glassboro, it was not until a year later, on July 1, 1968, after repeated pressure by Johnson, that the two superpowers announced their intention to enter into "near-term" talks "on limitation and reduction of offensive strategic nuclear weapons delivery systems as well as systems of defense against ballistic missiles." Frenzied work then ensued within the administration to prepare a U.S. position. What came out of this effort, which was centered in the Pentagon, was an outline for a brief treaty proposal that would have imposed a quantitative, but not a qualitative, freeze on strategic missile launchers and an agreement to limit ABMs to an equal, but as yet unspecified, number. An ominous limitation of the proposal was that it would not have restricted MIRVs (multiple independently-targetable reentry vehicles).* Thus, while the number of missile launchers would have been limited under this proposal, the number of warheads could still have increased significantly, since individual missiles, if MIRVed, might carry as many as ten warheads.

On August 19, 1968, the Soviet Union finally agreed to schedule a summit conference to initiate the talks. The date was to be in the first ten days of October, the site probably Moscow. A joint announcement was to be released on the morning of August 21. On the night of August 20, however, Soviet and other Eastern bloc nations invaded Czechoslovakia, and President Johnson felt obliged to cancel the summit meeting announcement just hours before it was to be issued. It was a cruel disappointment for Johnson, and he persisted in

---

* The first U.S. MIRV test took place a week after the administration adopted the treaty outline. At the meeting of the Committee of Principals where final discussion of the treaty outline took place, Secretary of State Rusk, presiding, asked specifically whether anyone present wanted to suggest that MIRV testing be postponed. There was no response.

hoping that the atmosphere might improve sufficiently to allow missile talks to start within the few remaining months of his term. For their part, the Soviets were willing to go ahead. But it was not to be. After the 1968 election President-elect Nixon and his representatives made it clear that they would not look kindly on any attempt to begin the talks before the new administration assumed office.[2]

ACDA'S PROPOSALS

From its inception the Nixon administration was under heavy pressure to initiate the missile talks. The pressure came from the media, from elements in Congress, and even from some of the president's own appointees in the executive branch. But Nixon and Henry Kissinger, his national security adviser, were in no hurry. They felt it was important to prepare thoroughly. They also emphasized the idea that the decision on whether or not to begin the talks depended on the world situation, particularly Soviet behavior, an application of the doctrine of linkage to which both Nixon and Kissinger consistently adhered as a part of their arms control policy.[3] At length, on June 11, 1969, the United States notified the Soviets that we were willing for the talks to begin.

Soon after there began an intensified effort to reframe the opening U.S. position. The ACDA put forward a series of options. Option A banned mobile intercontinental ballistic missiles (ICBMs), limited the number of fixed ICBMs and ABMs, and froze the number and characteristics of intermediate-range ballistic missile (IRBM) launchers. Option B included all of A and, in addition, froze the number of fixed ICBMs and limited the number of submarine-launched ballistic missiles (SLBMs). Option C included all of B plus one all-important further step: it banned the deployment and flight testing of MIRVs. It thus went further than the draft treaty prepared in the Johnson administration. Option D went still further; it included all of C and, in addition, froze the number and characteristics of SLBMs, limited missile improvements and missile confidence firings, and froze strategic bombers. In essence, Option D amounted to an across-the-board freeze of the numbers and characteristics of strategic weapons. It came to be known within the administration as "Stop Where We Are" (SWWA).

The new ACDA director, Gerard Smith, made no effort to conceal his partiality for SWWA. He offered the following compelling arguments for it in an "Information Memorandum" circulated within the administration on May 9, 1969:

It would leave both sides with strategic "sufficiency," but without a first-strike capability, an essentially stable situation.

It would ban MIRVs on both sides, eliminating a feared threat to our Minuteman ICBMs from Soviet MIRVs.

By freezing Soviet ABMs, it would eliminate a prime reason for U.S. MIRVs.

It would permit active research and development programs, thus insuring that the United States would retain its technological lead.

It would be easier to verify than less restrictive proposals.

It would release great sums from military expenditures for other needs. Largely for this reason, it seemed likely to be acceptable to the Soviet Union.

Smith concluded his memorandum with this challenge: "If both the U.S. and USSR are serious about halting the strategic arms race, SWWA might be the way to do it."

I lunched with Smith on June 4 and told him I was in favor of going as far as possible, even to the extent of adopting SWWA. We agreed, however, that Option C was as far as the administration was likely to go, if that far. Secretary of State Rogers was more hopeful. I encountered him at a dinner party on June 14 and recorded this impression in my diary:

> Rogers is very optimistic that a meaningful U.S. position will evolve from the NSC meetings beginning next week. In fact, he indicated that he has already cleared a good, solid U.S. position with President Nixon. Rogers said he thought the position of "Stop Where We Are" has a good chance of being adopted.

Rogers was probably deluded. It is doubtful that SWWA was ever seriously considered by Nixon and Kissinger.

NIXON CONSIDERS THE OPTIONS

The first of the National Security Council meetings on Strategic Arms Limitation Talks (SALT) policy to which Rogers had referred took place in the Cabinet Room of the White House on June 18. I was invited to sit in.

> President Nixon said that the two sides were in approximate strategic balance. The choice was to keep building or stop—we might not have that choice much longer. It was apparent to him

that an "*appropriate*" *arms control agreement would be in the security interest of the United States.*

The reliability of U.S. intelligence was discussed. The president expressed great displeasure that the intelligence community's estimates of what the Soviets had done or were doing had erred on the low side. He added that, although many honest individuals in government wanted to get on with disarmament, he wanted it understood, clearly and loudly, that they should not bias intelligence reports in order to prove their arguments. The proper use of intelligence was to help come to a conclusion, not to prove a conclusion. He asked sternly whether that was understood and Helms said it was.*

Verification was discussed at length, the main issue being whether we should insist on some onsite inspection in a strategic arms treaty or rely entirely on our own national technical means. Smith thought we should feel the Soviets out on this as a tactical measure. The president said it might be better to include a demand for onsite inspection at the beginning; then we would be in a position to trade it away later for something that would be to our advantage. Rogers felt that a demand for inspection might scare off the Soviets. The president said it was an unfortunate fact of life that we had to assume that the Soviets would cheat on any agreement and that we could not do so. He doubted that our bringing up the verification question would upset the Russians. Helms said our national verification ability was adequate as long as the Soviets didn't interfere with it. He thought onsite inspections would be useful but not necessary.

---

* In the background of this colloquy was a controversy about whether the Soviets had, like ourselves, been testing MIRVs. Secretary Laird, supported by Kissinger and his NSC staff, believed that a recent Soviet test in the Pacific had involved MIRVs. The CIA's opinion, which under White House pressure they refused to revise, was that the three warheads atop the tested missile were not independently targetable; in other words, that what the Soviets had tested were not MIRVs but MRVs (multiple-reentry vehicles, but not independently targetable) such as the United States had deployed for several years. We now know that the CIA was correct. Gerard Smith (*Doubletalk*, pp. 160-61) quotes Laird as having said on a number of occasions: "I don't make the distinction between MIRVs and MRVs," although all other U.S. military planners did.

*Deputy Defense Secretary David Packard then described the
four options proposed by ACDA. President Nixon quickly indicated that he thought Option D (SWWA) was the least desirable
of the four. He dismissed it as a "propaganda gimmick." General
Wheeler agreed on behalf of the Joint Chiefs. He said that a ban
on the testing of MIRVs (Options C and D) would make it
impossible for the Chiefs to meet their targeting objectives—reliable MIRVs were needed to hit hardened Soviet targets. He went
on to say that the Soviets had probably already tested their MIRV
successfully whereas we had not.**

*There was an attempt at counterargument from those sympa-
thetic to SWWA, or at least Option C. Smith asked that we
consider where we might be in ten years if both sides continued
with MIRVs. Rogers asked which side would benefit most from
MIRVs. Secretary of Defense Laird conceded that the benefits
might be about even. He then disclosed the wellspring of Defense
Department anxiety—the Soviets, he said, were trying to develop
a first-strike capability. Under Secretary of State Elliot Richardson questioned this—it would not be sensible, he said, since our
studies indicated that our retaliatory second strike after a Soviet
attempt at a first strike would kill 30 percent of the USSR's
population. The president also doubted that a successful first
strike was possible.*

Following the meeting of June 18, Kissinger issued a very remarkable
memorandum, which is worth quoting in full. Entitled "Criteria for Strategic
Sufficiency," it read as follows:

As a result of the June 18, 1969, National Security Council meeting,
the President has made the following decision:

For planning purposes, strategic sufficiency as far as nuclear
attacks on the United States are concerned should be defined
as follows:
1. Maintain high confidence that our second strike capability is sufficient to deter an all-out surprise attack on our
strategic forces.

---

* We know now that this was not true—the Soviets were well behind us in
MIRV development.

2. Maintain forces to insure that the Soviet Union would have no incentive to strike the United States first in a crisis.
3. Maintain the capability to deny to the Soviet Union the ability to cause significantly more deaths and industrial damage in the United States in a nuclear war than they themselves would suffer.
4. Deploy defenses which limit damage from small attacks or accidental launches to a low level.

Pending further studies, the President has directed that these criteria be used by all agencies in considering issues relating to the U.S. strategic posture.

As the Cold War recedes in time, it is worth having this reminder of how grim the calculations were that animated its principal participants.

The four SALT options were discussed again at a June 23, 1969, meeting of a SALT steering group put together for the purpose of preparing a report requested by Kissinger. Science Adviser Lee DuBridge and I had both been appointed to this group.

General Royal B. Allison, representing the Joint Chiefs of Staff, indicated straight out that Stop Where We Are (SWWA) was unacceptable to the Chiefs, mentioning specifically that they opposed any limitations whatever on the development of technology. DuBridge and I took issue with this stand, contending that without some limitation on technology there could be no progress in arms control. Smith asked Allison if the Chiefs could accept SWWA if there were a perfect verification system. Allison evaded the question—he said it was not realistic. Packard took a milder position than Allison—he thought that, with proper definitions, SWWA might perhaps be possible. [This was the only such expression I recall hearing from a Pentagon spokesman.] *DuBridge, with a little show of exasperation, asked Packard whether the Joint Chiefs were against all arms control. Packard thought their stand was not that extreme.*

Another full National Security Council meeting on SALT occurred on June 25. DuBridge and I were again invited.

The president began by stating, quite forcibly: "There is only one person responsible for the security of our nation, and I am that person. My actions, in addition to their immediate impact, will greatly affect the options available to our next president at a period when some of these armament matters may be even more critical. I shall listen carefully to all the viewpoints expressed, but in the end, when I lay it down, I expect it to be followed."

Smith argued again for SWWA. He said that it alone among the options would result in money savings; also that it would have propaganda advantages as a U.S. proposal even if the final agreement were more limited. General Wheeler again expressed his opposition. Wheeler then challenged optimistic conclusions reached by the Verification Panel* that a MIRV agreement could be verified. He wanted another review by a group of "independent" technical experts. A sharp discussion ensued. Smith noted that the Panel's analysis had been done by people who would actually be responsible for verification monitoring, and that they were professionals who were better qualified to make those judgments than were their detractors. The president acknowledged that the members of the Verification Panel were technically competent but said that they might have used their hearts and not their heads in coming to their optimistic conclusions. [This was similar to what he had said at the June 18 meeting about those whose intelligence findings underestimated Soviet capabilities.] DuBridge contended that the Verification Panel had done a very thorough job, looking very hard at the photographic evidence. When Wheeler argued that it was impossible to monitor the development of MIRV techniques, DuBridge countered that we could indeed see MIRV tests. The president asked what I thought and I said I agreed generally with DuBridge.

---

* Originally established by Kissinger to review only verification issues, the Verification Panel's oversight was in time broadened by him to include other SALT issues as well, although the group's name was never changed. It was chaired by Kissinger and included ACDA director Smith, Under Secretary of State Richardson, Deputy Secretary of Defense Packard, Joint Chiefs Chairman Wheeler, and CIA Director Helms. Most of the work of the panel was done by a working group representing the same agencies, which undertook or sponsored specific analyses assigned by Kissinger. The Atomic Energy Commission, which had capabilities that might have been of substantial help to the panel, was not asked to contribute.

Next came a discussion of how we would handle consultation with the Allies. President Nixon wondered whether consultation wasn't a matter of "therapy" for the Allies and therefore whether we needed to do any more than indicate to them the options we were considering. If we later needed their support in order to go ahead, then would be time enough to sell them on a specific course of action. In any case, we should make it clear to the Allies that it was our decision to make after we consulted with them. Kissinger interposed a caution that the NATO countries were legitimately concerned about the future of the nuclear umbrella that protected them.

Laird made the point that within 15-20 hours after we consulted with our Allies all the information would be in the hands of the Soviets. The president agreed, saying, "My God, with the Norwegians, Danes and Swedes sitting there, what else would you expect?" [There was a certain pardonable imprecision here; the Swedes, not members of NATO, would not be "sitting there."] *He went on to say that everything leaks also at the Senate Foreign Relations Committee and that it would not be safe to give them anything but a sanitized version of our position. He said we could give more to the Senate Armed Services Committee. It was then pointed out that Stuart Symington (D-MO) sat on both committees, and the president admitted this was a problem. He said it was more important that the negotiations succeed than that Congress be briefed. The president concluded that the discussions with NATO should be kept rather loose and that they probably should include two or three ridiculous things in order to throw off the Soviets. He said this might also be the way to handle Congress.*

The president asked whether we needed to open the negotiations by making a definite proposal. Smith said he would certainly be more confident as our negotiator if he knew what our position was at the start, even if it was not revealed. Nixon pressed Smith on why it was desirable to make a full proposal at the start if all we could expect from the Soviets was a propaganda proposal. Smith replied that there were two reasons: (1) it was the United States that, under Johnson, had proposed SALT in the first instance; and (2) the Soviets historically start such discussions with broad, propaganda-oriented proposals. The president alluded to the thesis of Ambassador Llewellyn Thompson that the Soviets would lose interest if we did not start out with a definite proposal and said he disagreed with Thompson. He thought a

*better reason for starting with a substantive proposal was the
favorable effect this might have on American public opinion.
Secretary Rogers suggested that perhaps a good way to start would
be by tabling a very comprehensive agreement, including verification requirements that the Soviets wouldn't accept. We could
then fall back from these requirements later on if we wished.
Kissinger objected that the history of American verification proposals was that in falling back from our opening positions we
tended to fall back too far. Richardson suggested that we beat the
Soviets to the punch by doing what they do—start with our best
propaganda position of broad, general principles.*

*Vice President Agnew said that, whatever position we adopted,
some people would find it unreasonable. The president said that
whether this was important depended on who it was who thought
the position was unreasonable. He said he would be horrified if
the New York Times endorsed our position and that we mustn't
try to be fashionable. Rogers said we weren't talking about the
New York Times but about the American people. Agnew replied
that the situation was so complex that perhaps it was not reasonable to expect the American people to understand it.*

What we who participated in the various administration strategy sessions on
SALT did not know at the time was that they may have been to some extent a
sham. We have Henry Kissinger's testimony to this. He writes:

> Nixon took a keen interest in the strategy for SALT and in what
> channels it should be negotiated. But the details of the various plans
> bored him; in effect he left the selection of options to me. Yet if the
> bureaucracy had become aware of this, all vestige of discipline would
> have disappeared. I therefore scheduled over Nixon's impatient
> protests a series of NSC meetings where options were presented to
> a glassy-eyed and irritable President so that directives could be issued
> with some plausibility on his authority.[4]

Gerard Smith has commented that the Verification Panel meetings were
similarly devoid of genuine consultation. He writes:

> A standard feature of Verification Panel meetings was a note passed
> to the chairman [Kissinger], and his abrupt departure and absence
> for up to half an hour during which many top government officials
> wasted time in small talk. Then a hurried return [by Kissinger] after

presumably an urgent presidential session of great import. Usually the break in the SALT discussion was followed by a short resumption and a quick adjournment as it became clear that Kissinger had some different preoccupation weighing on his mind. My impression after leaving Verification Panel meetings was that they were perfunctory and made little contribution to solving problems, but rather were recitals of departmental positions fairly well known to all hands before the meeting.[5]

This rather contemptuous treatment of high administration officials was a hallmark of the Nixon-Kissinger way of doing business. It contributed in the end to a lack of unity and a general sense of disarray in the administration (see the discussion of reorganization proposals in chapter 14). As revealed at the June 25 meeting, Nixon had a similar attitude toward the NATO allies and members of Congress.

A LAST CHANCE TO STOP MIRV

The discussion of SALT options was taking place at a pivotal time for the near future of the arms race. As of June 1969, MIRVs had not yet been deployed by either side, nor had there even been a successful MIRV test, although testing by the United States had been going on for some ten months. (The first successful test was to occur in August 1969.) It was therefore still possible to arrest the headlong rush into this new technology.

Nixon and Kissinger were subject to competing pressures during this critical period. On June 17, 1969, Senator Edward W. Brooke (R-MA), supported by forty other senators, introduced a resolution calling for a unilateral moratorium on MIRV testing. A similar recommendation was made by the president's own General Advisory Committee on Arms Control and Disarmament, a distinguished group that included John J. McCloy (chairman), Dean Rusk, Cyrus Vance, Harold Brown, William W. Scranton, and William J. Casey. Also leaning toward this view were key officials in the administration, notably Secretary of State Rogers, Under Secretary Elliot Richardson and, of course, Gerard Smith. What all these supporters of a MIRV agreement feared—and what actually happened in the ensuing decades—was that if the United States deployed MIRVs, the Soviet Union, perceiving our deployment as a first-strike threat, would soon follow suit. Soviet MIRVs would then pose a severe threat to the survival of our principal land-based deterrent, the Minuteman missiles, leading to the requirement for a new generation of less vulnerable and more powerful missiles, and both sides would be committed to new rounds in an accelerating, destabilizing, and fearfully expensive arms race.

Although the hour was late, there was still time in June 1969 to head off these developments. As indicated earlier, the Pentagon—specifically, Secretary of Defense Laird and the Joint Chiefs of Staff—was adamantly opposed to any agreement limiting the testing or deployment of MIRVs. For reasons that were never entirely clear, President Nixon joined the Pentagon in opposing a MIRV agreement as part of the U.S. position. A clue to his thinking might be found in this statement in his memoirs: "I believed that the only effective way to achieve nuclear arms limitation was to confront the Soviets with an unacceptable alternative in the form of increased American armaments and the determination to use them."[6] In this context I am reminded of something that former Soviet ambassador Anatoly Dobrinin told me in an informal chat at the Soviet embassy in 1981. He said that the strategy of first building up U.S. supplies of nuclear weapons in order later to cut back on them made no sense. He cited as examples the U.S. adoption of MIRVed weapons and the introduction of the Trident submarine system. In both cases the Soviet Union had matched the U.S. buildup and no cutback followed—on either side.

SALT PROCEEDS—MIRV CONTINUES

As indicated in the next chapter, neither I individually, nor the AEC collectively, participated in the latter stages of the SALT story. For the sake of completeness, I will present here only a brief summary of what took place. For those who wish to go into the subject more deeply, excellent accounts are available.[7]

The SALT negotiations with the Soviets did not, in fact, get under way until November 1969, nearly three years after Lyndon Johnson first proposed the idea. When the Nixon administration finally indicated it was ready to proceed—this was in June 1969—the Soviet side waited another five months before assenting.

When the SALT negotiators finally got together in November 1969, there was early agreement on the desirability of limiting ABMs, but the asymmetry between the forces of the two sides led to difficulties in reaching an agreement involving offensive weapons. The Soviets then sought to limit the negotiations to ABMs. The United States, fearing further growth in the Soviet Union's already burgeoning ICBM arsenal, insisted that offensive weapons be included as well. After a prolonged deadlock, it was decided to negotiate a permanent treaty limiting ABMs and, as a holding action, to add an interim agreement restricting the growth of offensive arms for five years.

The ABM Treaty and the Interim Agreement on Strategic Offensive Arms were signed by Presidents Nixon and Brezhnev on May 26, 1972, in Vienna. The Senate gave its consent to ratification of the ABM Treaty on August 3, 1972, by a vote of 88 to 2. The Interim Agreement, being an executive agreement rather than a treaty, required only majority approval by both houses of Congress, which was obtained on September 30, 1972. The treaty and the agreement then both entered into force on October 3, 1972.

The ABM Treaty limited each side to two systems of 100 launchers each, one to protect the national capital, the other to protect a missile complex. By later amendment, each side was limited to only one of these choices. The Soviet Union elected to retain its Galosh system, defending Moscow. As indicated in the last chapter, the United States first elected to defend only the Minuteman missile site at Grand Forks, North Dakota, but later, in 1976, decided to phase out that installation and not to substitute another.

The Interim Agreement essentially froze at existing levels for a five year period the number of intercontinental ballistic missile (ICBM) launchers, operational or under construction, on each side. It permitted the increase of submarine-launched ballistic missile (SLBM) launchers up to an agreed level for each side only with the destruction of a corresponding number of older ICBM or SLBM launchers. Within limits, modernization and replacement were permitted. The agreement placed no limits on strategic bombers, forward-based systems, mobile ICBMs, or MIRVs. Accordingly, while the number of launchers was limited, the number of warheads that could be launched was not. Thus, one of the principal purposes Johnson and McNamara had had in mind in proposing missile talks—to prevent a major escalation in the arms race—was to a large extent defeated. It was defeated by two factors. One was the delay in getting the talks started. As Dean Rusk put it in a conversation in March 1986:

> If those talks had started in, say, early September 1968, the state of the art in MIRVs was such that we might have been able to get them under control. But that move into Czechoslovakia delayed the talks. And then when the Nixon administration came in they had to spend nearly a year getting their ducks in a row so that by the time serious talks could begin with the Soviet Union the MIRV problem had gotten out of control—the horses had cleared the stable.

Even with the delay in starting SALT, it might still have been possible to avoid the MIRV escalation by adopting some variant of the Stop Where We

Are (SWWA) option, as advocated by Gerard Smith and supported by others, including Secretary of State Rogers and me. When President Nixon, without serious consideration, brushed SWWA aside as a "propaganda gimmick," that opportunity was lost.

MIRV arguably exacerbated the nuclear arms race more than any development since the H-bomb. When the Soviets proceeded to load their ICBMs with up to ten warheads each, many on our side felt that our land-based deterrent was threatened. President Reagan spoke of the threat in the 1980s as a "window of vulnerability." In response, he ordered a buildup of U.S. strategic weaponry and initiated the ill-conceived Strategic Defense Initiative ("Star Wars"). The Soviets kept pace, in quantity if not in quality. Defense expenditures on both sides ballooned to new heights. Perhaps, in retrospect, we will one day be able to think of MIRV as the crowning folly that helped bring both sides in the superpower arms race to their senses, thus making possible the arms control initiatives of the '80s and early '90s.

NOTES

1. Johnson, *The Vantage Point*, pp. 479-81.
2. I have written in greater detail about these developments during the Johnson administration in my book, *Stemming the Tide*, pp. 413-40.
3. Kissinger, *White House Years*, pp. 132ff.
4. *Ibid.*, p. 148.
5. Smith, *Doubletalk*, p. 111.
6. Nixon, *RN*, p. 524.
7. See, in particular, Smith, *Doubletalk*, and John Newhouse, *Cold Dawn*.

5

The Advice of Scientists

You can lead a horse to water but you cannot make him drink.

—Proverb

PROPOSED SEABED TREATIES

During the 1960s many nations began to show increased interest in tapping the vast resources of the ocean floor. This led to concern that in the absence of clearly established rules of law, some nations might use the seabed as a base for military operations.

In November 1967 a movement started within the United Nations recommending that study be given to the "reservation exclusively for peaceful purposes of the seabed and the ocean floor." An ad hoc committee was established to conduct studies and make recommendations. Largely because the United States was using bottom-dwelling listening devices to monitor Soviet submarines, the responses of this country and of the Soviet Union took divergent paths. The Soviets proposed a sweeping resolution "solemnly calling upon all states to use the seabed . . . exclusively for peaceful purposes"; their proposal would thus have outlawed the U.S. listening devices. A more modest ACDA proposal discussed within the U.S. government was to ban the emplacement of "weapons of mass destruction" on the ocean floor; this proposal would not have disturbed the listening devices.

The ACDA proposal encountered a surprising amount of Pentagon resistance. One opposition argument, as presented by Joint Chiefs chairman Earle G. Wheeler and Deputy Defense Secretary Paul Nitze in the spring of 1968, was that although the United States had no plans at that time to deploy nuclear weapons on the ocean floor, and envisioned no such plans in the future, it still might one day prove advantageous to do so and therefore should not be foreclosed. This position was so extreme that it outraged the usually imperturbable Dean Rusk. Referring to the seabed debate in a conversation not long afterwards, Rusk deplored the growing influence of the military on U.S. foreign policy and observed that President Eisenhower had been right when he warned the American people against the "acquisition of unwarranted influence . . . by the military-industrial complex."

In due course the pro-seabed treaty position won out within the Johnson administration. In June 1968 the Soviet Union and the United States presented resolutions expressing their respective points of view to the ad hoc UN committee, recommending at the same time that that body give way to the Eighteen Nation Disarmament Committee (ENDC) as an organization better able to take effective action.

On April 30, 1969, I attended a meeting convened to consider whether to reaffirm the Johnson administration's position regarding a seabed treaty. Many of the big guns of the administration were present, including the president, Vice President Agnew, National Security Adviser Kissinger, Secretary of State Rogers, Secretary of Defense Laird, Joint Chiefs Chairman Wheeler, CIA Director Helms, Attorney General John Mitchell, ACDA Director Smith, White House Science Adviser DuBridge, and many subordinates, including a Colonel Alexander Haig of the National Security Council staff.

> Smith said we should make this moderate proposal in the ENDC to prevent the matter from being considered by the General Assembly, which was likely to approve the Soviet idea of complete demilitarization of the seabed.
>
> Laird reaffirmed the Pentagon's resistance to any seabed treaty. He said such a pact would work to Soviet advantage because they had a great land mass and only limited access to the oceans, whereas we had extensive shorelines. DuBridge countered that our shorelines would make us more vulnerable to seabed weapons—therefore a treaty prohibiting such weapons would be to our advantage. General Wheeler, repeating the stand he had taken during the Johnson administration, said that while the United States had no plans for seabed weapons, we didn't know very much about the oceans and should keep our options open.

Laird said he was thinking of the future and didn't want to trade away any political advantage. It was his feeling that it was best to begin tough with the Soviets—you never gained anything if you gave away too much. Rogers asked why having a seabed treaty would be giving away anything at all. He added that the United States had already expressed itself at the ENDC as being in favor of such a treaty. At this point Vice President Agnew said he would be remiss if he didn't express his concern that we seemed always to be reacting to Soviet suggestions. Why didn't we have initiatives of our own?* Smith and Rogers answered that the discussion of a seabed treaty at the ENDC had in fact been initiated by us, not by the Soviets, and that, for the sake of its world image, the United States sorely needed to show some interest in disarmament.

Laird suggested we make a seabed treaty part of a package deal that included strategic arms limitations. Smith said that there had been various attempts at package deals in the past, with no success. It was only when a single item was broken out, as in the case of the test ban treaty, that we got anywhere. President Nixon said he wanted to be sure of the value of such arms control agreements with the Soviets. He recalled that it had been a close call with him to come out in favor of the Limited Test Ban Treaty and he still wasn't sure this had been the correct decision. He asked me what I thought. I said that the test ban had been clearly to the advantage of the U.S. and the world, since it slowed the arms race and halted atmospheric fallout. The president next asked me what I thought about the Seabed Treaty. I said I favored it and that it would be a mistake to reverse our position at the ENDC after having spoken out in favor of the treaty there. The president said then [in words I was not soon to forget] *that he was more interested in my technical judgment than my political*

---

* I attended several meetings at which Agnew was present. I generally found his interventions to be quite vacuous, frequently off the subject. Nixon appears to have developed a low opinion of him over time, finding him useful almost solely for delivering hard-line, biting speeches written for him by others. Stephen Ambrose (*Nixon, The Triumph of a Politician,* p. 586) writes that Nixon spoke to both John Mitchell and H. R. Haldeman about dropping Agnew from the ticket for 1972 in favor of John Connally, but was discouraged from doing so because Agnew had wide support among conservative Republicans.

> *judgment. I said it was difficult to separate the two in this case*
> *but that, speaking from the technical point of view, the treaty*
> *would not impede our development of nuclear weapons.*

The Pentagon appeared at this meeting to have persisted in the negative attitude that so outraged Dean Rusk. But Rogers told me later that Laird acknowledged after the meeting that he had not been well prepared and regretted having been so negative.

Shortly after this meeting President Nixon reaffirmed the previous U.S. position in support of a seabed treaty. In May 1969 Adrian Fisher introduced at the ENDC a U.S. draft treaty prohibiting the emplacement of weapons of mass destruction on the seabed and ocean floor beyond a three-mile coastal zone. Two months earlier the Soviets had submitted their draft treaty providing for complete demilitarization of the seabed beyond a twelve-mile coastal zone. In addition to differing on what was to be prohibited, the Soviet and U.S. treaty drafts had different provisions for verification. In a curious reversal of historical roles, the Soviet Union contended that all structures on the ocean bottom should be subject to on-site inspection, whereas the United States argued that violations would be easy to detect without any on-site inspection. The Soviets obviously wanted to inspect the American bottom-dwelling monitoring devices and we, just as obviously, did not want them inspected.

In due course the Soviets, in a demonstration of apparent reasonableness, came around and accepted the more limited American approach. On October 7, 1969, the superpowers jointly submitted to the Conference of the Committee on Disarmament (CCD)—the new name given to the ENDC after it was enlarged from 18 to 26 members—a joint draft of a Treaty on the Prohibition of the Emplacement of Nuclear Weapons and Other Weapons of Mass Destruction on the Seabed and the Ocean Floor and in the Subsoil Thereof. The principal obligation of the treaty is described in its lengthy title. There was protracted discussion of this draft treaty at the CCD, leading to several amendments. The discussion focused on the definition of the exempt coastal zone—the Soviet proposal of a twelve-mile limit was finally adopted—and on means of verification. As to the latter, it was decided that parties suspecting a violation could use their own means of verification, or they could apply to other parties for assistance, provided they did not interfere with legitimate seabed activities.

A final draft of the treaty was approved by the UN General Assembly on December 7, 1970, by a vote of 104 to 2 (El Salvador and Peru), with two abstentions (France and Ecuador). It was opened for signature in Washington, Moscow, and London on February 11, 1971. The treaty cleared the Senate without difficulty, although consideration was delayed for about a year. It entered into force on May 19, 1972, the Big Three and the required total of 22 nations having by then deposited their instruments of ratification.

A NEW FOREIGN POLICY APPARATUS

The president's comment to me at the April 30, 1969 meeting—that he was more interested in my technical judgment than my political judgment—gave me much to ponder. During the Eisenhower, Kennedy, and Johnson administrations, the chairman of the Atomic Energy Commission had been an active participant in the formulation of arms control policy. This came about in large part from his membership on the Committee of Principals. The committee had been established by President Eisenhower in 1958 to coordinate the executive branch's review of arms control policy. Under Eisenhower its membership included the secretary of state, who acted as chairman, the secretary of defense, the director of central intelligence, the AEC chairman, and the president's science adviser. President Kennedy expanded the membership from five to nine by adding the chairman of the Joint Chiefs of Staff, the president's national security adviser, the director of the U.S. Information Agency, and, after establishment of the Arms Control and Disarmament Agency, its director. The end result of the Principals' consideration of an issue tended to be a recommendation to the president, conveyed by the committee's chairman, the secretary of state.

The Committee of Principals was highly valued by Kennedy. He underscored this by participating personally in several of the group's meetings. While the Principals continued to meet regularly during the Johnson administration, President Johnson appeared to place less value than Kennedy had on their recommendations, preferring to thrash things out personally with the less numerous group of intimates with whom he met regularly at the "Tuesday lunches."*

The Committee of Principals never met under Nixon. I was unprepared for this turn in events. On February 12, 1969, during a get-acquainted meeting I had with Gerard Smith, the new director of ACDA, I suggested that he try to arrange meetings of the Principals to discuss some proposed nuclear weapons

---

* When the Tuesday lunches began in February 1964, attendance was limited to the president, the secretaries of state and defense, and the national security adviser. Later, the chairman of the Joint Chiefs of Staff, the director of CIA, and the White House press secretary were added.

cutbacks. Smith then told me that Henry Kissinger might have knocked out the committee in his operational plan. I protested that there would be a need for the same senior people to get together on key issues no matter what one called the group. Smith appeared to agree and stated that he would urge that Kissinger and Secretary of State Rogers plan to use the Principals as in the past. But a few months into the Nixon administration the committee was abolished. Nor did it turn out to be the case, as I had surmised, that "the same group of senior people" would come together on key issues. Nixon and Kissinger had something quite different in mind.

Even before the inauguration, Kissinger had devised and obtained Nixon's approval for a thorough overhaul of the executive branch's way of doing business in foreign affairs. Under the new dispensation the consideration of important foreign policy matters was centralized in the White House. The main instrument that Nixon and Kissinger used to accomplish this was a revitalized National Security Council (NSC) apparatus, with Kissinger himself at the helm. In the new organization the NSC was buttressed by a series of interagency subcommittees, which, on assignment from Kissinger, would draft analyses of policy. Kissinger himself chaired a review committee that screened these review papers and decided which ones were to be put before the full NSC and/or the president. Kissinger used this structure not only to obtain needed review and analysis but also as a way of keeping the bureaucracy busy while preventing it from putting forth an agenda of its own. As Tom Wicker points out, Kissinger ordered at least 35 different studies during the administration's first month.[1] Secretary of State Rogers tried unsuccessfully to resist this development, which greatly reduced the influence and morale of his department.[2] The very appointment of Rogers, however, an attorney with virtually no previous experience in international affairs, was a portent that Nixon intended to diminish the importance of the State Department in the formulation of foreign policy.

Also devalued in the reorganization process was the CIA. One of Nixon's early actions was to remove the director of CIA from the NSC.[3] Nixon's attitude toward State and CIA, as explained by Kissinger, was as follows:

> He had very little confidence in the State Department. Its personnel had no loyalty to him; the Foreign Service had disdained him as Vice President and ignored him the moment he was out of office. He was determined to run foreign policy from the White House...He [also] felt it imperative to exclude the CIA from the formulation of policy; it was staffed by Ivy League liberals who behind the facade of analytical objectivity were usually pushing their own preferences. They had always opposed him politically.[4]

In addition to the motives Nixon may have had for excluding certain groups from foreign policy making, Kissinger had an apparent one of his own. This was to eliminate competitors with himself in this function. He sought, and obtained, a controlling role in international affairs second only to that of the president. In accomplishing this he feuded with and succeeded frequently in humiliating Secretary of State Rogers.

REDUCED ROLES

The abolition of the Committee of Principals was a clear indication that Nixon and Kissinger wished to narrow the circle of people regularly consulted about arms control. In 1972, Kissinger spelled out the somewhat convoluted thinking behind this approach:

> One reason for keeping the decisions to small groups is that when bureaucracies are so unwieldy and when their internal morale becomes a serious problem, an unpopular decision may be fought by brutal means, such as leaks to the press or congressional committees. Thus, the only way secrecy can be kept is to exclude from the making of the decision those who are theoretically charged with carrying it out.[5]

The implications of all this for my personal participation were quickly made evident in the consideration of policy regarding SALT. Following the two meetings I attended in June, there were no further large interagency meetings on SALT during the summer of 1969. Then on October 18 my arms control assistant, Allan Labowitz, reported to me that a new and more restricted group was being established to help resolve the continued serious dispute between the CIA and the Department of Defense on verification capabilities. This subject was no longer to be considered by the Steering Committee of which Science Adviser DuBridge and I were members. Instead, at the president's direction, Kissinger was limiting discussion to representatives of Defense, the CIA, the Joint Chiefs of Staff, and ACDA. The new group represented the same agencies as the previous one except that DuBridge and I had been dropped. The change therefore seemed to have been adopted for the specific purpose of dropping us. I speculated in my diary:

> *It seems likely that DuBridge and I are being by-passed due to the strong stands we took in favor of arms control at the meetings in*

June—the president seemed a little displeased about this at the time.

DuBridge's explanation was different. When he and I were both again excluded from an NSC meeting on SALT, this one held on November 10, 1969, a week before talks with the Soviets were to get under way in Helsinki, we discussed the matter on the telephone:

> *DuBridge said that his being shut out was a very mysterious business to him. He had tried politely, and then pretty firmly, to get through to National Security Council channels, but without result. He thought Kissinger didn't believe that scientists were any use on matters like this and that he, Kissinger, had persuaded the president to adopt a similar view.*

I subsequently learned a little more about the exclusion of DuBridge and me when Philip J. Farley and Spurgeon Keeny of ACDA came to my office on May 30, 1970, to brief me on the status and progress of SALT since the previous summer. Apparently, Farley had to seek specific permission from the White House to talk to me. They told me that DuBridge had not been brought into any of the discussions and was not to receive even the briefing I was being given. This was on specific instructions from Kissinger, who wanted to keep people with a scientific portfolio, including all members of the President's Science Advisory Committee, out of the process of formulating SALT policy. The reason given for excluding me was "to keep to a minimum the numbers who have this sensitive information." But I continued to receive briefings on SALT progress from time to time.

In a 1992 conversation Spurgeon Keeny, now president of the influential Arms Control Association, shed additional light on why I may have been treated less harshly than DuBridge. Both a member of Kissinger's staff and DuBridge's assistant early in the administration, Keeny believes that Kissinger excluded DuBridge because he didn't want any competition or any dissident voice *in the White House.* Consequently, Kissinger treated DuBridge in what Keeny considers "a very shameful way," totally ignoring him and refusing to let him get involved in matters where he could have been helpful. Keeny is less confident about the reasons for my exclusion, but believes Kissinger probably decided that the AEC, like NASA, was a specialized agency whose advice wasn't needed in determining security policy.

After a series of futile attempts to gain some recognition in the White House, DuBridge resigned in September 1970. He was replaced by Edward E.

David, Jr., an engineer recruited from industry. In announcing David's appointment, Nixon was at pains to describe him as "a very practical man." Although his appointment disturbed some members of the scientific community, David's performance, as far as I could judge it, was very creditable.

Although I retained a full slate of responsibilities as AEC chairman, my exclusion from an active part in the formulation of arms control policy was very hurtful to me. I had regarded the ability to make a contribution in this field as probably the most rewarding aspect of my position.

NIXON AND SCIENCE

While there may well have been other factors, as indicated earlier, one should consider in passing the extent to which the AEC's loss of prominence in national security policy making may have derived from attitudes Richard Nixon harbored about science and scientists in general. There had been several indications at the start of his administration that Nixon was quite favorably disposed toward science. DuBridge was among his first appointments, and Nixon devoted one of his first press conferences to announcing the appointment, extolling both DuBridge and science in the process.[6] DuBridge also told me that, in his presence, Nixon had suggested to Secretary of State Rogers that a new position of assistant secretary of state for science be created. We have also referred (chapter 1) to Nixon's avowed enthusiasm for AEC's Plowshare program. This case suggests the possibility that Nixon's interest in science may have been restricted to what have been called science spectaculars, grandiose undertakings such as the moon landings or the supersonic transport that would enhance the nation's prestige. He did not seem to have much interest in the accumulation of scientific knowledge in the many thousands of research projects taking place in AEC facilities or in universities and private laboratories across the country.

Both Nixon and Kissinger appeared to feel—and what Nixon said to me at the meeting on the Seabed Treaty was evidence of this—that scientists could offer a means of getting things done but that their specialized knowledge did not endow them with any insights that were useful in the making of high policy. There may also have been another, more personal aspect to this. On the few occasions when I discussed scientific matters with Nixon, I detected in him a sense of discomfort, as though he didn't want to acknowledge that he was having difficulty understanding what was being said. In a similar situation, President Kennedy used to ask questions, challenging the scientist to explain more clearly. I think Nixon's unwillingness to do this stemmed from a basic lack of self-confidence. It is interesting that Spurgeon Keeny, in our recent conversation, noted that Kissinger also seemed uncomfortable in the presence of scientists and for reasons not dissimilar to those I believe applied to Nixon. So Nixon and Kissinger may well have shunned scientists both because they did not believe they were the appropriate people to have in high places and because of the personal discomfort they felt in scientific company.

Whatever may have been Nixon's initial disposition, relations between his administration and scientists both in and out of government deteriorated when it became evident that many members of the scientific community opposed Nixon's prosecution of the Vietnam War. Nixon also tended to identify scientists with the war-born unrest on campuses across the nation where most of the basic scientific research was undertaken. Relations approached the breaking point when individual members of the President's Science Advisory Committee publicly opposed deployment of the Safeguard antiballistic missile system and the development of a commercial supersonic transport (SST). The testimony of one PSAC member, Richard L. Garwin, contributed to the defeat of the SST in Congress.

By 1973, the White House, from the top down, was persuaded that the science mechanism was not serving the administration as the administration wished to be served. As DuBridge has written, "Nixon's staff became unhappy that PSAC did not always support Presidential policies and were also unhappy that PSAC did not seem to be an adequate political asset to the President."[7] In January 1973, the entire apparatus—science adviser, PSAC, and the Office of Science and Technology—was summarily abolished. The nominal task of coordinating government science policy and advising the government as a whole on scientific matters then fell on H. Guyford Stever, director of the National Science Foundation, reporting not to the president but to Secretary of the Treasury George Shultz in his capacity as chairman of a Council on Economic Policy.*

---

* This arrangement was short-lived. On assuming the presidency, Gerald Ford restored the position of science adviser to the president. Also during Ford's presidency, Congress, with his assent, established an Office of Scientific and Technical Policy.

AN ISOLATED PRESIDENT

Scientists were by no means the only group from whom Nixon chose to distance himself. As his administration progressed, he became more and more inaccessible even to members of his own cabinet, preferring to filter departmental business through a corps of White House assistants.

In time, I, along with others, found it increasingly difficult to gain the president's attention. I had been able to have direct access to both Kennedy and Johnson when a problem warranted it, although I tried not to abuse the privilege. During the Nixon administration an ever increasing number of walls were erected, until near the end my day-to-day direct access was to Will Kriegsman, who reported to John C. Whitaker, who reported to Peter Flanigan, who reported to John Ehrlichman, who reported to Nixon. One of Nixon's abiding complaints was that he found it difficult to control the bureaucracy. It is clear to me that he contributed to this situation by walling himself off from those who worked for him. I have always felt that the ultimate course of the Nixon administration might have been different had Nixon chosen to hear the opinions of a wider circle of advisers.

NOTES

1. Wicker, *One of Us,* p. 435.
2. An account of the reorganization, unfriendly to Kissinger, is found in Hersh, *The Price of Power,* chapter 2.
3. Kissinger, *White House Years,* p. 44.
4. Ibid., p. 11.
5. Quoted in Newhouse, *Cold Dawn: The Story of SALT,* p. 52.
6. William G. Wells, Jr., in William T. Golden, ed., *Science Advice to the President,* p. 208.
7. In Golden, ed., *Science Advice to the President,* p. 11.

PART III

FUROR OVER RADIATION STANDARDS

6

Monticello

On the mighty Mississippi, near Monticello, Minn.,
They're building a nuclear power plant and
they're committing mortal sin,
They'll contaminate our river with radioactive waste,
With insidious poison that no one can see or smell or taste.[1]

CONFRONTATION WITH MINNESOTA

In December 1965, the management of Northern States Power Company (NSP) reached an internal decision that a new generating unit in the 500-electrical-megawatt range would be required by 1970 to meet anticipated service demands.[2] Having just faced protracted public criticism regarding the predicted environmental effects of a large fossil-fueled plant then being completed, the company reasoned that it could avoid further criticism by making its next major addition a nuclear plant.[3] A nuclear plant would neither produce the soot, smoke, and noxious chemicals nor be subject to the fuel transportation and fuel storage problems of a fossil-fueled plant. NSP reached the decision to "go nuclear" despite an analysis indicating that a coal-fired plant would be economically superior.

Early in 1966, NSP held discussions with the AEC regulatory staff and with Minnesota state officials regarding the suitability of a site near Monticello, Minnesota (population about 1,500), on the Mississippi River, about 40 miles upstream from the water intakes for the twin cities of Minneapolis and St. Paul. No objections having been expressed to the site, the utility contracted in August 1966 with the General Electric Company for installation of a 545-megawatt boiling-water reactor (BWR) nuclear power plant.*

Directly after ordering the plant from General Electric, NSP applied to the AEC for a construction permit. The AEC then began its normal review processes. There was, first, an analysis of the proposed plant by the AEC regulatory staff to determine whether in its opinion a reactor of the proposed design and power could be operated safely at the selected site. The staff's finding, contained in a long and comprehensive "safety analysis report," was affirmative. While the staff was studying the application a second, parallel study was being undertaken by the congressionally established Advisory Committee on Reactor Safeguards (ACRS), a group of fifteen recognized experts in the various technical disciplines involved. The ACRS too found, and issued a public report stating, that the application met the AEC's criterion for issuance of a construction permit, namely, that there was "reasonable assurance that the proposed facility [could] be constructed and operated at the proposed location without undue risk to the health and safety of the public." After issuance of the favorable staff and ACRS reports, the next step was a public hearing by an independent three-man Atomic Safety and Licensing Board (ASLB), where any person affected had the right to intervene as a party to the proceeding. There was no intervention in the Monticello case at this stage and the ASLB duly approved issuance of a construction permit.† The AEC issued the permit on June 19, 1967; construction began the same day.

As construction proceeded, there were also state requirements to be met, and it was at this stage that strong opposition to the plant first manifested itself. As

------

* As the name implies, water entering a BWR is heated under pressure to a very high boiling point, producing steam that is used directly to drive a turbine. The BWR, predominantly produced by General Electric, is one of two types of reactors most commonly employed in U.S. nuclear power plants. The other, predominantly produced by Westinghouse, is the pressurized-water reactor (PWR). In PWRs water passing through the reactor is heated under pressure to a very high temperature but does not boil. Instead, it passes in pipes through a separate chamber, called a steam generator, heating that chamber's water to produce steam, which is then passed to the turbine.

† Following the ASLB's approval, the decision could still have been appealed by any party and could have been subject to further review by an appeal board and/or by the commission itself. There was no such appeal or further review with regard to Monticello's construction permit.

required by state law, NSP applied to the Minnesota Pollution Control Agency (MPCA) for a waste discharge permit, including permission to discharge radioactive effluents into the Mississippi River. The MPCA held a public hearing on the application on February 13, 1969. At this hearing considerable opposition to NSP's request was expressed by scientists from the University of Minnesota. They maintained that the contemplated discharges would contaminate the drinking water of Minneapolis and St. Paul and that technical means were available whereby NSP could reduce its discharges significantly. NSP acknowledged that it could make the changes but argued that to do so would be time-consuming and costly and that, in any case, the planned releases were well within limits established by the AEC.

Eight days later I received a phone call from Earl Ewald, chairman of the board of NSP. He had just returned from a luncheon meeting with the mayors of Minneapolis and St. Paul and reported that both mayors were quite agitated about the dangers to the twin cities' water supply. The AEC also learned at about this time that the state of Minnesota, confused by the conflicting arguments of the utility and the university scientists, had retained a consultant, Dr. Ernest C. Tsivoglou of the Georgia Institute of Technology,* to advise whether current AEC regulations governing radioactive discharges were strict enough to protect the public. In a 192-page report, Dr. Tsivoglou concluded that they were not. He noted, for example, that the AEC's standards failed to take into account the likelihood that there would soon be many additional reactors in the upper Mississippi region, NSP alone having announced plans for four more. He recommended that Minnesota take upon itself the task of establishing statewide standards that would limit radioactive discharges to about one-third the level permitted by the AEC. In addition, he recommended that individual plants be required to keep discharges as far below the statewide limits as was practicable. Recognizing that such actions might be subject to legal contest, Dr. Tsivoglou further recommended that the state assert "with vigor" its right to set pollution standards stricter than those of the AEC. He acknowledged that the state had no legal right to establish standards more lenient than those of the AEC.

The Minnesota controversy soon attracted national attention. In April 1969, Senator Edmund S. Muskie (D-ME), in his capacity as chairman of a House Subcommittee on Air and Water Pollution, wrote to the AEC asking its opinion of Dr. Tsivoglou's recommendations. In a sharply negative reply, I told Muskie that some of the recommended restrictions were too vague to

---

* Tsivoglou was a professor of sanitary engineering. From 1956 to 1966 he had been chief of radiological water control, U.S. Public Health Service.

be administered effectively and that others would be unduly burdensome. I pointed out that the AEC restrictions the consultant thought inadequate were based on guidelines of the Federal Radiation Council, a cabinet-level group, and that these had been approved by the president for the guidance of federal agencies. In general, I stated that the restrictions Dr. Tsivoglou was recommending would entail a major effort not justified by any gain. Furthermore, I questioned the legal authority of any state to regulate the radiological aspects of an AEC-licensed plant. On advice of counsel, I contended that in the Atomic Energy Act Congress had given the AEC preemptive jurisdiction over such regulation.

Notwithstanding the legal doubts, the MPCA on May 20, 1969, issued its waste discharge permit severely limiting NSP's discharge of radioactive effluents in the manner recommended by Dr. Tsivoglou.

STATES' RIGHTS

The AEC's first inclination was to seek legal intervention by the Nixon administration against Minnesota's action, which we considered unwise and, based on AEC's preemptive jurisdiction, illegal. It soon became apparent, however, that our position was not widely shared within the administration. The Department of the Interior, for example, which had also received a letter of inquiry from Senator Muskie, responded that, in its opinion, the standards recommended by Dr. Tsivoglou were both reasonable and achievable. Science Adviser Lee DuBridge expressed to me his opinion that if a state wished to impose regulations more severe than those of the federal government, the state had the right to do so. He believed that the courts would so decide if a test case were brought. In reply, I told DuBridge that if there were many different standards, it would lead to chaos in the nation's nuclear power program; also, if it were left to the states, levels could be set so low it would be impossible to meet them. I warned that the Joint Committee on Atomic Energy (JCAE) felt very strongly about this, so that the matter would inevitably be brought to a head.*

---

* In thus raising the specter of the JCAE, I was employing a time-honored AEC stratagem: steering a course between the often-conflicting urgings of the administration on the one hand and the JCAE on the other by playing one off against the other.

Late in August 1969 NSP decided to challenge Minnesota's legal right to impose restrictions on radioactive effluents. The rest of the industry, wanting early clarification about where it stood with respect to the threat of state regulation, had been pressing the utility to take this step for some time. The AEC had joined in the pressure because we also wanted the issue to be settled speedily. NSP, concerned about an adverse effect on its public relations if it seemed to be opposing steps to protect the environment, delayed taking action for several months, but at length it filed suit in both federal and state courts.

The court case soon disabused the AEC of any impression we might have had that Minnesota was off on its own in contesting AEC regulations. Within a short time, seven states indicated their wish to appear as intervenors or friends of the court in support of Minnesota. (By the time the case opened, on October 5, 1969, this number had increased to twenty.) In its 1969 meeting, the National Governors' Conference unanimously passed a resolution supporting Minnesota's right to establish stricter standards than those of the AEC.[4] The AEC briefly considered intervening on the side of the utility. We hung back, however, because of our uncertainty about the administration's position. We still hoped that, after mature reflection, the Department of Justice might itself see fit to intervene, a reasonable expectation in a jurisdictional dispute between a state and a federal agency. Our point of view was well expressed by California congressman Craig Hosmer, the most active Republican member on the Joint Committee, when he wrote to President Nixon on October 9:

> My position is that the U.S. Government ought to get in and get a decision establishing Federal preemption and that there are many good reasons for this, including the fact that the issue ought to be cleared up as rapidly as possible if we are going to have a viable nuclear power industry in this country. It is both my sincere hope and my strong advice that the Justice Department be instructed to intervene in this case as a friend of the court on behalf of the principle of Federal preemption.

But the word that reached us from administration sources was not encouraging. For one thing, it was established Republican ideology to encourage states' rights. The administration also recognized that, in accord with an environmentalist wave that was sweeping the country, public sentiment seemed much in favor of strict radiation controls, even if that meant higher electric bills. One very vocal citizens group in Minnesota was, in fact, demanding that the state withdraw the Monticello waste disposal permit and substitute for it one that would allow no radioactive discharge whatever. It was also probably the case that the drumfire of criticism then being directed against the AEC, the nuclear industry, and the Joint Committee (more about this criticism later) had diminished our collective influence in the White House.

Still the Joint Committee did not give up. On October 20 I learned from Hosmer that he and other members of the committee had discussed the Monticello matter with Assistant Attorney General William Ruckelshaus. Ruckelshaus readily agreed that Congress had intended in the Atomic Energy Act to reserve regulation of radioactive discharges to the federal government. He indicated, however, that whether the Justice Department would intervene on the side of NSP was not a matter of law but a "policy question that would have to be resolved in the White House." On October 28, at the Joint Committee's hearings on the environmental effects of producing electric power, Science Adviser DuBridge testified that the administration had as yet reached no decision on this "policy question." But we learned from other sources that Ruckelshaus had been instructed by the White House to stay out of the case.

On October 29, 1969, the Commission and top AEC staff met with Minnesota governor Harold LeVander in a last-ditch effort to reach an agreement by compromise. We sought to appease the governor by suggesting alternative activities the state could undertake in the atomic energy field. It could, for example, enter into an agreement, such as we already had with several states, whereby Minnesota would assume authority over the licensing of radioisotope use and production in the state, or it could participate in the monitoring of radioactive effluents from nuclear power plants. (The latter activity was one no state had yet undertaken.) The governor did not take the bait. He said that neither suggestion was a satisfactory substitute for what the state wanted to do, which was, quite simply, to set its own standards for radioactive discharges.

Later that same day LeVander met with Vice President Agnew. According to the next day's *Washington Post,* the governor said he was pleased with the meeting. After reading this newspaper account, I called presidential assistant Peter Flanigan, who was then the AEC's principal White House contact on day-to-day business.* Our conversation, as noted in my diary, gave the AEC little comfort.

> *Referring to newspaper accounts of LeVander's talk with Vice President Agnew, I told Flanigan I wanted to be sure that the vice president wasn't being painted into a corner on the Minnesota*

---

* Flanigan had been Nixon's deputy campaign manager, second only to John Mitchell, and had been responsible after the election for political appointments. In his position on the White House staff he had succeeded Robert F. Ellsworth, who was appointed ambassador to NATO in April 1969.

Minnesota Governor Harold LeVander with the author and Commissioner Ramey in
October 1969. The governor came to Washington in a futile attempt to resolve differences with the AEC over the regulation of radioactivity releases from nuclear power
plants.

matter. Flanigan replied that he knows the vice president's general feeling on the subject and it is this: it is right and proper for the AEC to set minimum standards and no state government has the right to issue standards that are more lenient. Furthermore, a reasonable state government would be likely to accept the AEC regulations. On the other hand, if an unreasonable state government wished to impose regulations stricter than those of the AEC, then the federal government should not attempt to prevent the state government from being foolish on the side of strictness. Eventually, this action by the state would increase the cost of electricity, and this would soon force the state back to the AEC position. I protested that such an approach could lead to a less safe condition because intensifying one aspect of a reactor's operation (reduction of effluents) could cause more frequent shutdowns, with resulting possibilities of accidents. Flanigan responded that, if a plant's operation raised questions of safety, this presumably would violate AEC's safety standards and the AEC could then choose not to license the plant. I tried to point out that this became very complex and that the utility got caught in the middle. He replied that it was unfortunate but not at all unusual for a utility to feel it was being placed in an untenable position by a regulatory agency. I said that we could think of a number of outlandish requirements established by states. Flanigan replied that our federal system assumed states could be foolish.

This conversation made me realize that I had not previously understood the full implications of the Nixon administration's "new federalism."

AFTER LONG DELAYS, A LICENSE

As NSP's lawsuit against Minnesota made its way slowly through the courts, the AEC was considering whether to issue an operating license for Monticello.*

---

* When an application for an operating license was received, the AEC staff and the Advisory Committee on Reactor Safeguards again conducted comprehensive reviews to determine whether the plant, as constructed, could be operated safely. A hearing was not mandatory at this stage, as it was at the construction permit

After further technical reviews, the Advisory Committee on Reactor Safeguards concluded on January 10, 1970, that the plant indeed met its test, that is, it could be operated "without undue risk to the health and safety of the public." The AEC thereupon published in the Federal Register a notice of intent to issue an operating license. Petitions to intervene were promptly filed by the Minnesota Environmental Control Citizens Association (MECCA), by three University of Minnesota graduate students, and by a high school student. The AEC then in its discretion scheduled a public hearing before an atomic safety and licensing board (ASLB). It is noteworthy that Monticello's operating license application was the first to be contested or to be made the subject of a public hearing in seven years. The last previous contest had been over the Enrico Fermi Atomic Power Plant near Detroit, a fast breeder reactor that involved novel questions about safety.

The ASLB hearing was dominated, and subjected to long delays, by an unprecedented request made by MECCA at the outset of the proceedings. They asked to see the inspection reports prepared by the AEC's division of compliance regarding five other nuclear power reactors. The issue was a difficult one for us. As I noted in my diary:

> *If this request is complied with, it will open the doors to our furnishing reports, confidential information, etc. in great quantities, thereby overwhelming the regulatory staff* [which at this time was severely understaffed in relation to its workload] *with work and embarrassing vendors and utilities. If it is not complied with, the AEC will be accused of withholding information and we may be required to furnish the information anyhow under the Freedom of Information Act.*

The issue was discussed at a Commission meeting three days later:

> [AEC General Counsel Joseph] *Hennessey explained that the Commission's decision should be based on whether it was contrary to the public interest to release the information. The major concern was that an uninformed reader might become unduly alarmed by safety issues raised but not fully discussed in the reports.*

---

stage, but one could be requested by persons affected, or one could be scheduled by the AEC on its own initiative.

The commission finally directed the staff to make the reports available after deleting certain information we regarded as privileged.* The intervenors promptly protested the deletions, and the matter was then referred to a specially convened Atomic Safety and Licensing Appeals Board.

Meanwhile, much time had elapsed and NSP was feeling the pinch. On June 19, 1970, we received an outraged letter from chairman Ewald. He reminded us that the scheduled date for Monticello to be in operation had been the previous month, and that construction had been completed in accordance with that schedule. He estimated that the regulatory delays were now costing NSP $1,100,000 per month, were costing General Electric $500,000 per month, and were exposing utility customers to the risks of power curtailments. He then added this warning:

> If the delays encountered in this licensing procedure are duplicated in connection with the other nuclear power plants scheduled for commercial service in the next few years, it can safely be asserted that the splendid promise of nuclear power will have had a very short life.

Ewald concluded by calling on the AEC to get its regulatory act together through "strong and innovative leadership."

The matter of the privileged documents nevertheless dragged on all summer, finally being resolved in a series of complicated rulings that, in effect, ruled on the documents case-by-case. This controversy, which was to be replicated in subsequent hearings about other plants, was doubly unfortunate: not only did it cause delay but it also added to mistrust of the AEC by giving the false impression that we had something to hide about the safety of the plant.

On September 8, 1970, the AEC issued a limited license for Monticello authorizing the loading of fuel and low-power startup testing. This action was upheld in a state District Court despite an appeal by Minnesota's attorney general. Then on December 22 a federal district judge in St. Paul ruled in favor of NSP in its court case against Minnesota. The judge stated: "The fact that [in the Atomic Energy Act] Congress has directed, and not merely authorized, the AEC to effect a comprehensive licensing program for atomic energy is a strong indication of preemptive intent." (The Supreme Court, hearing the case on appeal, affirmed this decision in 1972.)

---

* We proposed to delete: (1) names of the inspectors and of people talked to by inspectors; (2) copies of internal regulatory correspondence with inspectors; and (3) references cited in the inspection reports.

On January 19, 1971, the AEC finally issued a license authorizing operation of Monticello. It had been more than a year since the AEC's Advisory Committee on Reactor Safeguards had voted its approval of such an action. Even then, the authorization was temporarily restricted to low- power operation until acceptable performance of feedwater pumps could be verified. This hurdle was passed a month later. The plant reached full design power and entered commercial operation in June 1971, more than a year behind schedule. From then until now Monticello has had one of the best operating records of any reactor of its type.*

SEQUELS

The Atomic Energy Act limits the term of operating licenses to 40 years, subject to renewal upon expiration. In 1985 Monticello became one of two plants— Virginia Electric Power Company's Surry-1 was the other—involved in a joint Department of Energy-Electric Power Research Institute study to evaluate the technical and economic feasibility of such renewals. The study concluded that there were no major obstacles to either plant's continuing to operate well beyond the initial 40 years. Monticello also served for a while as a pilot plant to demonstrate for other utilities the regulatory and technical path leading to renewal of an operating license. The Nuclear Regulatory Commission, meanwhile, has been developing the regulatory requirements for license renewal, and a final rule for extending operations an additional twenty years was issued in November 1991.[5] NSP expected at one time to submit an application for license renewal in December 1992, but this has more recently been held in abeyance. It is significant, moreover, that the utility has apparently decided that its next major power plant addition will be fueled by coal.

The Monticello case has been worth recounting in some detail because it was a harbinger of the rising tide of environmental opposition faced by the AEC as it sought to fulfill its responsibilities for regulating the licensing, construction, and operation of nuclear power plants. We shall now consider that opposition on a broader front.

---

* It is interesting to note that Bill Clinton has selected Hazel O' Leary, president of Northern States, to be secretary of energy.

NOTES

1. Folk song by Mike Murphy of the Hill-Dillies, a Minnesota satirical song duo.
2. I am indebted to NSP for much of the chronological detail in this account.
3. Foreman, ed., *Nuclear Power and the Public,* p. viii.
4. Walker, *Containing the Atom,* p. 315.
5. "Nuclear Plants: Life After 40," *EPRI Journal,* October/November 1990, pp. 20-29.

7

The Environmental
Onslaught

Nuclear energy is the most extreme case where public fear of
technology goes beyond what seems reasonable in the light of
actual experience.

—Spencer R. Weart[1]

THE MOVEMENT

The Monticello case was symptomatic of a new phenomenon for which we
in the AEC were ill prepared: the rise of a generalized opposition to nuclear
power plants on environmental grounds. Prior to 1969 there had been local
opposition to certain proposed plants. It had been rooted either in concern
about despoiling natural values, such as the scenery and beaches of the Pacific
coastline, or in questions about the safety of individual plants, such as those
situated near earthquake faults or near the centers of populated areas. By
contrast, the new opposition that began to appear early in 1969 was concerned
with more fundamental ecological problems, such as the pollution of air and
water. Furthermore, it was nationwide in scope, as demonstrated by the fact,
noted in the last chapter, that twenty states intervened on Minnesota's side in
the legal action brought by Northern States Power Company.

Environmental awareness had received strong impetus from the 1962 publication of Rachel Carson's epochmaking book *Silent Spring,* the first publication on ecological matters to reach a large audience. This noteworthy book, which has been compared in its influence with Harriet Beecher Stowe's *Uncle Tom's Cabin,* exposed in overwhelming detail and eloquent phrases the havoc being wrought on the natural environment by the widespread use of pesticides in agriculture. Carson's revelations aroused indignation, not only against the chemical and agricultural interests that caused the damage but also against the government departments that might have prevented it. The indignation was heightened by the attacks made on *Silent Spring* by some in government and industry.[2] Such attacks conveyed an impression of powerful interests intent on suppressing the truth.

Other experiences apparent to the average citizen also contributed to the spread of environmental consciousness. These included the acidification of water near coal mines, the profusion of solid waste, the littering of streets and highways, thickening layers of smog above Los Angeles and some other cities, the Love Canal community in New York State allegedly made uninhabitable by industrial waste, the spoliation of lakes and forests by acid rain, the blowout of an offshore oil drilling rig in the Santa Barbara Channel, and the fouling of rivers and lakes by industrial waste, including one river that actually caught fire.

While environmental consciousness had been growing throughout the 1960s, it experienced an exponential growth in the early Nixon years. In his recent book on Nixon, *One of Us,* Tom Wicker cites surveys showing that in May 1969 only 1 percent of respondents believed that the environment was the most important issue facing the president, whereas two years later this number had climbed to 25 percent.[3] The surge in opinion was both exemplified and stimulated by the first Earth Day, April 22,1970, in honor of which some 20 million people participated in rallies in dozens of cities, environmental teach-ins were conducted in some 200 colleges and universities, Congress took the day off (in order that members so disposed could participate in environmental observances in their home jurisdictions), and part of New York's Fifth Avenue was closed to traffic. At this point, environmentalism had truly become a mass movement.

Increasingly, environmental confrontations began to involve energy facilities—pipelines, refineries, offshore drilling platforms, transmission lines, and, especially, power plants of all kinds. The confrontations grew in number and intensity when it was proposed to increase the capacity of power plants to as much as 1,000,000 kilowatts, as opposed to the 60,000 to 100,000 kilowatts common in earlier decades. These huge facilities caused questions to be asked about the sources and transportation of their fuel, the disposal of their residues, their discharges of waste heat and radioactivity, the scarring of landscapes by transmission line corridors, and whether there were not more benign alternatives such as the use of geothermal or solar power. A new question was also being asked: whether society as a whole might not be better off if it reined in its seemingly insatiable appetite for energy.

NUCLEAR POWER AS A TARGET

Nuclear power provided an especially inviting target for environmentalist agitation during the Nixon years. A number of large new nuclear plants had reached or was nearing completion. The prospect was for many more such plants—in 1967, for the first time, more than half of the new generating capacity ordered by U.S. utilities had been nuclear. In the public mind there was an association between nuclear power and nuclear weapons. This association exacerbated the fear of serious accidents that would release lethal amounts of radiation. The nuclear community—the AEC, the Joint Committee, and industry—tried to minimize this fear by emphasizing the extreme improbability of such an event. What we were to discover, however, was that the public was not disposed or equipped to deal with probabilities. What many people seemed to demand of nuclear power was zero risk, never mind the comparison with other risks. This was frustrating to technical people trained in numerical analysis, but there it was.

There was another worrisome factor with which we had to contend in the public arena. This was a growing suspicion of and hostility to the AEC as an institution. To some extent this was a reflection of public attitudes toward science and technology in general. A public which had only recently regarded scientists and technologists with awe and admiration was becoming increasingly critical and mistrustful of them. In part this was a transfer of the resentment caused by technology-induced depredations to those believed to be responsible. As Spencer R. Weart has written: "The leading opponents...opposed nuclear energy as a way of opposing all complex centralized power—of fighting military, industrial, bureaucratic authority in general."[4] There was also an association of nuclear energy with the radioactive fallout from atmospheric tests which, until all but ended by the Limited Test Ban Treaty of 1963, were thought to have damaged the health of persons near test sites and threatened much wider injury. The AEC was held responsible for these alleged consequences and for its less than completely candid public accounting for them. In addition, there was mounting resentment of the alliance between the AEC and the Joint Committee on Atomic Energy, an alliance that seemed to insulate nuclear programs from some of the normal give and take to which other programs were subjected in the processes of government. Finally, there was widespread criticism of the apparent conflict of interest involved in the fact that the AEC was at the same time both regulating the use of nuclear power and promoting its development.

Antinuclear and anti-AEC sentiment was exacerbated by a wave of books and articles addressed to the general public. One of the most influential of the books was *The Careless Atom* by Sheldon Novick, a protégé of the prominent Washington University (St. Louis) environmentalist Barry Commoner and a very skilled writer. Novick's all-encompassing indictment mentioned every conceivable unfavorable aspect of nuclear power. He emphasized the possibility of accidents and what he considered the uncertainty of the technology for preventing them. As an indication that the industry itself expected catastrophic occurrences, he pointed to the Price-Anderson amendment to the Atomic Energy Act, which limited a utility's liability from a single accident to $500 million. Nor did Novick neglect the alleged hazards of routine radioactivity releases and other reactor wastes, the regulation of which he considered inadequate. Assessing the nation's energy future, Novick questioned the need for introducing nuclear power at the pace then existing. Another widely circulated book was *Perils of the Peaceful Atom* by Richard Curtis and Elizabeth Hogan. These authors went further than Novick in recommending that the entire nuclear program be dropped as a costly mistake.

Regarding the approaches adopted in this whole genre of publications, I had the following to say in a speech to members of the Edison Electric Institute in June 1969:

> Many of these publications use the effective propaganda technique known as "stacking the deck"—the technique of taking all the detrimental, isolated facts and information about a subject, misinterpreting other factual material, adding numerous statements— taken out of context—by authorities in the field, and placing all this material in a story that gives a completely one-sided viewpoint. Specifically, every fact and statement in such a story may be true, while the article as a whole, and the conclusion it draws, may be invalid and misleading. Such dishonesty is made more harmful by the fact that these articles are written as exposes and crusades in the public interest.

In another context, Dean Rusk once characterized this technique as "selective truth-telling." Two, of course, could play at this game and the AEC was guilty of some selective truth-telling of its own. Take this statement that appeared in an AEC report entitled "The Nuclear Industry—1969":

> No member of the general public has received a radiation exposure in excess of prescribed standards as a result of operation of any type of civilian nuclear power plant in the United States.

As the *New York Times* (January 16, 1970) pointed out, this statement was "not entirely frank." It was, in fact, so hedged about with qualifications that if examined in detail it became quite unimpressive. "No member of the general public" excluded those working in industry, and there had indeed been some excessive exposures in industry. "Exposure in excess of prescribed standards" begged a question, since the standards themselves were under attack as inadequate. "Civilian nuclear power plant" excluded military and research reactors, and there had been an accident at an army reactor in 1961 that killed three workers. "In the United States" excluded problems encountered in other countries, for example, the very serious accident to England's Windscale reactor that had caused a regional public health emergency. This kind of disingenuous oversell did further damage to the AEC's credibility among knowledgeable people. We had a good story to tell, and it would have been better to tell it with complete candor.

FIGHTING BACK

By May 1969 the AEC recognized that it and the nuclear power program it espoused were facing an unprecedented public acceptance crisis. The Commission therefore decided that the time had come to take active initiatives on the public relations front. A high-level staff group under the leadership of Assistant General Manager Howard C. Brown, Jr., was given the assignment of mounting a coordinated campaign to answer the critics. The other commissioners and I made a number of speeches, gave numerous press interviews, and made many appearances on television news programs to refute specific charges, sometimes engaging critics in face-to-face debate.

In my own speeches, which were unusually frequent in 1969, I endeavored to make the following points:

1. Continued increases in electricity supply were necessary to meet the needs of a rapidly expanding world population and the expectation of improved standards of living by people in both developed and developing nations. (I found it particularly frustrating that people with whose humanitarian objectives I readily identified seemed to feel that those objectives could be furthered by cutting back on the use of energy. This seemed to me to be wholly illogical and I said so on more than one occasion.)[5]

2. The only practical means of providing needed amounts of electricity in the near term were fossil-fueled (principally coal) and nuclear-fueled plants.

3. Nuclear plants were environmentally superior to coal plants, which spewed forth large amounts of noxious chemicals into the air. The mining and transportation of coal also had deleterious health and environmental effects that use of nuclear plants might obviate.

4. The use of nuclear plants could help conserve limited supplies of fossil fuels for essential uses in transportation and manufacturing.

5. Nuclear power plants, while not risk-free—all energy production involved some risk—were acceptably safe. As for the dread fear of radiation, I argued that the standards set by AEC on radiation exposure were based on years of scientific inquiry and reflected the recommendations of leading authorities around the world.

Generally I was low-key in my presentations, as characterized by my introduction to one speech: "Come, let us reason together." On one occasion, however, I felt provoked into some rather agitated comment. On October 29, 1969, I testified before the Joint Committee as one of the leadoff witnesses during their hearings on "Environmental Effects of Producing Electric Power." My testimony was, to say the least, vigorous, eliciting some surprise from the *Washington Post*'s reporter, who thought of me as "ordinarily a quiet, soft-spoken man." I accused foes of nuclear power of "engaging in unsubstantiated fear-mongering" and "hysteria" likely to bring on power shortages in years to come. Indulging, perhaps, in a little fear-mongering of my own, I added: ". . . a city whose life's energy has been cut, whose transportation and communications are dead, in which medical and police help cannot be had, and where food spoils and people stifle or shiver while imprisoned in stalled subways or darkened skyscrapers—all this also represents a dangerous environment."

Despite the occasional hyperbole, I would still maintain that the points I was making were essentially valid. Granted that the risk of building more nuclear power plants may not have been zero, I was arguing that such a course involved less risk than the available alternatives, namely, doing without the electricity or supplying the electricity by alternative means. Unfortunately, large segments of the public seemed unwilling to go along with this approach. Studies have shown that the public tends generally to be illogical in its evaluation of risks. Special fear seemed to be attached to the hazards of radiation, in part based on an association with the havoc wrought by nuclear weapons, in part on the unseen insidious nature of radiation, and perhaps also on the growing distrust of government and large-scale, government-sponsored technology. There was also an irrational sliding scale that people applied to different sources of radiation, being relatively far more accepting of medical X rays, transcontinental flights, and radon gas, for example, and far less accepting of routine power plant releases than the statistical risk estimates justified. One calculation, for example, indicated that a round-trip transcontinental jet flight exposed a person to 250 times as much radiation as did living for a year within twenty miles of a nuclear power plant.[6]

REACHING A LARGER AUDIENCE

One problem the AEC had in its public relations campaign was that many of our speaking engagements were before government, industry, or technical groups who were likely to be sympathetic; we were, in effect, preaching to the choir. We did, however, have a few opportunities to appear before a wider public. One such occasion took place on September 11, 1969, when Commissioner Ramey, Commissioner Thompson, and I appeared at a day-long public meeting at the University of Vermont in Burlington. The meeting had been suggested by Vermont senator George Aiken, a member of the Joint Committee on Atomic Energy. It received national attention.

The feature event of the day was an afternoon panel discussion presided over by Vermont governor Deane C. Davis, in which four nuclear critics squared off against Ramey, Thompson, and two other nuclear defenders.* The audience

---

* The other nuclear defenders were Dr. John Storer, head of the pathology and immunity section of Oak Ridge National Laboratory's biology division; and Stanley Auerbach, also from Oak Ridge, a specialist in the effects of radiation on ecology. Arrayed against them were Dr. Arthur R. Tamplin (more about him in chapter 8), Dr. Ernest Tsivoglou (Minnesota's adviser), Dean E. Abrahamson (professor of anatomy and physics at Washington University, St. Louis), and Clarence A. Carson (professor of fishery biology at Cornell).

was clearly on the side of the critics, and the performance of the defenders did little to win converts. Generally, their scientifically cautious responses to questions seemed technical, stiff, and full of qualifications. One of the problems that beset our side of the argument was that although we were convinced that existing radiation standards involved little risk, we could not prove this. Given that there was some uncertainty, it was difficult to argue that the small group of scientists who established the standards should have exclusive control over the public's exposure to radiation. The critics, on the other hand, gave answers and made statements that, while often inaccurate or exaggerated, were more confident, intelligible, and emotional.

In my own remarks, given in the evening to a smaller audience, I pointed out that to meet the physical needs of a growing population in an industrial civilization, a certain amount of pollution was unavoidable and that nuclear power was a way of meeting needs for electricity with relative safety and reliability while protecting the environment. As to the last point, I gave an extended analysis of how effluent releases from nuclear power plants were regulated and of how minimal they were compared with background radiation exposures from natural causes. My presentation was reasonably well received, but it did little to retrieve what one industry representative interviewed by *Nucleonics Week* termed "a disaster."[7]

The pronuclear forces had an opportunity to recoup a month later in a symposium held by the University of Minnesota. At this meeting, Commissioner Ramey represented the AEC and Congressman Craig Hosmer (R- CA) the Joint Committee. The format was more scholarly than it had been in Vermont, featuring a number of prepared papers and published proceedings that still make interesting reading today.[8] The pronuclear side did well in this format, but as with most scholarly symposia, the public relations impact was minimal.

On October 23 and 24 it was back to Vermont to face hostile audiences in Brattleboro and Bennington, respectively. At these meetings, the pronuclear side took off the gloves and slugged it out a bit more with the critics, with results certainly no worse than were obtained from the more reserved presentations in other meetings. This seemed to emphasize a point made by an industry public relations manager, namely, that technical facts by themselves did not hold their own against the emotional currents that underlay many of the opposition's arguments.

Believing that nuclear power was taking more than its deserved number of hits from the environmental movement, the Joint Committee attempted to right the balance by holding two extensive sets of hearings on "Environmental Effects of Producing Electric Power" in 1969 and 1970. Joint Committee chairman Congressman Chet Holifield (D-CA) was characteristically frank and unabashed in stating the motivation for the hearings in his opening statement on October 28, 1969:

> The JCAE's responsibility is to encourage the development of nuclear electric generating plants. A proper evaluation of the environmental impact of a nuclear electric plant can only be made by comparison with a conventional electric generating plant . . . They must be compared to be properly evaluated.[9]

Holifield obviously expected that such a comparison would show nuclear plants to an advantage over fossil-fueled ones. Part 1 was conducted during eight days in October and November 1969 and heard as witnesses government officials involved in the problem. Part 2 was conducted early in 1970 and heard nongovernmental witnesses. The hearings provided a wealth of information both about technical matters and about governmental processes for controlling environmental damage. They attracted very large audiences, particularly on the first few days.

Some good news for nuclear advocates came in December 1969 with the release of a study by the Department of Health, Education, and Welfare showing that there was almost no radioactivity in environmental samples collected in the vicinity of Commonwealth Edison's Dresden nuclear plant near Chicago. It was the most detailed and comprehensive study of a nuclear power plant's operation ever undertaken. To have a non-AEC, non-industry source confirm what we had been saying might have helped slightly to narrow AEC's "credibility gap."[10] But a new challenge was arising from within AEC's own organization.

NOTES

1. Spencer R. Weart, "Images of nuclear energy: Why people feel the way they do," *IAEA Bulletin,* March 1991, p. 30.
2. These are described in Frank Graham, Jr., *Since Silent Spring.*
3. Wicker, *One of Us,* p. 509.
4. Weart, "Images of nuclear energy," p. 35.
5. JCAE, *Hearings on Environmental Effects of Producing Electric Power,* Part 1, p. 89ff.

6. R. Wilson and E. A. C. Crouch, "Risk Assessment and Comparisons: An Introduction," *Science,* April 17, 1987, p. 268.

7. *Nucleonics Week,* September 18, 1969, p. 13.

8. Harry Foreman, ed., *Nuclear Power and the Public.*

9. JCAE, *Hearings on Environmental Effects of Producing Electric Power,* Part 1, p. 2.

10. The complete HEW report was reproduced as an appendix to the JCAE *Hearings on Environmental Effects of Producing Electric Power,* Part 1, pp. 824ff.

8

Challenge from Within

There is little doubt that the AEC is determined to rid itself
of Gofman and Tamplin or, at least, render them voiceless.

—Ralph Nader[1]

THE STERNGLASS EPISODE

The criticisms of AEC that drew the most attention in 1969 and 1970 were
those leveled by two research associates in the agency's own Lawrence
Radiation Laboratory at Livermore, California,* Dr. John W. Gofman and Dr.
Arthur R. Tamplin.

Gofman had been one of my graduate students at Berkeley in the early 1940s,
earning his Ph. D. in nuclear inorganic chemistry. He was as bright a graduate
student as I have ever had. He was a co-discoverer of the fissionable isotope
uranium-233, this work being presented as a very brilliant doctoral dissertation.
Then, rather abruptly, he changed course and went to medical school. I
remember being disappointed about this—it was during World War II and I
felt that a talent like Gofman's was sorely needed in the work on the nuclear
weapon. But in medicine as well he made a brilliant and important contribution, being one of the first, I believe, to associate phospholipids in the blood
with heart problems. After earning his medical degree, he became a full professor

---

* Now named Lawrence Livermore National Laboratory.

at Berkeley, teaching medical physics, and was given the rank of associate director at Livermore.

Tamplin also had an impressive background. He earned a Ph.D. in biophysics, studying under Gofman at Berkeley, and worked at the Rand Corporation on problems concerned with the space program. The two were charter members, Gofman being the director, of a biomedical division set up at Livermore early in 1963. As originally announced, the new unit was to concentrate on assessing the biological effects of radioactive fallout from nuclear tests. But after the achievement of the Limited Test Ban Treaty later in 1963, the group gave increased attention to the biological effects of other AEC programs. Gofman conducted a cytogenetics program that dealt in particular with the relation between cancer and the chromosomal makeup of cells. Tamplin, working under Gofman's supervision, concentrated on methods for predicting the distribution within the biosphere of radionuclides produced in nuclear explosions. Gofman gave up the leadership of the biomedical program in 1966 so that he could return to laboratory research, but Tamplin continued in the program.

In March 1969, on a visit to my old laboratory, the Lawrence Radiation Laboratory in Berkeley,* I conferred with Gofman, John R. Totter, director of AEC's Division of Biology and Medicine, which supervised and allocated funds for Gofman's work at Livermore, and Michael M. May, director of Livermore. At that time, all was peaceful between Gofman and the rest of us; there was no hint of the storm to come.

It all began in a rather roundabout way. Ernest J. Sternglass, Ph.D., a professor of radiation physics at the University of Pittsburgh's medical school, had been attracting a lot of media attention since about 1963 with writings and television appearances in which he argued that radioactive fallout from nuclear weapons tests had caused 375,000 infant deaths and uncounted fetal deaths. His reasoning seemed quite tortured. Noting that a gradual decrease in the number of infant deaths, which had been going on since the early 1940s, had been suddenly arrested beginning in 1952, he attributed the change to the increase in atmospheric nuclear testing that had occurred at that time. He then estimated the number of infants who might have survived had the previous rate of decrease in infant deaths continued past 1952 and claimed that this number of deaths was attributable to nuclear testing. The AEC's position was that Dr. Sternglass's conclusions were unsupported by the wealth of scientific information on this much-studied question and that they were based on a misinterpretation of the data and an incorrect use of statistics. (There was no justification for claiming that two events were necessarily connected just because they

---

* Now named Lawrence Berkeley Laboratory.

At the new Bio-Medical Building of the Lawrence Radiation Laboratory, Livermore, California, on March 6, 1969. From left, laboratory director Dr. Michael May; Dr. John Gofman, director of Livermore's Bio-Medical Division; Dr. John R. Totter, director of AEC's Division of Biology and Medicine; and Seaborg. Before long, Gofman would be embroiled in some bitter disputes with the rest of us, but all seemed well at this stage.

occurred at the same time.) Nevertheless, his conclusions obtained very wide publicity and the AEC decided that they could not be ignored.*

In a paper prepared for a Livermore seminar in April 1969, Tamplin criticized Sternglass's methods and assumptions. He then went on to state his own estimate of infant deaths from atmospheric tests: not 375,000, but 4,000, as well as 8,000 fetal deaths. When word got out about Tamplin's paper, the *Bulletin of the Atomic Scientists* invited him to submit it for publication. This prospect alarmed Livermore and AEC management because there had never been any acknowledgment or belief within the organization that fallout had caused infant or fetal deaths anywhere near Tamplin's estimates. Accordingly, Tamplin was asked by Dr. Totter, first by telephone and then in writing, to separate out the part of his paper containing his own estimates and send it "to a refereed journal, i.e., Health Physics , where other scientists would have an opportunity to comment on your lines of reasoning." Tamplin, reinforced now by Gofman, indignantly refused, and his paper was published by the *Bulletin* in its December 1969 issue.

THE GAUNTLET THROWN

This brush with AEC and laboratory management appeared to sharpen the interest of both Gofman and Tamplin in the question of how the AEC regulated the radioactive discharges from nuclear power plants. They soon formulated a position that was sharply critical. At the time, following guidelines established by the Federal Radiation Council (FRC), AEC had adopted a standard requiring that power plants endeavor to keep routine releases of radioactivity from nuclear power plants "as low as practicable" and, in any case, so low that members of the general public would be exposed to no more than 170 millirem of radiation in a year, an amount roughly equivalent to the average amount received from

---

* Seeking to explain this publicity, Philip M. Boffey wrote in Science (October 10, 1969, p. 199): "How could Sternglass achieve such wide exposure for his views when so many scientists believe he is wrong? Part of the answer probably lies in the fact that Sternglass makes good press copy—he has a startling theory that relates to important public issues. Another explanation is that Sternglass is in tune with a number of deep public moods—the revulsion against the military, the desire to end contamination of the environment, and the tendency to disbelieve the rosy reports emanating from government agencies."

natural sources in the United States.* Tamplin, now joined by Gofman, who had become personally interested in the controversy, concluded that this permitted level was too high and that it constituted a serious health hazard.

Roughly speaking, their reasoning was as follows: They assumed, contrary to some scientific argument, that there was no threshold below which radiation has no adverse biological effect and that the "damage is directly proportional to the dose *right down to the lowest doses.*"[2] They then extrapolated the often damaging dose-effect relationships observed at high doses to estimate the effect on the entire U.S. population if every person was exposed to AEC's maximum permissible dose.

Beginning in the fall of 1969, Gofman and Tamplin began to seek opportunities to publicize their position. While some of their presentations had a professional tone, others were more polemical. Gofman in particular was very effective in persuading lay audiences. His talks and his writings were well expressed, emotional, combative, and confident.

In the autumn of 1969 Tamplin appeared at two of the public forums on nuclear power mentioned in the last chapter, the Burlington, Vermont, conference in September and the University of Minnesota symposium in early October. He later told a *Washington Post* reporter that Livermore management did not want him to accept these invitations.[3] In the afternoon debate at Burlington he appeared as part of the environmental group critical of AEC's regulations.

By mid-1969 the AEC had become accustomed to public criticism from outsiders, but the appearance of a challenge from well-qualified and persuasive members of its own organization was a novel situation. Questions immediately arose as to whether there should be steps taken to inhibit further criticism by the two scientists. On the evening before the Minnesota event I had to cross a sort of personal Rubicon on this issue:

> *Mike May* [director of Livermore] *called me at home concerning the paper that Tamplin is to give tomorrow in Minneapolis at the symposium on "Nuclear Power and the Public." May said that*

---

* Both the International Commission on Radiological Protection (ICRP) and the National Committee on Radiation Protection and Measurements (NCRP) had concluded in the 1950s that 5 rem (5,000 millirem) per year should be the maximum permissible dose for atomic energy workers and that the general population should be exposed to no more than 10 percent of this amount, or 500 millirem. In issuing its guidance to federal agencies, the FRC divided the latter amount approximately by three.

Commissioner Thompson was quite upset about the Tamplin paper, which makes rather extreme assumptions concerning the potential concentration of reactor-emitted cesium-137 in milk. I told May that the paper, about which I had been informed earlier in the day, seemed to be very biased, but that Tamplin had the right to present it.

The conclusion of Tamplin's paper in Minnesota threw down the gauntlet in unmistakable fashion:

> In summary, as a member of the scientific community, I view the burgeoning nuclear power industry with a great deal of anxiety. My impression is that these power plants should be designed so as to approach absolute containment of the radioactivity . . . As the situation stands, aside from the bland reassurances of spokesmen for the Atomic Energy Commission and the nuclear power industry, there is no reason to assume that nuclear reactors will not jeopardize the public health and safety.[4]

The double negative with which Tamplin couched his last conclusion was symptomatic of a difficulty that plagued this entire debate. Although many scientists believed that the Gofman-Tamplin assumption of a linear relationship between the effects of radiation at high and low doses was incorrect, there was insufficient evidence either to prove or disprove this on scientific grounds. The same was true of AEC's opposite conclusion that the low levels of radiation permitted by its regulations were all but harmless—this could not be proven either. In the end the AEC had to fall back on its core assertion that the benefits of nuclear power plants far exceeded their adverse consequences. This threw the whole issue into the public arena, for as Harold P. Green has well maintained, "[r]isk-benefits decisions are not scientific problems. They are political concerns and should be debated in the rough and tumble of the political process."[5]

Later in October 1969, Gofman and Tamplin, in a joint paper to a meeting of the Institute for Electrical and Electronic Engineers (IEEE) in San Francisco, made the most definitive statement of their position to date: "If the average exposure of the U.S. population were to reach the allowable 0.17 rads [170 millirem] per year average, there would, in time, be 32,000 extra cases of fatal cancer plus leukemia per year, and this would occur year after year."[6] Their proposal was that allowable limits be reduced by a factor of ten.

Among the most widely noticed of the duo's public appearances was one in November 1969 before the Senate Subcommittee on Air and Water Pollution chaired by Senator Edmund S. Muskie (D-ME), who had recently earned much favorable attention as Hubert Humphrey's running mate in the 1968 presidential election. They made this appearance, according to Gofman, after being urged by Mike May not to do so.[7] They contended on this occasion, as they had previously, that a tenfold reduction in AEC's limits for radioactive discharges was urgently necessary.

FIRST REACTIONS

Following their testimony before the Muskie subcommittee, both Gofman and Tamplin were "called on the carpet" and interviewed at some length by Chairman Holifield and others on the Joint Committee. Gofman and Tamplin described the exchange as "some two hours of frank and substantive discussion." Holifield told me about the meeting during a telephone conversation some ten days later:

> *Holifield said he asked them why they were speaking out the way they were, citing the appearances in San Francisco, Vermont, Minnesota, and before the Muskie subcommittee. Gofman said he had sent his paper to the AEC but couldn't get any reaction, and was therefore forced to go to the public. Holifield said he told them it was a mistake to take their theories to laymen rather than to their scientific peers. Holifield said that Ed Bauser* [staff director of the Joint Committee] *later told him that Gofman and Tamplin seemed a little contrite about the methods they had pursued. Holifield suggested that, if I see them, I might assure them that I will arrange for the presentation of their theories before the very best people.*

On November 28, Gofman wrote to me complaining bitterly about how he and Tamplin were being treated. He referred particularly to the Joint Committee's "insult, veiled and unveiled intimidation, ridicule, sarcasm, and jokes." In this letter he also accused the AEC staff of bias and suggested the need for greater objectivity by the AEC "to solve this thorny problem."[8] So much for the contrition Ed Bauser had thought he detected!

The subject of what to do about the Gofman-Tamplin attacks on AEC's radiation standards now became a regular topic at Commission meetings. As to the meeting on December 11, 1969, I noted in my diary:

The other Commissioners appear to want to take some action in the way of rules against such statements. I am afraid that our only recourse is to answer the Gofman-Tamplin arguments logically in the public forum.

On December 17, Livermore director Mike May called to report two suggestions by Carl Walske, assistant for atomic energy to the secretary of defense. The first was that someone make a statement that the attacks being made by Gofman and Tamplin were simply expressions of personal opinion not backed by any evaluation. The second was that a technical working group be convened for about a week to review the scientific questions at issue, particularly whether there was any evidence justifying extrapolation of high-dosage radiation effects to low dose rates. I presented this suggestion at an executive meeting of the Commission that afternoon. There was general agreement that some sort of meeting or review was desirable and it was decided that AEC's Advisory Committee for Biology and Medicine would be the most suitable body to conduct it. Commissioner Ramey reported that Tamplin was planning to present a paper in which he would request a moratorium on nuclear power plants because of questions about the danger of reactor accidents. Commissioner Thompson questioned Tamplin's competence to be sounding off on an aspect of nuclear power so far afield from his specialty. Commissioner Johnson revived the suggestion that all AEC laboratory employees be required to publish their views in scientific journals or be required to clear them with the responsible AEC division. At this point, according to the secretariat's minutes of this meeting:

> The Chairman and Commissioner Larson voiced grave concern about any attempt to censor laboratory employees and particularly in this situation where Dr. Gofman was a full professor at the University of California. It was agreed that the best solution to the problem was to have individuals in such matters be criticized by their peers rather than restricted by the supporting agency.

CONTROVERSY ON THE MERITS

While the question of possible administrative restraints was being discussed, the AEC was also taking advantage of any opportunities to mount a refutation of Gofman and Tamplin on the merits of their scientific and technical contentions. A chief burden of our argument, as I communicated it to Senator Muskie following his subcommittee's hearings in December 1969, was that to reach the number of additional cancer deaths that Gofman and Tamplin were positing from exposure to reactor effluents, they had to assume that the entire U.S. population was being exposed continuously to the maximum levels allowed by AEC regulations. The fact was that no one—not a single person—was being exposed to such levels.*

Commissioner Thompson presented AEC's argument in a more extended fashion in an appearance before the Federal Radiation Council (FRC) on May 8, 1970. Thompson produced data showing that calculated exposures at plant perimeters were generally about 1 to 2 millirem per year; and that the number of people exposed to such levels would reach about 1 percent of the total population at some unspecified time in the future. He therefore concluded that for every citizen of the United States to be exposed to 170 millirem per year from nuclear power plants was a "physical impossibility" and that there was "no . . . threat to the health and safety of the public from present or planned nuclear power plants."[9] He later estimated that radioactive discharges from the nuclear plants then operating or under construction might be responsible for 1 extra fatal cancer case per year, not 32,000 as estimated by Gofman and Tamplin.

The FRC nevertheless decided at this meeting to review its basic guidance for radiation protection, which was the basis for the AEC regulations that had come under attack. They may well have had in mind the argument used by Gofman in responding to such points as Thompson and I were making: If the allowable limits are never approached, why not lower them?

The publication of AEC's views seemed only to incense Gofman and Tamplin. They now became quite abusive in public, calling AEC's refutations of their claims "blatantly stupid" and describing AEC officials as immoral and dishonest.[10] Moreover, their criticisms of the AEC and nuclear power began to attract persistent attention in the popular media. In the summer and autumn of 1970 articles about the two appeared in *McCalls, Esquire, Atlantic Monthly, Newsweek, National Geographic, Reader's Digest, Life, Barrons,* and the *National Journal.* During the same period, there were feature articles in several newspapers, including the *Philadelphia Enquirer* (a series of seven articles), the *Christian Science Monitor* (a three-part series), the *New York Times,* and the *Washington Post* (the last two with several articles each). In addition, all three television networks did special programs, one on ABC giving the subject of "Nuclear

* Gofman and Tamplin acknowledged that "few" people would be exposed to the maximum allowable radiation, but they argued that the limit might be approached as nuclear plants became more numerous.

Energy and the Environment" two hours. Ever present in these media presentations was the allegation about 32,000 extra cancer deaths per year, a statistic that by its very repetition began to achieve a semblance of reality. Gofman and Tamplin themselves made a number of public appearances at forums where the nuclear power issue was debated. Gofman, in particular, was much in demand for appearances on television news and talk programs.

As the public debate proceeded, Gofman and Tamplin hardened their position. No longer advocating a tenfold reduction in AEC's allowable limits, they now maintained that "the laws should read that the acceptable limit is zero . . . and that the privilege of releasing a pollutant to the environment must be negotiated." [11] They later backed away, however, from the specific prediction of 32,000 extra fatal cancer cases. When a number of other investigators who shared their basic premises came up with lower numbers, Gofman said that the fact that "the precise numerical estimates of hazard differ among investigators is highly secondary. The real issue is that the hazard is large rather than negligible."[12] And indeed, when the newly formed Committee on the Biological Effects of Ionizing Radiation (BEIR)* concluded in 1972 that the Gofman-Tamplin estimate of deaths from reactor effluents was too large by a factor of five, it was still widely interpreted as a vindication of their work.

ADMINISTRATIVE ACTIONS

The scientific argument the AEC had with Gofman and Tamplin was all but obscured in late 1970 and 1971 by a running fight over some administrative actions taken at Livermore to reduce the size of the two men's budgets and staffs, particularly those of Tamplin. On January 14, 1970, while I was in Spain on official travel, word came down that President Nixon had directed that an additional cut of $100 million be made in AEC's budget for fiscal year 1971, the makeup of the cut being left largely to us. In due course Livermore was notified that its activities would have to be cut by about 10 percent. Discussions then ensued between laboratory management and AEC program directors about how these cuts should be allocated.

It should be noted that under the contracts for management of AEC facilities, direct responsibility for personnel decisions rested with the contractor,

---

* The BEIR Committee was established by the National Academy of Sciences at the request of HEW Secretary Robert Finch, with the request that investigation of the Gofman-Tamplin thesis be a first order of business.

in this case the University of California. AEC, of course, exercised influence through the program management and budgetary processes, but if Livermore director Mike May had been determined to fire Gofman and Tamplin, there was no direct action AEC could have taken to prevent this. I was therefore relieved when at a meeting with the Commission on April 17,

> *May brought up the Gofman-Tamplin matter, making recommendations that were essentially identical to those I had been making to my fellow Commissioners. He said that it would be very counterproductive to fire them and that the only real solution lay in answering their accusations, no matter how intemperate, in open and public debate.*

Yet Gofman's provocations were such as to cause May to waver in this tolerant attitude. The episode that all but drove him over the edge was a letter that Gofman wrote to the Atomic Industrial Forum after the AIF printed a critique by Victor Bond, associate director of Brookhaven National Laboratory. In his letter, Gofman wrote:

> The AIF, AEC, and Dr. Bond all seem to believe that a stupid set of lies will enable them to ram ill-considered atomic programs down the throats of the American public. The more you all lie, hide the facts, and deliberately and unashamedly distort every responsible criticism, the earlier will be the demise of your outrageous activities.[13]

After reading this letter May told me that Gofman's practice of writing "libelous letters" had reached the point where it seemed necessary to terminate his relationship with the laboratory unless he promised to desist.

This added provocation may well have added to the severity of the staff cuts imposed on Gofman and Tamplin by the laboratory. The cuts were the subject of an article in the *Washington Post* on July 5, 1970. The article appeared to be written entirely from the Gofman-Tamplin viewpoint.* It disclosed that Gofman's staff of twelve had been reduced by two but that a far heavier blow had fallen on Tamplin. He had lost ten of his twelve research assistants and his secretary. Gofman told the *Post* that he did not consider the reduction in his

---

* The reporter, Thomas O'Toole, told me later that an additional portion based on an interview with Livermore's Roger Batzel had been "bitten off in the composing room" and that this was "overlooked in the editorial department." "That was unfortunate," O'Toole said, "because Batzel's remarks gave the story some balance."

staff a reprisal ("others were cut more," he acknowledged). Tamplin, on the other hand, felt that the action against him was too pointed to be explained away in terms of an overall budget cut. He interpreted it as an invitation to quit. "That would make it too easy for them," he said. "They're going to have to fire me."

Enter now Ralph Nader. The day the *Post's* article appeared, Nader wrote a hard-hitting letter to Senator Muskie, accusing the AEC of being "a cliquish technocracy keeping the public at bay and dissenting . . . scientists wrapped in invisible chains for fear of . . . job loss." He said that we were suppressing scientific freedom and that, if we succeeded, Congress would be deprived of information needed to evaluate programs. Noting that Gofman and Tamplin had testified at Muskie's invitation, Nader implied that the senator owed them protection against any unjust treatment that followed such testimony. Senator Muskie passed Nader's letter along to the AEC, asking for our comments. Nader had evidently also sent a copy of his letter to the *Washington Post*, and they published large excerpts from it.

Gofman appeared to have been emboldened by the support and publicity being given to his complaints. On Friday, July 10:

> *Commissioner Thompson called me at home at about 6:45 P.M. He said he had just received a call from Roger Batzel, who was very agitated as the result of another confrontation with Gofman. I called Roger immediately; he told me that Gofman had demanded that all of Tamplin's people, including his secretary, be restored to him, and that if this was not done within 36 hours, he, Gofman, would take some drastic, irreversible action. I told Batzel that it would be impossible to comply with such a demand on such a time scale (which would mean by Sunday morning, July 12) and that he should make no attempt to do so.*

Tamplin's people were not restored. Gofman took no drastic action.

We replied to Muskie's letter two weeks after receiving it. The interim period had been spent compiling a chronology of administrative actions at Livermore, giving the reasoning behind each move. The compilation showed, we contended, that the actions taken were not "in reprisal for criticism" but "in the interest of scientific productivity and in order to reflect changes in priorities." We then concluded:

> There are approximately 21,000 scientists engaged in the national atomic energy program. We could not hope to recruit or retain scientists of outstanding competence if they were not free to engage

in open and critical discussion of the scientific issues. Of course, this freedom, like all our cherished freedoms, carries with it a corresponding responsibility. For scientists—in whom society entrusts so much in its future health and welfare—it carries a special responsibility for careful, reasoned, and accurate accountings to the public of their findings.

Muskie wrote to the AEC again on August 5. Our report, he said, did "not appear to be an unbiased review of the allegations made by Drs. Gofman and Tamplin" because it was produced by people who disagreed with their scientific conclusions. He felt the need for a review by an unbiased third party. "For that reason," he concluded, "I intend to propose that the American Association for the Advancement of Science, or another appropriate, independent group, undertake a complete review of this situation and report to the Subcommittee on Air and Water Pollution at a public hearing." True to his word, Muskie wrote to AAAS president Athelstan Spilhaus on August 12, inviting the association to review "this potential threat to the free and open discussion of scientific issues." Five days later, Livermore director Michael May issued a statement in which he said he would welcome an independent investigation.

Late in October Gofman was informed that a routine review of his program was to occur in November, and the several scientists who were to conduct the review were identified. He then wrote me a highly emotional letter objecting to the procedure. He considered it to be a "further reprisal" against him by John Totter (director of AEC's biology and medicine division), whom he accused of persistently "slandering my person, my work, and my scientific competence." Totter knew full well, Gofman contended, that two of the reviewers were "antagonistic." Gofman then accused me of hindering cancer research by condoning the actions of Totter and his staff and bitterly reproached me for a lack of fairness. He averred that he would not object to an unbiased review of his work, and Batzel informed me by phone that Gofman had named five individuals who he believed could conduct such a review.

In my reply I told Gofman that I accepted his comments "as a sincere attempt to be very frank" in making known his views. I pointed out that it was a common AEC practice to review contractor programs and identified several recent or ongoing reviews of other programs in the biology and medicine field. I then stated that we would take "the unusual step" of adding to the review team three of the five individuals he had mentioned to Batzel. We declined, however, to remove any "members already engaged in the task." In conclusion, I expressed hope that all of us would be able to rest on the conclusions reached in the forthcoming AAAS review of his disagreements with the AEC.

In due course the technical reviews of the Livermore programs were completed, and at a Commission meeting on March 19, 1971:

> *We discussed whether we should send a letter to Livermore encouraging them to reduce the programs of Gofman and others based on the critical reviews of their programs. We decided that we would meet with Batzel and discuss this further in view of the sensitivity of taking any Commission action connected with the work of Gofman, despite the merits of the case.*

The meeting with Batzel occurred a week later. It was agreed that Gofman's research would be cut back on the basis of the critical reviews. The one concession we made to the "sensitivity" problem was the decision that Batzel would merely inform us that he was making the cut. Normally, AEC (Totter) might have written to him suggesting that he do it, but by now we were reluctant to have the record show such direct involvement.

REVIEWS AND REACTIONS

Later in November 1970 Tamplin and Gofman's delicately titled book, *"Population Control" Through Nuclear Pollution* (this time Tamplin was listed as the primary author), was published and the authors made appearances before different groups around the country on its behalf. The book, written in popular style, was in part a diatribe pushing the authors' views on the various scientific issues between them and the AEC, in part an account of their alleged abuse at the hands of AEC and laboratory authorities, and in part an alarmist attack on AEC programs across the board. They followed this book the next year with another one, *Poisoned Power: The Case Against Nuclear Power Plants.* Published in paperback only, it was distributed to student and environmental groups as a sort of handbook. Using much of the same material as in the previous book, it provided arguments and counterarguments for use in debate about the merits of nuclear power and suggested tactics to use in pushing the environmental cause.

In December 1970, in response to the request by Senator Muskie that it investigate charges that the scientific freedom of Gofman and Tamplin had been abridged by the AEC and Livermore, the AAAS established a Committee on Scientific Freedom and Responsibility. I do not recall, however, that any specific investigation ever took place. Gofman left Livermore on or about January 1,

1973. His relations with laboratory management towards the end of his tenure seemed cooperative, and he continued to serve Livermore as a private consultant. Tamplin left Livermore on September 1, 1973, to join the Natural Resources Defense Council, a prominent nongovernmental public interest organization that has done some excellent work, particularly in the field of arms control.

The prolonged encounter with Gofman and Tamplin further scarred the already bruised image of the AEC and the nuclear power program. Although we sought to justify our positions as being rationally based on scientific merit, it was widely perceived that an element of personal reprisal had crept in. The encounter also raised new questions in the public mind about the adequacy of AEC's controls over radioactive emissions from nuclear power plants and added significantly to the pressure on the agency to make those controls more stringent.

NOTES

1. In a letter to Senator Edmund S. Muskie, July 5, 1970.
2. Gofman and Tamplin, *Poisoned Power*, p. 297. Italics in original.
3. Thomas O'Toole, "Two Physicists Bucking AEC on Safety Report Squeeze," *Washington Post*, July 5, 1970.
4. Foreman, ed., *Nuclear Power and the Public*, pp. 64-65.
5. Harold P. Green, *Science*, February 26, 1971, p. 783.
6. Quoted in Gofman and Tamplin, *Poisoned Power*, p. 97.
7. O'Toole, "Two Physicists Bucking AEC."
8. Quoted in Walker, *Containing the Atom*, p. 345.
9. Federal Radiation Council Meeting, Minutes and Record of Actions, May 8, 1970.
10. Walker, *Containing the Atom*, p. 348.
11. Tamplin and Gofman, *"Population Control" Through Nuclear Pollution*, p. 48.
12. *Nucleonics Week*, November 26, 1970, p. 3.
13. Quoted in Walker, *Containing the Atom*, pp. 352-3.

9

Lowering the Limits

SEVERAL POINTS OF VIEW

The charges by Gofman, Tamplin, and others that the AEC's restrictions on radioactive releases from nuclear power plants were too lenient presented more than a public relations challenge. We had to decide on a substantive response: Did we wish to reaffirm the existing standards or to amend them; if the latter, how?

The issues were discussed several times at Commission meetings in the fall of 1969, without agreement. At first I was alone among the commissioners in wanting to adopt lower numerical limits. I had not advocated making such a change in prior years, but in the circumstances of 1969 I felt that the AEC's position of holding to the higher limits when utilities could meet lower ones with relative ease was logically weak and that it detracted further from the agency's already declining image.

The other side of the argument was much as expressed by Congressman Craig Hosmer, who took occasion to speak to me about the matter at a luncheon for visiting Brazilian officials on October 27.

> Hosmer told me that he thought the current uproar concerning radioactive effluents from nuclear power plants would diminish. He hoped, therefore, that we wouldn't be stampeded into requiring lower radioactivity levels since costly apparatus would be required to meet such standards, unnecessarily burdening the nuclear power industry.

I nevertheless persisted in my position at meetings of the Commission and as the year wound down, I began to get some support from Ramey.

Pressures soon began to mount from outside the AEC. On February 5, 1970, we presented the issue at a meeting of the AEC's Advisory Committee on Reactor Safeguards. The committee was unanimous in believing that the standards should be made more stringent. We also learned at about this time that the President's Science Advisory Committee (PSAC) might soon suggest that we tighten our standards and that Health, Education, and Welfare Secretary Robert Finch had requested that the Federal Radiation Council look into the possibility of tightening its guidelines, which were the basis for AEC's standards. These outside opinions seem to have influenced the positions taken by commissioners such that, on February 20:

> *We finally approved, by a vote of 4 to 1, with Thompson dissenting, amendments to AEC regulations (10CFR Parts 20 and 50) that will tighten the control of effluents in light water reactors. This will now be discussed with members of the JCAE.*

While we expected some lack of enthusiasm from the Joint Committee, we were not prepared for the virulence of its opposition. On February 26:

> *Ramey and I, along with others from the AEC, met with Holifield, Hosmer, and principal staff people from the JCAE. Ramey described our proposed action, namely, that we wanted to add to our regulations the requirement that radioactive effluents be kept as low as practicable and that, in order to make this meaningful, we wanted to define what this meant in numerical quantities. Holifield felt, and Hosmer agreed, that this would be letting the Joint Committee down after all its support of the AEC. Holifield thought any change in standards should come through action by outside bodies such as the Federal Radiation Council or the International Commission on Radiological Protection, not from the AEC itself. I argued that it was time for the AEC to show some leadership in the national movement toward cleaning up the environment. I noted that the recommended changes in regulations represented the unanimous view of our regulatory people and the Advisory Committee on Reactor Safeguards and that, if we meant what we said about our regulatory function operating independently of our development function, we had to take such views very seriously. I pointed out further that increased stringency was being urged by the President's Science Advisory Committee, the Office of Science and Technology, many members of Congress, the Council on Environmental Quality, and the*

Federal Power Commission, and that it behooved the AEC to move when it would seem to be on our own initiative rather than to wait until it was clear we had been forced to move by outside pressures. We didn't succeed in convincing Holifield, and the meeting ended with an emotional statement by him in which he said that if we took this step we would so undercut his effectiveness that he would no longer be our supporter in Congress on any matter that required his help.

While Holifield's position in this case might seem to have been headstrong and unreasonable, one had to be sympathetic with what was at stake for him. He had served on the Joint Committee since its inception in 1946 and, by dint of extremely hard and dedicated work, had become probably its most knowledgeable and influential member on nonmilitary matters.* Holifield was among those on the Joint Committee who believed that the group could be creative in the making of policy and the development of programs, as opposed to the more traditional view that a congressional committee's role should be limited to review and oversight. In answer to those critics who argued that the Joint Committee was usurping the executive branch's prerogatives in creating policy and pushing programs, Holifield was forthright and unyielding, saying on one occasion: "Sometimes we feel that maybe the Congress should set some policies in this Nation, and the administrative agencies should carry them out."[1] He believed deeply that furtherance of the peaceful uses of nuclear energy was in the best interests of this country and the world. He clearly recognized the public pressures that were building up to threaten the future of the technology and the institutions that upheld it, including the AEC and the Joint Committee, and he seemed to feel that stubborn and consistent combat against all such pressures was the wisest course of action. I shared Holifield's enthusiasm for the peaceful atom but differed with him in being more willing than he to concede that our critics might be right in some particulars and to countenance compromise and concession in trying to reach the goals we both espoused.

Meanwhile we were receiving divided counsel from industry. Officials from the General Electric Company, whose boiling-water reactors constituted a significant fraction of the reactor market, told us that they could without difficulty reduce radioactive effluents to less than 5 percent of our existing

---

* In their 1963 book on the Joint Committee, *Government of the Atom*, Harold P. Green and Alan Rosenthal wrote about Holifield (p. 49): "In order to study on weekends and until eleven or twelve most evenings, he has given up golf, hunting, and fishing."

With three chairmen of the all-important Joint Committee on Atomic Energy. From left, Congressman Melvin Price, Congressman Chet Holifield, and Senator John O. Pastore. Pastore and Holifield alternated as chairman during my ten years at the AEC. Holifield, a member of the JCAE since its beginning in 1946, was probably its most dedicated and influential member until he resigned in December 1974. Price, also one of the original JCAE members, became chairman during the 93rd Congress, 1973-74.

limits, and they urged us strongly to set actual numbers in any modifications of those limits. They felt that the element of certainty that numbers would introduce would be important to their design efforts. On the other hand, top officials of the Atomic Industrial Forum (AIF), the nuclear industry's trade association, contended, just as Hosmer had in the conversation reported above, that our proposed stricter standards could add significantly to the cost of nuclear power plants. The AIF officials agreed that power reactors in routine operation discharged only a small fraction of the radioactivity permitted by AEC regulations. Still, contingencies could be foreseen in which a much higher release would take place, and the lenient limits in the current regulations were thought to provide a cushion to absorb such incidents.[2] An example given was a possible failure of fuel element cladding.* If regulations were tightened so as to eliminate this cushion for contingencies, plants might have to be designed, built, and operated to a more exacting and, the AIF thought, much more costly standard. The AIF therefore requested that we not publish our proposal in the Federal Register for public comment until the nuclear power industry had been given an opportunity for further assessment and comment.

FIRST PROPOSALS

At Holifield's request, JCAE and AEC staffs got together early in March 1970 to see whether a compromise solution could be reached. Our people described the meeting as "stormy." The solution reached amounted pretty much to a full retreat by the AEC. We decided on a new version of our regulation in which, in accordance with the Joint Committee's wishes, numerical limits for radiation exposure would not be lowered. Instead, the proposed amendment would merely require licensees to make reasonable efforts to keep such exposures "as low as practicable" and to present evidence that they had done so in periodic reports to the AEC. The as-low-as-practicable criterion had long been an implicit part of our regulatory philosophy, but now we proposed to formalize and strengthen it. We hoped that the new requirements would assure further improvements in radioactivity control as advances in technology were made.

---

* Sheldon Novick cited a 1966 instance when the Pacific Gas & Electric Company asked for temporary relief from AEC standards because of a failure of cladding at its Humboldt Bay plant. The request was denied and PG&E was forced to operate the plant at a reduced power level until the defective cladding could be replaced. (*The Careless Atom*, pp. 111 ff.)

The proposed rule was duly issued for public comment on March 28, 1970. Minor changes were made as a result of comments received, and the rule became effective on January 2, 1971.

But the issue would not go away. Environmentalists and some members of Congress continued to press for lower numerical limits. Somewhat to our surprise, we received complaints from industry that the AEC's new guidelines were not specific enough. It also became clear that if the AEC did not on its own lower its numerical standards such action might well be imposed on us by the new Environmental Protection Agency (EPA). The EPA came into existence pursuant to the National Environmental Policy Act of 1969, which became effective on January 1, 1970. It swiftly became the largest independent regulatory agency in the Federal government. It took from the Interior Department responsibility for clean water; from HEW clean air and waste disposal programs; from the Food and Drug Administration pesticide research and standards; from Agriculture pesticide registration; and from AEC radiation monitoring. It also completely absorbed the functions of the Federal Radiation Council, whose guidance the AEC had followed in large measure in setting its own standards.

There was also international example to consider. At an International Atomic Energy Agency symposium in New York in August 1970 it became evident that most countries with nuclear power plants were setting lower legal limits for radioactive effluents than those of the AEC or those recommended by the ICRP.[3]

As a rearguard action, Holifield and Hosmer sponsored and steered through the House a bill, one of whose provisions would, in effect, have removed control over radiation standards from the EPA and placed it instead in the hands of the National Committee on Radiation Protection and Measurements (NCRP). The legislation passed the House by a vote of 345 to 0 on September 30, two days before the EPA was to come into existence. Dwight Ink, assistant director of the Office of Management and Budget, called me about this bill the day after it was passed to say that the House's action could be subject to strong criticism on grounds that the NCRP was considered by some to be a creature of the AEC.* Indeed, the Senate, eager to buoy up the EPA, amended the bill to delete

---

* The NCRP was a statutory body of 65 members chosen for their expertise in radiation measurement and radiological effects. The members served for staggered six-year terms. As of late 1969 2 of the 65 were AEC employees chosen not because of their affiliation but for their competence as individuals. While the committee used data obtained from AEC research, it also used information from a wide variety of other sources in a number of countries. AEC research undoubtedly had an influence on the committee's work, but it was an almost

the provision transferring authority over radiation standards, and the Senate's version was accepted by the House-Senate conference committee.

At a Commission meeting on April 1, 1971, we discussed a proposal that in effect would have required that annual exposure of individuals living near the boundary of a nuclear power plant site be kept to less than 5 millirem, an enormous reduction from the existing maximum of 170 millirem. It took three meetings before all of the commissioners were ready to go along with such a reform, but this finally occurred on April 12.

Once more the AEC presented its proposal to the Joint Committee and once more we encountered an extremely emotional adverse reaction from Holifield. Just as he had in February 1970, Holifield indicated that he would cease to support the AEC if we took this step. We had also to contend this time with opposition from Senator John Pastore, who, under the Joint Committee's scheme for rotating the chairmanship between House and Senate with each new Congress, had succeeded Holifield as chairman in January 1971. Momentarily we once again hesitated, asking the AEC staff to look into the possibility of setting radioactivity limits as a range, such as 5 to 10, or 5 to 15, millirem per year and also of drafting the instruction as a guide rather than as a regulation. Ramey, in particular, was reluctant to proceed in the face of Joint Committee opposition. But on May 6:

> *We finally obtained Ramey's concurrence in the proposed amendments. The force of the argument is so great that the Commission feels it simply must go ahead and make this improvement. An important factor is that EPA is pressing to set similar criteria on their own. We are hoping to coordinate our announcement with them.*

Coordinating with EPA didn't turn out to be so simple a matter. A disagreement quickly developed as to who should issue the numerical guides, we or they. On June 1, a large meeting was held between top officials of the two agencies. It quickly became apparent that on both sides the issue was in large part one of image with the public.

> [EPA Administrator William J.] *Ruckelshaus felt that EPA should do it first in order to establish credibility with the public that EPA was taking the initiative as a standard-setting agency acting independently of the AEC. I objected, pointing out that*

---

libelous exaggeration to contend that this large group of highly-esteemed and well-trained experts would surrender their independent judgment. Yet, Dwight Ink was faithfully representing a widely held opinion.

> *the AEC was known to have had this matter under study for more*
> *than a year and that, if we deferred now to EPA, it would create*
> *an adverse impression that we had delayed acting until pushed*
> *into it by EPA.*

The issue was not settled at this meeting, but within the next few days compromise wording was concocted that allowed AEC to issue a *Federal Register* announcement of a proposed regulation. In our biweekly report to the White House we noted that "the proposed radiation guidelines . . . would limit exposure to persons living near the plants to less than 5 percent of the average natural background radiation."

Our issuance brought a call from Holifield to Ramey restating his adamant opposition. It brought also a visit from 26 utility chief executives.

> *The visitors expressed their strong disapproval of our recent action. I*
> *tried to impress on them that in the long run this would be to the*
> *advantage of the utilities as well as of the AEC and the American people.*
> *They were concerned that our action amounted to a capitulation to the*
> *demands of Gofman and Tamplin. We tried to convince them that we*
> *had acted with more in mind than that. They also expressed concern*
> *that this action would result in demands by unions for impossibly low*
> *exposure levels for utility employees. I believe that the meeting was useful*
> *in allowing the industry people to blow off steam.*

This was as far as the matter had proceeded when I left the AEC in the summer of 1971.

SEQUELS

The proposed amendments were the subject of a rule-making hearing that convened for seventeen days spread over the first five months of 1972. Active participants in the hearing included the AEC regulatory staff, 3 power reactor manufacturers, an intervenor group representing some 20 electric utilities, another intervenor group representing more than 50 individuals and environmental groups, and the states of Minnesota and Vermont. One of the contentions discussed was that the restrictions in the proposed guidelines were too severe; another was that they were too lenient. The hearing recessed on May 6, 1972, pending the preparation by the AEC of an environmental statement on the likely effects of the proposed numerical guidance.

The final environmental statement was issued in July 1973. Hearings on the proposed numerical guides then resumed late in the year. When the AEC passed out of existence in January 1975, there had been no formal issuance supplanting the old standard of 170 millirem. Ultimately, on January 13, 1977, the EPA issued a standard (40CFR190) establishing the maximum exposure at 25 millirem per year, not 5 millirem per year as the AEC had recommended more than five years earlier. To provide for the contingency situations that so concerned the industry in 1970, the regulation provided that "[t]he standards may be exceeded if . . . a temporary and unusual operating condition exists and continued operation is in the public interest."

One reason—perhaps the main reason—why the final issuance was so long delayed was that public pressure for it had diminished. Long before the new regulations became effective, routine emissions of radioactivity, once the focus of such intense controversy, had ceased to be much of an issue. Indeed, in his maiden speech as AEC chairman on October 20, 1971, my successor, James Schlesinger, stated his belief that "the argument over radioactive discharges is pretty well off the boards." (As noted above, Hosmer had predicted two years earlier that this would occur.) Antinuclear forces had long since switched their emphasis to questions of safety, particularly the adequacy of emergency core cooling systems to shut reactors down safely in the event of a malfunction.

NOTES

1. Quoted in Green and Rosenthal, *Government of the Atom*, p. 12.
2. Similar arguments on the need for a cushion had been offered by Thompson in testimony before the Joint Committee in October 1969. (JCAE, *Hearings on Environmental Effects of Producing Electric Power*, Part 1, pp. 153ff.)
3. *Nucleonics Week*, August 20, 1970, pp. 4-5.

Part IV

RISE AND FALL OF THE BREEDER

10

Getting Off the Ground

BEGINNINGS

It was the conviction of scientists who worked in the World War II atomic energy project that the energy content of uranium, if it could be fully realized, promised a huge new source of low-cost electricity as well as the conservation of fossil fuels for uses for which they were peculiarly suitable, such as in transportation and as industrial raw materials. The scientists were further convinced that the development of breeder reactors—those that would produce more fissionable material than they consumed—was essential to making available this full potential.

The latter conclusion was implicit in the process by which breeding occurs. In any nuclear reactor, the fissioning of each atom of a fissionable material, such as uranium-235, produces not only energy but also two or three neutrons. To continue the chain reaction, one of these neutrons must go on to cause another fission. The remaining neutrons may either escape the reactor completely or be absorbed by nonfissionable nuclei within the reactor. In a breeder reactor, one or more of the "extra" neutrons is absorbed by a fertile nucleus, a nucleus that is itself not fissionable but that becomes so when it absorbs another neutron. This new fissionable material can then be used to fuel the same or another reactor. More specifically, in a reactor employing the thorium cycle, fertile thorium-232 is transmuted into fissionable uranium-233. In a reactor employing the uranium cycle, fertile uranium-238 is transmuted into fissionable plutonium-239.* Breeding thus makes possible the utilization in energy production not only of the fissionable material in uranium ore but of the far more plentiful fertile material as well. For each atom of fissionable uranium-235 in nature there are about 140 fertile uranium-238 atoms that can be bred into plutonium.

In the early stages, soon after World War II, many types of breeder reactor were visualized. Some would employ the uranium cycle, some the thorium cycle. Some, the "fast breeders," would employ neutrons traveling at the speed at which they are liberated in fission. Others, the "thermal breeders," would employ neutrons slowed down by some moderating material such as water. Another important differentiation involved the type of coolant employed to carry off the heat of fission and deliver it to a power-generating system. Among the coolants proposed for thermal breeding were water and molten salts; among those proposed for fast breeding were inert gas (such as helium) and liquid metal (such as sodium).

In the United States and several other countries, decisions were made quite early that a reactor employing fast neutrons, utilizing the uranium cycle, and cooled with liquid sodium, the so-called liquid metal fast breeder reactor (LMFBR), was the most attractive concept to pursue. Utilizing fast neutrons seemed preferable because nonproductive absorption of neutrons is less in fast breeders than it is in thermal breeders; thus, the breeding ratio would be greater in fast than in thermal breeders. The uranium cycle was selected in preference to the thorium cycle largely because it had become familiar in work with the wartime plutonium production reactors, whereas little was then known about the physical and nuclear properties of thorium. In addition, fast breeders were thought to work better on the uranium than on the thorium cycle. Liquid sodium was selected as the coolant because of its excellent heat-transfer and small neutron-absorption properties and because it had little moderating effect on the speed of the neutrons.

Experimental breeder reactors were built at AEC facilities beginning in the late 1940s to demonstrate the feasibility of the LMFBR concept. One of these, the Experimental Breeder Reactor 1 (EBR-1) at the AEC's Idaho reactor testing station, produced the world's first electricity from the fission process when a small generator was hooked on in December 1951. The amount produced was estimated at 200 electrical kilowatts. To indicate how secret even civilian

---

* Such transmutation occurs in conventional (nonbreeding) light water reactors as well, but in these the amount of new fissionable material produced is less than the amount consumed. Even so, the plutonium-239 resulting from the transmutation accounts for some 40 percent of the energy these plants produce.

nuclear activities were at this time, this accomplishment was not made publicly known until nearly a year later. EBR-1 was disabled in a 1955 meltdown accident. It was designated as a National Historic Landmark in August 1966, President Johnson himself conducting the ceremony at the site.

In 1963, a larger fast reactor, EBR-2, began operation in Idaho. It had a capacity of 16.5 electrical megawatts (MWe) and quickly became the workhorse of the AEC breeder program. It was used primarily for testing fuels and materials under fast reactor conditions. A zero power plutonium reactor (the ZPPR), which went into operation in 1969, also in Idaho, was large enough to allow full-scale mockups of the fuel arrangements expected to be used in commercial breeder reactors.

In 1955, the AEC initiated a program under which private utilities were invited, with substantial government help, to design, build, and operate experimental nuclear power plants. One of the projects accepted for this program was a fast breeder plant proposed by a consortium of utilities under the leadership of the Detroit Edison Company. Called the Enrico Fermi Atomic Power Plant, it proved to be the only fast breeder built on a U.S. utility system. Its initial operation was vigorously opposed in the courts by labor unions and others who felt that its location, near the western end of Lake Erie, was too close to an urban area to be safe. The operating permit was ultimately upheld by the Supreme Court, and Fermi went critical (achieved a self-sustaining nuclear chain reaction) in 1963. In October 1966, during tests to bring the reactor to its full power of 61 MWe, it suffered a partial core meltdown.

The accidents to EBR-1 and the Fermi plant served to underscore a conclusion reached by the AEC's General Advisory Committee in 1947, namely, that translating the breeding principle into practical hardware would be a "long, complicated, and difficult process."[1]

During the 1950s the emphasis in the AEC's nuclear power program was on developing types of converter (nonbreeder) reactors that promised relatively soon to be economically competitive with plants fueled by coal, oil, or natural gas—the three "fossil fuels"—and on bringing private industry into the nuclear power picture. Development of breeder reactors continued but was considered a secondary, long-range goal.

It appeared for a while in the late 1950s that nuclear power might fall short of its goal of becoming economically competitive. Optimism gradually returned, however, as the costs of fossil fuels increased and as pioneering plants succeeded in bringing nuclear power costs down. Then, in 1964, an apparent breakthrough occurred when the Jersey Central Power and Light Company announced that it had decided to install a 500 MWe nuclear power plant in preference to a coal-fired plant, having made this choice on the basis of economics alone.* Other utilities soon climbed on the nuclear bandwagon, such that roughly half of the large-size commercial power plants ordered in 1966 and 1967 were nuclear.† All at once the economic future of nuclear power seemed to be transformed. In a 1962 report to President Kennedy the AEC had predicted that there would be 40,000 MWe of installed nuclear capacity by 1980, representing about 10 percent of total utility capacity. By the beginning of the Nixon administration in 1969, we had raised the estimate for 1980 to 150,000 MWe, representing one-fourth of total utility capacity. Looking further ahead, we predicted that the capacity of nuclear plants would constitute half the U.S. total by the year 2000 and that essentially all generating capacity built in the 21st century would be nuclear.

ECONOMIC URGENCY

Paradoxically, the predicted success of nuclear power seemed to threaten its future. This was because the predictions raised questions about whether the nation would have enough economically recoverable uranium to meet the needs of the large number of expected nuclear power reactors. These were almost all expected to be of the light water reactor (LWR) type, so called because they would use ordinary water as their primary coolant. Since they would be fueled primarily by the fissionable uranium-235 isotope, these reactors would be able to extract only between 1 and 2 percent of the energy potentially available in their uranium fuel. They therefore would depend on the availability of low-cost uranium ore if they were to supply energy at affordable rates. But the Edison Electric Institute, the electric utility industry's trade association, estimated that under a LWR regime the United States would have used up all of its low-cost uranium by 1995.

---

* When he telephoned me to impart this news, Albert Tegen, the president of Jersey Central's parent company, could scarcely conceal his elation. He confidently predicted that coal-fired plants would henceforth no longer be economical on the Eastern seaboard.

† Not fully appreciated at the time was the fact that General Electric had priced the Jersey Central plant below its cost. GE hoped to make up its losses as further plants were ordered, making it possible to spread development costs over several plants.

Breeder reactors seemed to be the missing ingredient that would rectify the situation. As I stated in Congressional testimony:

> [Breeders] would multiply the energy that it is possible to obtain from uranium as a minimum by a factor of 100 or more, that is, the ratio of the abundance of the uranium-238 to that of uranium-235. But, in actuality, the factor is much more than that, thousands and tens of thousands, because the cost of the fuel is so much less when you use all of it that you can afford to mine much lower grade uranium.[2]

Based on such calculations, breeders seemed able to meet U.S. energy needs for hundreds, perhaps thousands, of years. Further, by drastically lowering fuel costs, they offered the potential of much lower electricity prices to consumers. The economic benefits that might flow from anticipated lower electricity costs seemed to place a premium on having breeder reactors as soon as possible. Accordingly, the AEC early in 1967 sharply upgraded the LMFBR program from its previous secondary status. In a report to President Johnson we now identified it as our highest-priority nuclear power development activity.

STATUS IN 1969

As the Nixon administration began, the AEC was quite far advanced in its LMFBR development efforts. A comprehensive technology development plan had been formulated. Consistent with this plan, the detailed engineering of major or technically difficult components and systems was already underway. We were also well along in the preparation of facilities required for testing the many first-of-a-kind components that would be needed for a full-scale LMFBR plant. Existing facilities, such as the Experimental Breeder Reactor 2 (EBR-2), had been modified and upgraded for this purpose. New testing facilities, such as a huge (400 thermal megawatts*) Fast Flux Test Facility (FFTF) at Richland, Washington, were in various phases of design, construction, or initial operation.

---

* It is customary for the output of reactors that produce electricity to be measured in terms of electric power and for the output of reactors that do not produce electricity to be measured in terms of thermal power. Approximately three megawatts of thermal power are required to produce one megawatt of electric power.

Programs had been established to gather the technical knowledge emanating from these efforts and to compile them in the form of codes and standards to guide further efforts. Industry—including both manufacturers and utilities—was participating on a limited basis in all these programs and was also undertaking some supplementary work on its own.

These intensive technological efforts were expected to come together in the 1970s in the form of demonstration breeder plants. AEC plans as of early 1969 called for three such plants, each one to be built by a different manufacturer. Each was to be built on a utility system, with one or two utilities in a leading role, and was to utilize both private and public funds. A full-scale commercial LMFBR power plant was expected to be in operation by 1984.

This ambitious schedule seemed to fit hand in glove with the economic needs of the time. Thus, the AEC looked forward to a time, about the turn of the century, when LWRs and breeders would form together a completely self-sufficient fuel system. In such a system each breeder reactor would produce enough plutonium in seven to ten years to refuel both itself and one other reactor of comparable size.

The full implications of such widespread use of breeders were difficult to grasp at once, but, if one thought about it, some glittering possibilities came into view. For example, Alvin Weinberg, then director of the Oak Ridge National Laboratory and one of the most thoughtful of contemporary scientists, stated his belief that the breeder "would have to be ranked as of extraordinary importance in the history of mankind, only a little less important than the discovery of fission." Weinberg, in fact, went so far as to predict "a resolution through nuclear breeding of the competition between population and resources" and to conclude that the "new age of energy is here, and [that] the extravagant claims made for nuclear energy when it was discovered are really coming to pass."[3] The indications that nuclear energy might have such redeeming social values to counteract its destructive uses were exhilarating indeed to many who had worked in the wartime atomic bomb project.

Overlooked by many of us was the fact that the dizzying economic prospects being predicted for the breeder were dependent on the simultaneous fulfillment of a series of assumptions: (1) that demand for electricity would continue to increase at its current rate, approximately doubling every ten years; (2) that the increasing success of nuclear power in capturing the generating plant business would also continue; (3) that economically recoverable uranium would remain a scarce commodity; (4) that the technical difficulties of LMFBR development would be overcome without severe delays or escalations in cost; and (5) that adequate public and private funding would be available to see this development through to its conclusion. The nonfulfillment of any one, or at most two, of these assumptions might be sufficient to bring the whole edifice tumbling to the ground. In the actual event, none of the assumptions proved correct. But I am getting ahead of my story.

FUNDING PROBLEMS

If the breeder program was to fulfill the ambitious plans made for it, it was clearly essential that there be substantial government support. In 1969 I testified that a successful development effort would require that the AEC spend in excess of $2 billion over a fifteen-year period.[4] There was serious question whether such amounts would be appropriated. Already during the Johnson administration budgetary pressures had begun to be a serious restraint on the program. They had been an important factor, for example, in forcing us to choose a single breeder concept, the LMFBR, for priority emphasis instead of pursuing parallel development of several competing concepts to determine which was best. The Nixon administration signaled within its first week in office that it had no intention of being any more generous than its predecessor. President Nixon informed the heads of all executive departments and agencies on January 25, 1969, that the combined effect of an inflationary economic outlook, continued military operations in Southeast Asia, and a disappointing balance of trade would demand "decisive and substantial action to reduce the size of the budget and to keep Federal spending under strict control."

The stage for bruising budgetary struggles over the breeder program was set in correspondence between Budget Director Robert P. Mayo and the AEC in the autumn of 1969.* Mayo led off with a memo offering guidance for preparation of AEC's budget for fiscal year 1971 (the year beginning July 1, 1970). We had previously signaled the need for a government contribution of $240 million for the year to support the breeder program. Mayo expressed

---

* John Ehrlichman (*Witness to Power*, p. 90ff.) writes of Mayo that his "mannerisms and odd sense of humor thoroughly alienated Nixon during the development of the budget in the fall of 1969 . . . By late November, with only three weeks remaining to make all the final Federal budget decisions, Nixon refused to spend any more time with his Budget Director." Ehrlichman relates further how, after Mayo demanded a showdown in March 1970, he was told that he "lacked the President's confidence." Soon afterward he was gone. Amid the cruel caprices of the Nixon administration, one never knew who was in favor and who was not.

unhappiness with such a large amount. He suggested instead that "commercial users of the LMFBR technology . . . assume a greater share of the risk in this venture." Consistent with this approach, he asked several questions: How could utilities and manufacturers be made to compete for a role in the first plant so that they would increase their dollar investment? Could the government's contribution be limited to one demonstration plant instead of the three contemplated by AEC? If the government were to contribute to more than one plant, could the scheduling of these plants be more widely spaced? To decrease its capital cost, could the size of the first plant be held to 300 MWe or less?

In AEC's reply to Mayo's letter, we drew a parallel between what was occurring in the breeder program and the history of the development of light water reactors. We pointed out that the latter had been primarily a government program at first but that industry had then increased its support so that in the previous four years the government had invested only about $2 billion as against industry's $13 billion. We looked forward to a similar progression in the case of breeder reactors. We provided evidence that utilities and manufacturers were already committing substantially in funds, personnel, and facilities toward the breeder effort—we mentioned, for example, the financial participation of over 100 utilities in cooperative design studies with manufacturers. We argued against the suggestion that the breeder demonstration effort be stretched out. We pointed to the dollar benefits the AEC believed would accrue to consumers from an early introduction of the breeder. We noted also that further delays in the program, added to those already sustained for budgetary reasons, would have "a most serious psychological impact on industrial and utility management at a time when the AEC is urging that they commit substantial resources."

The skimpiness, from AEC's point of view, of government support for the LMFBR was mirrored by a similar lack of enthusiasm from industry. Manufacturers, while ostensibly eager to participate, were cautious in their approaches. For example, on March 27, 1969, the commissioners met with a number of General Electric officials to hear about their plans. A. E. Schubert (vice president, nuclear energy division) said that although GE hoped that AEC support for an LMFBR demonstration plant might be included in the fiscal year 1971 budget, a year's delay might not be too harmful in view of the many matters that the company would have to attend to before it was ready to proceed.

In November 1969 the AEC accepted proposals from three manufacturers, General Electric, Westinghouse, and Atomics International, to participate in the project-definition phase (PDP) of the LMFBR program. The purpose of this phase was to define the technical and economic risks of the total project and to determine whether there was sufficient basis for entering into a cooperative government-industry arrangement for the construction and operation of a demonstration plant. The total cost of the PDP effort was estimated at $8.2 million. AEC proposed that $4.2 million of this be contributed by the 3 manufacturers and the 85 utilities that were associated with one or another of them. Even this relatively modest assessment drew protests. At a meeting of the Atomic Industrial Forum in December 1969, industry officials complained that when manufacturers started their programs for breeder development it was on the assumption that government would bear the largest early expenses. It had now become clear that government support would fall substantially short of industry's expectations.

In March of 1970 Joint Committee chairman Chet Holifield stated his own view that attempting to finance the first demonstration plants by cooperative government-industry funding was not realistic. He predicted that the amounts forthcoming from industry would be disappointing.[5]

More bad news came the following month. In its April 21, 1970, issue *Nucleonics Week* reported that the prototype breeder reactor General Electric was contemplating would cost $400 million. At the time this seemed a shockingly high figure. On April 29, GE officials came in to explain. They had made a careful estimate of the cost of a 340 megawatt plant to be built in a remote area in upper New York State. They estimated that the direct cost of the plant would be only about $150 million, but that another $250 million had to be added for "contingencies and detailed engineering." No inflation allowance was included in these figures, so that if one were contemplating a plant to be completed in 1975, a realistic total cost could be not $400 million, but about $500 million.* I asked whether such a high cost did not place in doubt the viability of the whole breeder project, since I doubted that the Federal contribution could go much above the current allotment of $50 million. Where, I asked, would the rest of the money come from? The GE officials said they were looking into that.

All these cold dashes of financial reality caused some scaling down in approach. Within the same week in May 1970 we met separately with the leadership of two industry trade associations, the Atomic Industrial Forum and the Edison Electric Institute. The former group recommended informally, the latter formally, that there be only one demonstration plant, not the three the AEC thought necessary. The EEI issued a report a month later

---

* It seemed clear that GE, having lost a substantial sum on its "loss-leader" Jersey Central transaction, did not want to repeat the experience.

confirming that the utility industry would not be able to raise money for more than one plant, at least to start. The report added that there was new information indicating that there seemed to be enough uranium available to fuel nonbreeding light water reactors for a longer time than AEC and the industry had previously estimated, so that there was now less need for a crash effort on the breeder. (This early indication that the economic underpinning of the whole program might be a bit shaky passed relatively unnoticed.)

In August 1970 Milton Shaw (the chief operating head of the breeder program in his capacity as director of AEC's division of reactor development and technology) suggested that pushing back the start of work on the first demonstration plant for a year would be the best course in view of the financial problems. At the same time he expressed concern that such a postponement might convey the impression that the breeder program was being downgraded in emphasis or importance. He thought that would be most unfortunate because all the while these financial difficulties were occurring, research and development work was proceeding at a steady pace, with what he described as very promising results on such key components as pumps, valves, control rod drives, and fuel elements.

In September 1970 the LMFBR program came under renewed pressure from the Office of Management and Budget in the form of a letter from Deputy Director Caspar Weinberger, who had, in effect, replaced Mayo. Noting that the program would involve some $175 million of outlays in fiscal year 1971, he asked us to consider how this might be reduced prior to submission of our fiscal year 1972 budget. He noted that two of the conditions that had been assumed in arguing for an early development of the breeder, namely, rapid growth of nuclear power capacity and an impending shortage of uranium ore, were not materializing. He asked the AEC to reassess "the urgency and scope of the breeder reactor program." Specifically, he asked us to consider supporting only one demonstration reactor with government funds and deferring construction of the Fast Flux Test Facility.

The lack of industry support now began to draw critical comment from administration sources. A partial explanation was offered in early November 1970 in a letter from Federal Power Commission chairman John N. Nassikas to Deputy Budget Director Weinberger. After summarizing the environmental, conservation, and economic benefits of the breeder, Nassikas wrote: "The major share of this breeder development program which is being carried by the Federal Government cannot be shifted to private industry because the magnitude and time scale of the effort is well beyond their capacity to support . . . I trust you will weigh seriously these major considerations of national interest in sustaining this effort."

Later the same month Holifield reiterated his position that the bulk of funding had to come from government as "an investment in the future," that utilities and manufacturers were simply not set up in a way that could provide the sums needed. He again expressed the opinion that three demonstration plants, not just one, were needed to fully prove out alternative technical approaches.

On January 27, 1971, the commissioners, along with Milton Shaw and others from the AEC, met with a large delegation of utility executives and Edison Electric Institute leaders. The visitors told us they had come to the conclusion that industry could not raise enough money to build more than one demonstration plant. Commissioner Ramey and Shaw argued the desirability of having more than one, but the answer came back that there was no choice—the money simply wasn't there. There was talk of building a second plant later, but the industry people couldn't commit industry and we couldn't commit government to such a venture. There was then a discussion of how all three manufacturers could be involved in one project. It was suggested that each of the three, in its proposal to the AEC, should describe how, if it were chosen as principal contractor, it could involve the other two on a consortium basis.

Efforts to increase utility involvement in the LMFBR program led the AEC in the spring of 1971 to establish two industry-wide advisory boards. A Senior Utility Steering Committee of fourteen senior management executives was to advise on utility participation in a demonstration plant. A Senior Utility Technical Advisory Panel of twelve technical-management officials was to advise on how utilities might participate in supporting technical research and development.

First contacts with the latter group were discouraging. AEC General Manager Bob Hollingsworth learned from the panel members that utilities would not be able to raise the predicted $180 to $230 million for support of technical work but would only reach the range of $20 to $40 million. Further, Hollingsworth found that the only utilities that felt they could raise enough money to take the lead utility role in the demonstration project were TVA (the Tennessee Valley Authority) and the Commonwealth Edison Company (serving Chicago and vicinity). A venture in which these two would be joint owner-operators and the government's Oak Ridge reservation would be the site was beginning to emerge as the best, and perhaps the only, possibility for a demonstration project. But lack of both government and industry financial support made even this seem a dubious prospect.

PRESIDENTIAL BLESSING

With prospects for the breeder threatening to founder for lack of resources, a possible way to break the logjam occurred to Joint Committee Chairman Holifield, one of the most enthusiastic advocates of the program. This was to appeal directly to President Nixon in terms that might have strong political significance for him.

Holifield discussed such a move with me when we were together on a trip to Los Alamos in August 1970. His suggestion was that we try to get the president personally interested in the breeder program as something he could leave his mark on, suggesting to him, as Holifield put it, "that this great development to meet the energy needs of the future might be the equivalent of President Kennedy's man-on-the-moon program."

The most effective promoter of Holifield's idea turned out to be Holifield himself. He managed to get himself invited to travel to California aboard Air Force One on one of the president's trips to San Clemente. This occurred in late March 1971.* En route he had an opportunity for an extended conversation with Nixon. The following are excerpts from Holifield's own notes of this conversation, in which John Ehrlichman also participated:

> As soon as possible I started developing the case for the breeder reactor. I believe I made a strong presentation of the breeder goal and its possible cost of 2 billion dollars for three demonstration plants. I pointed out the goal if achieved, "an abundance of clean, cheap electricity for a thousand years." I then said, "Mr. President, you are a Republican, I am a Democrat but we are both Americans and this challenge for an abundance of clean, safe electricity goes far beyond partisanship. It involves the need for the future of our people and the people of the world. You can furnish the leadership which will supply that need."
>
> I then said, "Mr. President, President Eisenhower secured his place in history on two points: his military service in World War II and his initiation of the 'Atoms for Peace' program which I have supported for 18 years and which has had tremendous accomplishments. Mr. Kennedy pledged that he would place men on the moon and bring them back safely in ten years. This was accomplished

---

* By this time, following the Joint Committee's practice of alternating its chairmanship between Senate and House with each session of Congress, Senator John O. Pastore (D-RI) had become chairman and Holifield vice-chairman.

although he never lived to see it. It cost 50 billion dollars." I then said, "Mr. President, you too can secure a lasting tribute in the pages of history not at a cost of 50 billion dollars but at a cost of 2 billion dollars." . . .

The President listened intently as did John Ehrlickman [*sic*]. I became enthused as I explained the Breeder and [its] goals. The President said, "Chet, I can tell by your enthusiasm and conviction that you really believe what you are saying." I responded, "Mr. President I do believe. It is the culmination of 24 years of service on the Joint Committee on Atomic Energy. If I could see your Administration really committed to achieving the Breeder I would be ready to retire."*

The President turned to John Ehrlickman [*sic*] and said, "We should have a good briefing on this project." He then asked me who could give a proper briefing. I gave him the names. He asked me if I would attend and I said that I would be glad to attend, and suggested some other names of Joint Committee members who should be invited . . .

I left the office of the President and retired to my seat in the rear section of the plane.

In a phone call to me some days later, Holifield supplied further detail of his conversation with the president:

> Holifield said that he told the president he had a bear by the tail in Vietnam and that there was no way he could come out of that situation smelling like a rose because there were too many ramifications involved. He therefore badly needed an issue to take to the American people and the breeder was one to which the people would respond and that could be a big factor in his reelection. When the president asked how long it would take to get the breeder on the road, Holifield told him it would take ten to twelve years but that if there were a national commitment we could have three plants started and the program very well established by the end of a second Nixon term.

The briefing promised by the president was soon arranged. I learned about this in a phone call on April 10 from White House assistant Will Kriegsman. There was to be a Cabinet meeting on the thirteenth, and I was to do the

* There is a question whether Holifield, frequently a thorn in the side of Republican administrations, intended this offer to retire as an added inducement to gain administration support for the breeder.

briefing. He confirmed that this had come about as a direct result of the president's airplane conversation with Holifield. Kriegsman then told me that there was another dimension to this event from the White House point of view. It had to do with the fact that Holifield was chairman of the House Committee on Government Operations, to which the president's pending reorganization bills (see chapter 14) had been referred. Holifield's initial reaction to the reorganization, particularly the bill establishing a Department of Natural Resources under which the AEC would lose much of its independence, had been predictably hostile. The White House's hope was that the breeder matter might provide some basis for rapprochement between the president and Holifield on the reorganization. Kriegsman added that the White House hoped to avoid any confrontation between Nixon and Holifield at the Cabinet meeting and was looking to me to field any controversial questions that might come up.

Virtually the entire Cabinet was present at the meeting, which started at 8 A.M. Among many non-Cabinet officials present, in addition to Holifield, were Deputy Budget Director Weinberger, Economic Adviser Paul McCracken, Science Adviser Ed David, EPA Director William Ruckelshaus, Senators John Pastore and Howard Baker, Congressman John Anderson, and, from the White House, John Ehrlichman, Information Officers Herb Klein and Ron Ziegler, and Kriegsman.

> *I began by describing the role, present and projected, of nuclear power around the world. I described how reactors were regulated in the United States and said that there was no problem with radioactive effluents and that reactors could be built to operate safely. After describing the breeder and its advantages, I presented AEC's estimate that some $1 to $2 billion would be saved for every year that breeding on a commercial scale was brought into existence earlier. The immediate problem was to find funds to build the first demonstration reactor. I described the role of the three manufacturers and the utilities that would be associated with each of them, and said we had not yet made a choice among the three groups.*
>
> *Holifield followed with further comments on the importance to our economy and the environment of electrical energy in general and the breeder in particular. He repeated what he had told the president on the plane trip: it was more important to spend $2 billion this way than $50 billion to reach the moon. Joint Committee chairman Pastore chipped in with the important*

observation that all members of the committee supported the fast breeder.

The president then asked me how other countries were coming along on the breeder. I replied that the U.K. was building a 250 megawatt demonstration reactor to be put into operation in 1972 in Scotland; that France was also building a 250 megawatt demonstration plant to come into operation in 1973; and that the Soviet Union was well along in construction of a 350 megawatt demonstration reactor and was also building a 600 megawatt plant. All of these were to be of the LMFBR type. The president asked me how it happened that all these countries were ahead of us. I said it was because they had started construction on demonstration reactors before we did but that, if we speeded up our program, keeping in mind the 1980 objective for an economically competitive plant, we could reach that goal before the others. In answer to another question from the president I described the immediate U.S. objective as a 1,000 MWe reasonably economic demonstration reactor with a reasonably low doubling time [the time required to produce a surplus amount of fissile material equal to the amount required for the plant's initial fuel loading].

The president asked whether there would be significant scientific opposition. I said some scientists would oppose the breeder because of concern about radioactive effluents, which I said was not a serious problem, and that some would be concerned about safety, which was a more serious problem—there was a very low probability of a so-called catastrophic accident. In ending the meeting the president indicated he would discuss the matter further within the administration and would come up with some kind of a decision soon.

Later in the morning Holifield called to express general satisfaction about the way the meeting had gone. I told him he might have broken the Gordian knot in bringing all this about and that the power of his Government Operations Committee over the president's reorganization bill certainly didn't hurt.

The president's decision did indeed come soon, and it was all we in the AEC could reasonably have wished. On June 4, 1971, he sent to Congress a Special Message to the Congress on Energy Resources.[6] The message outlined "a broad range of actions to ensure an adequate supply of clean energy for the years ahead." These included sulfur oxide demonstration projects, coal gasification efforts, development of oil shale resources, a requirement for additional thermal insulation in federally insured homes, exploring the potential of geothermal energy, and efforts to encourage energy conservation. It was clear, however, from the space and emphasis given to the breeder, that the recommendations regarding it were the centerpiece of the message. The president said that the breeder represented "our best hope today for meeting the Nation's growing demand for economical clean energy." Fully adopting the AEC-Joint Committee line, he continued: "Because of its highly efficient use of nuclear fuel, the breeder reactor could extend the life of our natural uranium fuel supply from decades to centuries, with far less impact on the environment than the power plants which are operating today." Then followed these most welcome words:

> [T]here still are major technical and financial obstacles to the construction of a demonstration plant of some 300 to 500 megawatts. I am therefore requesting an additional $27 million in Fiscal Year 1972 for the Atomic Energy Commission's liquid metal fast breeder reactor program—and for related technological and safety programs—so that the necessary engineering groundwork for demonstration plants can soon be laid. . . .
>
> I believe it is important to the Nation that the commercial demonstration of a breeder reactor be completed by 1980. To help achieve that goal, I am requesting an additional $50 million in Federal funds for the demonstration plant. We expect industry— the utilities and manufacturers—to contribute the major share of the plant's total cost, since they have a large and obvious stake in this new technology. But we also recognize that only if government and industry work closely together can we maximize our progress in this vital field and thus introduce a new era in the production of energy for the people of our land.

Two weeks after the president's message, the AEC received an implementing letter from OMB assistant director Donald B. Rice granting us an increase of $36 million in budget authority for fiscal year 1962, as well as an increase from $50 million to $100 million in authorization for a first demonstration plant. Rice recognized our claim that further increases in federal funding would be required and indicated that OMB was prepared to consider such requests in later budget cycles "if AEC considers this to be unavoidable." He indicated a strong belief that the president's support for an accelerated LMFBR program "should be reflected in increased support of the program by American industry."

So it was that one of the essential props for successful achievement of the breeder, presidential support, fell into place. Still, it remained clear, as it had been from the beginning and as the president's message emphasized, that the program was not going to fly unless industry also rallied to its support. Nor did the improved political and budgetary situation alter the fact that formidable technical difficulties still barred the way to a successful LMFBR commercial plant.

APPROACHING THE FIRST DEMONSTRATION PLANT

The president's energy message, with its welcome infusion of more federal money, indeed brought about some change for the better in industry's willingness to get involved. This change was already noticeable at the Edison Electric Institute's annual meeting later in June 1971. Reports reached us that industry leaders who had been pessimistic about industry's willingness to contribute were now less so. It began to seem possible to raise an estimated $300 million needed for the first demonstration plant without relying primarily on TVA. (There had been concern that the White House would not look favorably on TVA, a federal agency, being a major contributor outside the budget process.)

On July 9, Commonwealth Edison's chairman, Thomas Ayers, perhaps the single leading utility figure on this matter, wrote to me announcing that within the next several weeks each investor-owned utility, regardless of size, would be asked by the Edison Electric Institute to pledge 0.25 mills per kilowatt-hour of its 1970 retail sales. The amount thus pledged was to be paid in ten equal annual installments, beginning in 1972. The total for the ten years was expected to reach $250 million. In a similar manner, the American Public Power Association would attempt to collect $50 million from publicly-owned utilities (mainly municipals and rural cooperatives). There seemed to be some optimism that these targets could be reached.

On July 21, Commissioner Ramey and I met with AEC general manager Hollingsworth and program director Milton Shaw to hear a report on discussions they had held with TVA and Commonwealth Edison. Both utilities appeared to agree on the need to locate the first prototype on the government's Oak Ridge reservation due to the fear of public resistance on safety grounds to location at any private site. The four of us also discussed how to allocate participation in this first, and perhaps only, demonstration plant among Atomics International, General Electric, and Westinghouse. Shaw indicated that having one manufacturer do the entire job would be simplest, but he cautioned that Atomics International could not survive without some involvement in the first plant, and he anticipated pressure to involve all three.

On July 29, the four of us (Ramey, Hollingsworth, Shaw, and I) met with Aubrey J. Wagner (chairman) and Jim Watson (manager of power) of TVA to discuss the arrangement between TVA and Commonwealth Edison. We made it clear again that Federal financing could not be increased beyond what had already been authorized, and that the plant would have to be owned by a utility, although the AEC could furnish the fuel and perhaps be responsible for part of the fuel cycle.

As my tenure as AEC chairman drew to a close in the summer of 1971, some new clouds were gathering. A congressional vote against authorizing funds for the LMFBR program was urged on each member in a letter from the environmental group Friends of the Earth. The letter raised the question of potential dangers to health, safety, and the environment. Another group, the Scientists' Institute for Public Information (SIPI), filed suit against the AEC for not having issued a statement under the National Environmental Policy Act on the long-range impact of the LMFBR demonstration plant program. The AEC then announced that a draft environmental statement had been prepared on two demonstration reactors, although not on the program as a whole. (In 1973 the U.S. Court of Appeals ruled in favor of SIPI and required the AEC to prepare an environmental impact statement on the entire breeder program.)

NOTES

1. Hewlett and Duncan, *Atomic Shield*, p. 29.
2. JCAE, *Hearings on Environmental Effects of Producing Electric Power*, Part 1, pp. 91-92.
3. Weinberg, *Reflections on Big Science*, p. 24.
4. JCAE *Hearings on Environmental Effects of Producing Electric Power*, Part 1, p. 93.
5. *Nucleonics Week*, March 19, 1970, pp. 4-5.
6. *Public Papers of Richard Nixon, 1971*, pp. 703-14.

11

Issues Along the Way

SAFETY

Early in 1969 Commissioner Johnson and I became concerned that in the headlong rush to develop an economical fast breeder reactor, the AEC program might be allowing insufficient time to resolve questions of safety. We were aware of some inherent features of the LMFBR concept that implied a certain hazard and of other features that argued for inherent safety. Implying hazard was the fact that breeders would operate at much higher enrichment levels than conventional reactors, increasing the likelihood that a partial melting of fuel could lead to a runaway chain reaction. Another possibility was the sequence that caused the EBR-1 meltdown in 1955, when heat was generated faster than it could be carried away by the coolant. Further, we knew that the liquid metal coolant would react violently upon any contact with air or water, so that a coolant leak could be a serious danger. These factors in combination raised the specter of a possible accidental explosion. Conducive to safety was the fact that the liquid sodium coolant would not be kept under high pressure, thus reducing the likelihood of leakage. It also appeared that LMFBRs would be self-regulating to the extent that any increase in the temperature of the fuel in the core would be accompanied by an increase in the rate at which neutrons were absorbed by uranium-238, thus reducing the rate of power production. Further, studies seemed to indicate that any explosion that might occur would be of small magnitude, likely to be contained within the reactor vessel and almost certainly within the walls of the reinforced concrete containment building.[1] Still, it was difficult at that time to come to firm conclusions about LMFBR safety since there did not yet exist any fully engineered plans for a specific full-scale plant.

Another who worried about the safety of fast breeder reactors was Edward Teller, then associate director for physics at the Lawrence Radiation Laboratory at Livermore, California. He had expressed his views publicly, with the media coverage that generally accompanied his pronouncements. I asked Teller about his concerns when I visited Livermore in March 1969.

> *Edward was adamant in his position, saying that he would continue to speak out against fast breeder reactors until it could be demonstrated to him that they were safe. He said that he would much rather have a fast reactor 700 feet under a large city than above ground 70 miles from the city. I observed that the engineering difficulties with underground siting were severe, considering such factors as heat dissipation. He asked if we had studied underground siting in detail. I said we had looked into it to some extent. I remarked that we had an extensive study of fast reactor safety under way, and he asked for any reports. He also made some statements about the possibility of a planned effort by saboteurs to cause a major release of radioactivity by first breaching the containment of a breeder reactor and then using a subversive reactor operator to mishandle the reactor controls to cause an excursion.*

The subject of safety was raised at a "stock-take" meeting of the Commission and the general manager on February 13, 1969, and it was decided to seek outside advice. The advice we got was reassuring. On March 26:

> *The commission heard a briefing on the safety of fast breeder reactors from Hugh Paxton of Los Alamos and Carroll Zabel, a professor of physics at the University of Houston and a member of the Advisory Committee on Reactor Safeguards. They seemed to think that the dangers of an explosion caused by a malfunction in presently planned breeders would be minimal and that, in any case, the size of the explosion would be very small, in the range of a few tons at most.*

Questioning the safety of the breeder did not go down well in some quarters, because much of the support for the program was very zealous, amounting almost to an article of faith. Such strong feeling was found in the Joint Committee, for example, and it had echoes also within the AEC. On one occasion in April 1969:

I had a somewhat stormy session with Commissioner Ramey, who feels that Commissioner Johnson and I are being a bit devious in questioning the safety of the LMFBR. I tried to convince him that my main objective was to satisfy myself that no serious nuclear explosion could result from any mishap.

As the program developed, safety continued to be a source of controversy. On the one hand, some of Milton Shaw's critics emphasized his perfectionist attitude, which, in this view, placed "excessive emphasis upon reliability rather than on economic performance."[2] On the other hand, a 1973 memorandum by Burns and Roe, the architect-engineer for the planned first demonstration plant, predicted that there would be problems with the plant because of a lack of agreement within the AEC on important safety considerations.[3]

THE FAST FLUX TEST FACILITY

It was recognized from the start that to make the LMFBR a commercial reality would be a task of great technical difficulty. The need to recover just about every atom meant that the reactor had to be built with materials that would absorb a minimum number of neutrons. Further, the fuels and materials used would have to withstand temperatures of 1,200 to 1,400 degrees Fahrenheit (as compared with 600 to 650 degrees for the nonbreeding light water reactors) and an intense bombardment of neutron radiation. There was an obvious need for a test facility that could simulate these extreme conditions. As an interim and partial solution, attention turned to the Experimental Breeder Reactor 2 (EBR-2), which had been in operation at the Idaho test station since 1963 as a breeder reactor demonstration plant. In 1965 its mission was changed to that of an irradiation test facility for breeder fuels and materials. To accommodate the new mission, modifications were made in the facility, and its operating power was increased from 45 to 50, later to 62.5 thermal megawatts.

An additional major test facility went into operation in 1969. This was the Liquid Metal Engineering Center at Canoga Park, California, which provided a complex of test facilities and supporting laboratories for evaluating LMFBR instrumentation, equipment, and components. There were also several facilities in which plutonium-fueled critical experiments were performed, the largest being the Zero Power Plutonium Reactor (ZPPR) at the Idaho testing station. (Zero power in this context means that the reactor did not generate a significant amount of heat.) In Fayetteville, Arkansas, the privately-owned 20 thermal megawatt Southwest Experimental Fast Oxide Reactor (SEFOR) performed experimental tests to demonstrate the operational safety of LMFBRs.

A need was felt, however, for a still more versatile and powerful testing facility, one that could more fully replicate the operating conditions of a commercial LMFBR. Accordingly, planning began in the mid-1960s for a huge Fast Flux Test Facility (FFTF), to be built at the Hanford Works near Richland, Washington. With a design power of 400 thermal megawatts and a neutron flux (defined as the number of neutrons passing through a square centimeter of area per second) more than double that of any existing test reactor, the FFTF was expected to have a testing capability unmatched in the world. There were some who claimed even that the experience to be gained from the FFTF would be so informative as to obviate the need for a demonstration breeder plant. Initial plans called for the facility to begin operation in 1974.

Overall system management responsibility for the FFTF was awarded to the Pacific Northwest Laboratory (PNL), a branch of Battelle Memorial Institute of Columbus, Ohio. Bechtel Corporation, San Francisco, was selected as architect-engineer responsible for general plant design. Westinghouse (advanced reactor division) was selected as the prime contractor for the reactor plant design, with Atomics International as Westinghouse's principal subcontractor.

As design work proceeded it became apparent that there was conflict between the management of PNL and AEC's division of reactor development and technology (RDT), headed by Milton Shaw. Shaw, who had handled nuclear propulsion for navy surface ships under Admiral Hyman G. Rickover, was a hard-driving manager in the Rickover tradition. He believed in tight central control, particularly of difficult projects. For a program as new, large, and diverse as the LMFBR, there were undoubtedly advantages to the type of direction that Shaw provided. On the other hand, there were large differences between the situations faced by Rickover and Shaw, to the latter's disadvantage. Rickover was able to obtain what funding he needed for his nuclear warships. The country was dedicated to his program—it was agreed to be an essential part of the effort to arm against the threat from the communist giants. Shaw, on the other hand, faced a constant struggle to obtain needed funding, whether from government or industry, and it was never sufficient to carry out the LMFBR program in the manner he thought technically required. As Francis Duncan, author of *Rickover and the Nuclear Navy*, put it in a recent conversation, "Shaw was trying to build a Rickover edifice on a foundation that didn't exist." It should also be noted that Shaw's approach contravened the basic organizational scheme of the AEC, which, following the organization inherited from the wartime Manhattan Project, involved a broad delegation of authority to contractors in the field, with headquarters employees functioning more as administrators than as managers.

I heard about PNL's side of the story periodically. For example, on April 29, 1969, Dr. Fred W. Albaugh, the laboratory's director, phoned to say that his problems with Shaw were becoming "almost intolerable."* Some of the details were explained to me by Dr. Bert Wolfe when he assumed his duties as PNL's project director for the FFTF in October 1969:

> *Wolfe stated that the supervision of PNL's work by RDT* [AEC's Division of Reactor Development and Technology headed by Shaw] *was far too detailed—he thought RDT did not have sufficient qualified people to exercise that kind of supervision. He noted that RDT had sent PNL 1,354 written directives thus far in 1969. Many of these instructions had the effect of changing the scope of the project, making it practically impossible to complete it within the budgeted amount, approximately $90 million.*

The budget problem was mentioned to me by Albaugh in a phone call in October 1969. He said that PNL had a "fighting chance" of staying within budget if they were "left alone and could be rescued from double- and triple-checking everything; if not, then the chances were zero." He noted that Bechtel was about to release a cost estimate on FFTF that would contain "all the Shaw goodies of balancing safety factors against safety factors," and they believed it would add up to double the budget.

On the other hand, there was also a continuing stream of complaints about PNL's performance. Some of the complaints emanated from the subcontractors, Westinghouse and Atomics International. From time to time in 1969 I heard from various sources about the lab's "lack of leadership" and "uncooperativeness." Much of the criticism focused on PNL's apparent inability to keep the FFTF within budget. Holifield called me on November 25, 1969, about problems with both PNL and Argonne National Laboratory, where much of AEC's technical work on reactor development was centered . He reported on a

---

* Fred was known to be a personal friend of mine, and this made it difficult for me to take a strong position in the matter. He had been a schoolmate at UCLA in the 1930s. I invited him to work with me at the Met Lab during World War II. While there he made a most important contribution in developing the REDOX process that was used after the war for separating plutonium from irradiated uranium in the Hanford plutonium production reactors. On the personal side, he ended up marrying my Met Lab secretary.

recent conversation with Shaw, whom he reported to be "very distressed and discouraged and about on the point of throwing in the chips."

As the FFTF fell more and more behind schedule, dissension over the project and the conflict between Shaw and PNL management infected the commission itself, resulting in some stormy discussions in which I tended to side with PNL whereas Ramey upheld the performance of Shaw.

The Bureau of the Budget also became involved in the controversy. BOB was apparently heavily influenced by comments made by Holifield critical of the performance of both PNL and Argonne. Budget Director Robert P. Mayo wrote to me on December 22, 1969, about a recent conversation in which Holifield had said it was "essential that the AEC laboratories perform effectively on development projects if they are to receive continuing support for basic research." Mayo concluded: "I would strongly urge that you take appropriate steps further to improve the situation."

The specific PNL-Shaw conflict was ended in January 1970 by a transfer of management responsibility for the FFTF from PNL to Westinghouse. The official explanation, as presented in AEC's Annual Report for 1970 (page 292), stated that Battelle (PNL's parent) had requested the move "to meet requirements of the 1969 Federal Tax Reform Act as it applies to nonprofit public foundations." This law placed limits on the amount of support a nonprofit organization could receive from a single source and still retain its tax-exempt status. It was reported that Battelle had to divest itself of some $15 million of AEC work in order to meet this criterion.[4] As I suspected at the time, and as Albaugh confirmed in a 1992 phone conversation, this explanation was merely a "legal crutch," a way of getting out of what had become for PNL an intolerable situation. The transfer of responsibility became effective on July 1, 1970, on which date some 1,000 employees transferred from PNL to Westinghouse.

But problems with the FFTF did not end with this change of contractor. On September 3, 1970:

> *Commissioner Thompson dropped in before lunch to tell me that he had come to the conclusion that we should stop the FFTF project, despite the great amount of money and effort that had gone into it. He felt that there was so much more yet to be spent that it would be better to stop it now than to continue to throw in good money after bad. He said that the present version had had its flux reduced by a factor of two from the original version and that the number of test loops had been decreased to two so that the facility was "only a whisper" compared to its originally planned capability. I said I thought it would be very difficult to make such a drastic decision at this late date.*

I was sympathetic with what Thompson was saying, but indeed there was no way of giving up on the FFTF at that point without derailing the entire breeder program because Shaw had made this plant the focus of the program's research and technology efforts.

As things developed, the new Westinghouse management was no better able than PNL had been to keep the FFTF within budget. The budgetary trail of the FFTF is not easy to follow in detail, in part because a lot of related research and development was performed elsewhere, but it was estimated in 1973 that the project would end up costing about $600 million, as compared to an initial (1968) estimate of $87.5 million.

The FFTF was finally completed in 1980, some six years behind schedule. After the demise of the U.S. LMFBR program (discussed in the next chapter), the facility continued in full-power operation performing tests for foreign organizations. The Department of Energy sought to close the FFTF beginning in 1990 but was deterred by Congress. In April 1992 the facility was placed on standby status in consideration of a possible future use in the production of plutonium-238 for spacecraft power plants.[5]

EXPLORING THE ALTERNATIVES

While giving priority emphasis to the LMFBR, the AEC had for a number of years been giving a modicum of support to breeder concepts other than the LMFBR. Underlying the Commission's thinking on this subject was an awareness that there might be technological difficulties with the LMFBR, which for a number of reasons seemed to be a high-risk endeavor. We were mindful also that in the development of other new technologies, such as the automobile, television, or, for that matter, light water reactors themselves, there had been a number of competing variants at the start, and that putting these through the process of comparative evaluation after each had undergone some early development had been very useful in identifying the best options. Also, to the extent that an alternative using the thorium cycle could be developed in addition to one using the uranium cycle, energy resources would be vastly extended since thorium was estimated to be much more abundant in nature than uranium.

In his autumn 1969 letter complaining about the cost of the breeder program, Budget Director Mayo asked whether the AEC could not reduce the number of alternative breeder concepts it was supporting. In reply, we pointed out that in the previous five years we had eliminated seven major alternatives to the LMFBR, reducing the number we still wanted to support to three very promising approaches. These were the light water breeder reactor, the molten salt breeder reactor, and the gas-cooled fast breeder reactor. I argued that any further elimination should be deferred until some very important technical information was forthcoming on the basis of which industry could determine whether it wished to support any of these three concepts.

The light water breeder reactor (LWBR) had been in development at Westinghouse's Bettis Laboratory near Pittsburgh under the direction of Admiral Rickover. For demonstration purposes, Rickover proposed to install a breeder core in the Shippingport Atomic Power Station near Pittsburgh.* A criticism of the LWBR was that it would have a very low breeding ratio and thus would not contribute much to solving any long-range problem of assuring the supply of nuclear fuel. Still, it had distinct advantages. It offered the only known way of increasing significantly the fuel utilization achievable in existing light water reactors. Further, since it proposed to use the thorium-U^{233} cycle, it could make available for power production a large part of the energy available in the nation's thorium reserves. Interest in the LWBR stemmed in part from the possibility that if the cost of uranium should increase significantly, many light water reactors might be converted to the use of thorium and eventually, after several loadings, reach the thorium breeding cycle. Finally, the LWBR was attractive because it would utilize proven technology with which utilities were already familiar.

The molten salt breeder reactor (MSBR) was being developed at the Oak Ridge National Laboratory under the direction of Dr. Alvin Weinberg, who lent his considerable prestige to efforts to promote it. Like the LWBR, it used the thorium cycle. As Weinberg pointed out, the MSBR had the advantage of very high heat-transfer capability. A drawback was that it employed slow rather than fast neutrons and so would not have a high breeding ratio.

Notwithstanding their advantages, neither the LWBR or the MSBR had much industry support. On the other hand, there was considerable support for the gas-cooled fast breeder reactor (GCBR), which employed the uranium cycle. More than forty utilities had joined Gulf General Atomic, Inc., in pursuing this concept. There was some analysis indicating that a GCBR's doubling time and

---

* This plant, on the Duquesne Light Company system serving the Pittsburgh area, became in 1957 the first civilian nuclear power plant to become an integral part of a commercial power network. It was built under Admiral Rickover's direction, employing the same type of pressurized-water reactor used in the early submarine reactors. It was built with very great attention to quality and, possibly as a result, had very high power costs.

its breeding ratio would be as good as those of the LMFBR, its capital costs less, and its coolant, helium, much easier to handle than liquid sodium.*

As Mayo indicated in his memorandum cited earlier, the Bureau of the Budget appeared from the first to feel that all the systems other than the LMFBR provided inviting targets for budget cuts. Consequently, it was necessary in each budget cycle to fight for their survival. In the Nixon administration's first markup of AEC's fiscal year 1970 budget, which occurred in March 1969, the LWBR was eliminated entirely, and both the molten salt and gas-cooled approaches were cut severely from the already low level of support advocated by the AEC. On March 17, 1969, we appeared before Mayo and his principal staff to appeal these and other proposed cuts. Admiral Rickover personally made the argument for the LWBR with a forceful presentation. The next day we learned that the LWBR had been restored at a reduced level, with the very difficult condition that we subtract an equal amount somewhere else in the AEC's budget.

The necessity to fight for survival or to limp along on small budgets did not, of course, go down easily with the sponsors of the alternative approaches, and AEC commissioners and top staff had to spend much time hearing and responding to their appeals. On April 2, 1969, for example, the commissioners met with representatives of some 37 utilities who felt that the gas-cooled approach offered the best potential for achieving a reliable, efficient, and economic breeder.

On November 10, 1969, we received the Budget Bureau's markup for the fiscal year 1971 budget. This time all breeder approaches other than the LMFBR were eliminated entirely. After I protested in a conversation with Mayo he relented a little; we could keep alive the LWBR or the MSBR, but not both. He left it to the AEC to make the choice. The Commission found this task a difficult one. The LWBR was close to the completion of its development program; it therefore represented the less costly budgetary choice and the quicker payoff. The MSBR had broader, long-range potential but would cost a lot to develop. When it came time to vote, Commissioners Johnson, Thompson, and Larson voted for the MSBR; Ramey and I for the LWBR. This outcome was made questionable, however, by Larson's former connection with the Oak Ridge National Laboratory, where the molten salt work was taking place. It was

---

* Gulf was also marketing the high-temperature gas-cooled reactor (HTGR), a thorium-cycle concept that, though not a breeder, offered substantial improvement in fuel utilization over existing light water reactors. A 40 MWe prototype plant employing this concept had been in operation in Pennsylvania since 1967, and a 330 MWe prototype was under construction in Colorado.

therefore agreed that I would have one more try at Mayo. I did so the same afternoon. I described to him the inconclusive results of our vote and suggested a possible solution, namely, to carry through the LWBR and also to carry the MSBR at a low level for a number of years just to keep it alive. I told Mayo that otherwise we might lose the team at Oak Ridge as well as a real chance for an eventual breakthrough on a very inexpensive source of nuclear power. Mayo reluctantly said BOB might make $5 million available for MSBR, as well as a larger amount for the LWBR, but, again, only if the AEC volunteered a compensating cut from some other program. We were able to do that.

On November 25, 1969, the Commission and members of the principal staff met with Alvin Weinberg. Unaware of our negotiations on his behalf two weeks earlier, he had come to plead for greater support for the molten salt approach. Learning from us that the project was still alive seemed a relief to Weinberg, but the reduced level was an obvious disappointment. Not long afterward, in a wide-ranging letter to Joint Committee chairman Holifield, Weinberg wrote: "I believe the country's almost single-minded commitment to fast breeder reactors, and its corresponding inability to support alternatives, particularly the molten salt breeder, is an error which I hope the Joint Committee can somehow correct in the not too distant future." This appeal was unlikely to produce results—nor did it—because the Joint Committee itself had a strong bias in favor of the LMFBR.

In its first markup of our fiscal year 1972 budget, in December 1970, the Bureau of the Budget moved again to eliminate the LWBR. Appealing this decision, I expressed the view that it would be a mistake to close down the LWBR after so much money had been spent on it and when it was so near its objective. This and other items on which AEC appealed from BOB's markup were reviewed by President Nixon and, as a result, the $10 million we had requested for the LWBR was restored. The molten salt approach continued to limp along at its reduced level of support.

In the 1970s, the government's commitment to the LMFBR became more exclusive, and budgetary support for the alternatives dwindled. After enduring near-starvation budgets for a number of years, the gas-cooled breeder zeroed out at the beginning of 1981. As of 1980 some utilities were cooperating on the design of a 300 MWe GCBR demonstration plant, but the project was not pursued. Preliminary designs were also prepared for molten salt breeder plants, but these, too, did not come to fruition. In February 1970 a reactors subcommittee of the AEC's General Advisory Committee classified the LWBR not as a breeder but as an "advanced converter." Among several such concepts that the subcommittee considered, it recommended that the LWBR "should be assigned lowest priority." Nevertheless, after several delays for technical and regulatory reasons, a light water breeder core utilizing the thorium-U^{233} cycle was brought to criticality at the Shippingport Atomic Power Station in August 1977. It operated well but was shut down because of budgetary restraints in October 1982, bringing to an end the pioneering Shippingport station's 25 years of service. An analysis completed in 1987 indicated that during the operation of the LWBR core a modest amount of breeding—1.39 percent—had indeed taken place.[6]

Alvin Weinberg may well have been right. The AEC, with the Joint Committee's active connivance, may well have erred in putting too many of its breeder eggs in the LMFBR basket. While correctly stating the case for alternative concepts in budget presentations, we gave them only token support compared to the massive emphasis on the LMFBR. When presidential support was sought, it was for the LMFBR only, and when the LMFBR was elevated to the status of a national goal with additional budgetary support, it all but assured that the alternatives would recede further into the shadows. Rather than throw such huge resources into a massive LMFBR program with short-term deadlines, the AEC might have done better to initiate a slower and broader program that would have afforded the opportunity to change course as difficulties arose. As later analyses would demonstrate (see chapter 12), there was not such great economic urgency to get breeder reactors on-line quickly as we first maintained. On the other hand, we did not fully appreciate this until the bulk of the program commitments had already been made.

NOTES

1. This analysis is based in part on "Breeder Reactors: The Next Generation," by Robert Avery and Hans A. Bethe in Kaku and Trainer, *Nuclear Power: Both Sides,* pp. 211-12.
2. Allen L. Hammond, "Management of U.S. Breeder Program Draws Criticism," *Science,* November 19, 1971, p. 809.
3. Deborah Shapley, "Engineer's Memo Stirs Doubt About Clinch River Reactor," *Science,* July 22, 1977, p. 351.
4. *Nucleonics Week,* February 5, 1970, pp. 1-2.
5. *Nuclear News,* April 1992, p. 99.
6. Duncan, *Rickover and the Nuclear Navy,* pp. 219-27.

12

Crash Landing

FORWARD MOVEMENT

The breeder effort in the United States was eventually to run aground, but not before it came much nearer to fruition. The final demise did not occur until mid-1983, some twelve years after I had left the AEC. Following is a summary of the major events during this period.

Strong forward movement on the demonstration plant occurred in 1972. A cooperative agreement involving AEC, TVA, and the Commonwealth Edison Company was signed in August. TVA was to provide a site on the Clinch River, adjoining AEC's Oak Ridge reservation, and was to operate and maintain the plant; Commonwealth Edison was to provide engineering, management, and purchasing services. The plant was to generate about 400 megawatts of electricity (MWe), to cost about $700 million, and to begin operation in 1979. Westinghouse, General Electric, and Atomics International all submitted proposals for providing the plant's nuclear system. Late in the year AEC selected the Westinghouse proposal. By the end of 1972, about $240 million had been pledged by 282 utilities toward the plant's cost.

In 1973 the demonstration plant acquired a name. It was to be called the Clinch River Breeder Reactor. Projected capacity was reduced from 400 to 350 MWe. During the year there was extensive site investigation; safety and environmental evaluations were started; preparations were made for procurement of major components and materials; staffing of the project organization was begun; and research and development on fuels and components continued.

In 1974 there was further progress on design, scheduling, and procurement; an environmental report was prepared; and Westinghouse began negotiating with General Electric and Atomics International to enlist their participation in the performance of specific portions of the project. In 1975 Congress was made aware that the estimated cost of Clinch River had more than doubled from the 1972 estimate of $700 million. The new estimate was $1.7 billion.* This revelation contributed to rising doubts about the project that were reflected in intense congressional debate. The Joint Committee rushed into the breach by initiating a year-long review of the entire LMFBR program, concluding that its continuation was essential to the nation's energy future. For the moment doubts were stilled and in December 1975 an authorization bill for AEC's successor, the Energy Research and Development Administration (ERDA)† included $171 million for Clinch River.

Even though the demonstration plant was having difficulty getting started, plans were initiated to move on to the next step. Three independent studies of a follow-on, full-scale (1,000 MWe) prototype were begun in 1975. The design work was to be finished in 1978, construction to begin in 1981, and operation to start in 1988. Design work for the first commercial breeder, the next phase, was to be initiated in 1983. (It will be recalled that at the beginning of the Nixon administration the plan was to have the first commercial plant *in full operation* by 1984.) The requested authorization for the entire breeder program for fiscal year 1977 was $655 million, of which $237 million was for Clinch River. An ERDA program plan indicated that future annual budgets to support the program would exceed $1 billion. All this activity seemed based on the continued assumption that there was a time urgency about bringing the breeder to commercial reality, that delay would cost the nation from $1 to $2 billion per year. But there was now increasing doubt about this proposition, including that expressed by a Ford Foundation report published in 1977. It concluded that "under most reasonable circumstances delayed introduction of breeders [would have] little economic consequence." This conclusion was based on estimates that, as compared to those made by the AEC but a few years earlier, were: (1) lower as to the number of LWRs that breeders would serve; (2) higher as to the amount of economically recoverable uranium that would be available for those

---

* The reader will recall from chapter 10 the shock that was felt in 1970 when General Electric estimated that its demonstration breeder mght cost $500 million.

† The AEC ceased to exist in January 1975, its operating functions being assumed by ERDA and its regulatory functions by the Nuclear Regulatory Commission. See chapter 14 for an account of these developments.

LWRs; and (3) much higher as to the costs of the breeders themselves, both as to capital costs and fuel costs.[1]

Enter now the Carter administration. From the first it was hostile to the breeder program in general and to Clinch River in particular. The president and his assistants argued that, in an economy awash with plutonium, some of it might fall into the wrong hands and lead to nuclear weapons proliferation. This was a concern much emphasized in the 1970s, especially after India became in 1974 the sixth country to test a nuclear device.

In April 1977 President Carter announced a policy of not using plutonium to fuel nuclear reactors. Since production of plutonium was the raison d'être of the LMFBR, the new policy, if perpetuated, would clearly have sounded the breeder program's death knell. Following Carter's pronouncement there was a battle back and forth between the president and the Congress about Clinch River that lasted through the end of his administration. Carter repeatedly requested authority to shut down the project, whereas Congress, while not supporting Clinch River sufficiently to permit strong forward progress, provided enough money to keep it alive.

Clinch River's fortunes seemed to revive with the advent of the Reagan administration. (Reagan was a strong supporter of nuclear power and was reported to have made a campaign pledge to the Atomic Industrial Forum that he would support Clinch River.[2]) In March 1981 he proposed that the project's budget be increased by $200 million. But the legislative strength generally enjoyed by Reagan in his early months as president did not extend to this issue. In May 1981 the House Committee on Science and Technology narrowly voted to deauthorize Clinch River and to spend an initial $20 million for its termination. Although the full House overturned the committee's recommendation in July, providing $228 million to begin construction, it was by an unconvincing margin—206 to 186—that boded ill for the future. Two proposals to cut back funding were defeated in the Senate. Not the least of the influences on the Senate was the personal interest of Republican leader Howard Baker in this huge undertaking on his home turf (Tennessee). President Reagan reaffirmed his support in October when he rescinded Carter's ban on the reprocessing of plutonium and issued a general order for all affected executive departments to get busy on Clinch River.

But the image of the program continued to be damaged by cost escalation and rising doubts about the various economic forecasts on which it was based. In addition, there were challenges of a legal and regulatory nature. The Department of Energy (DOE),* hoping to get construction started at long last,

---

* DOE succeeded ERDA on October 1, 1977.

applied to the Nuclear Regulatory Commission (NRC) early in 1982 for permission to let work start without the filing and review of environmental and safety-related reports. Such shortcuts, DOE estimated, might reduce the project's schedule by one to two years and save perhaps $10 million. Although the NRC rejected this request, its decision was reversed in federal court, and in September 1982 site clearing and excavation at the Clinch River site actually began.

Meanwhile, the economic justification for the breeder program received another major challenge with the release in July 1982 of a draft General Accounting Office (GAO) report that said the United States would probably not need breeder reactors until 2025 at the earliest. While the report did not recommend that the government terminate the Clinch River project, it did say that the project's high priority "might be misplaced." Later in the year, moreover, the GAO reported to the House that the project's final cost would be about $8 billion, not the $3.2 billion repeatedly stated by DOE, and certainly not the $700 million estimated by the AEC in 1970.

Notwithstanding the adverse reports, work on Clinch River had been moving steadily forward. As of September 1982, when excavation began, plant design was estimated to be 87 percent complete; more than $740 million worth of equipment had already been delivered or ordered; and total spending on the project had exceeded $1.3 billion.[3]

Another close brush with extinction came in December 1982. On the 15th the House voted, 217 to 96, to eliminate funds for Clinch River from a stopgap spending bill. On the 18th the Senate voted to retain the funds. On the 20th, the House-Senate conference committee agreed to keep the project alive.

TRAIL'S END

After the close brush with extinction in the congressional votes of December 1982, the Reagan administration itself began to see the handwriting on the wall. On February 13, 1983, Energy Secretary Donald P. Hodel acknowledged in congressional testimony that Clinch River might have to be scrapped if the nuclear power industry did not provide more money for it. At the same time, the administration began casting about for new means of sharing the cost with industry. Among the inducements reported under consideration were federal loan guarantees, tax-exempt bonds, and various contractual guarantees. But the case for industry support was critically wounded in April when it became clear that TVA, whose region Clinch River would have served, had no need for the additional electricity and had no interest in buying either the plant or its output.

DOE's budget request for Clinch River for the fiscal year to begin October 1, 1983, was $270 million. In May 1983 the House voted 388 to 1 to deny all funds unless there was a plan for sharing more of the cost with industry. The other side of this equation was made clear by Secretary Hodel, who testified that private investors might be willing to put more than $1 billion into Clinch River, but only if assured by the government that the plant would eventually be built. Such an assurance could, of course, not be given. It was another case of chicken and egg.

It did not take long for the logical implications of this impasse to be expressed. In June 1983 the Senate passed a $22.3 billion energy and water appropriations bill that set aside no money for Clinch River. What seemed like the final nail was driven on October 27, when the Senate voted 56 to 40 against a specific measure providing funds for Clinch River.

Thus came to an apparent end an undertaking of some twenty years duration on which well over $1.3 billion had been spent and to which hundreds of talented professionals in government and industry had devoted their knowledge, skill, and energies. At this writing (late 1992) there is under way a movement to revive the U.S. nuclear power industry through the introduction of standardized designs for a new generation of inherently safer light water reactors. An important argument for such a development is the need to reduce the amount of "greenhouse" gases and noxious chemicals that would otherwise be produced by the burning of fossil fuels. Whether the government and industry sponsors of the revival can gain the necessary amount of public acceptance is still open to question. But in any case, there seems to be no place in the planned revival for breeder reactors. For the United States, at least, the whole grandiose enterprise had been unrealistic.

WHAT WENT WRONG

It is worth stepping back a moment in an effort to decipher why the reality of the breeder effort differed so greatly from the expectations of its sponsors. Perhaps foremost of what went wrong was the fact that in spite of heroic efforts to overcome them, the breeder program encountered intractable technical problems. Those of us who had enthusiastically pushed the program—and I was certainly one of those—had underestimated the difficulties involved, for example, the need to have materials and components that could withstand extremely high temperatures and neutron flux levels with minimum absorption of neutrons. Consequently, the estimated cost of the breeder demonstration plant, as well as of other aspects of the program, was subject to continual escalation, and the schedule for different aspects of the program was repeatedly set back. By 1983 the estimated cost for Clinch River had risen to about $4 billion, with the utility industry still committed to contribute the same $240 million it had pledged in 1972. This contribution, once about one-third of the project's estimated total cost, was now one-sixteenth of the total. These developments all but made a mockery of the prediction that breeder plants would lower energy costs to the American people.

It might have been possible to overcome the difficulties over a period of time in a more moderately paced, smaller-scale program. Had such a modest effort indicated that the LMFBR was likely to be technically flawed, it might have been possible to pursue the benefits of breeding through one or more of the alternative concepts. But the LMFBR program's sponsors, including me, had persuaded themselves and eventually persuaded others, including the president, that there was an economic urgency to proceeding rapidly with an all-out effort on the LMFBR, culminating in the contention that every year of delay in bringing a commercial breeder plant on line would cost the nation from one to two billion dollars.

As indicated in chapter 10, the argument for pursuing the LMFBR on such a crash basis rested on a series of economic assumptions, each of which was to prove invalid. It was assumed, first, that the nation's demand for electricity would maintain its previous rate of advance. Since the end of World War I, electric power consumption had doubled approximately every ten years. There had been a consensus, both in and out of government, that this would continue. The forecast proved widely off the mark. Rather than doubling, utility sales of electricity increased only 50 percent in the 1970s and only 29 percent in the 1980s.[4] Several factors contributed to the erroneous prediction. Gross national product, to which electricity use has historically been closely tied, did not increase as much as expected. Next, the oil shock of the 1970s and the ensuing energy crises led to strong movements for energy conservation, including the introduction of more efficient electric appliances. Use of electricity was discouraged by rising costs. Finally, the forecasts may have overlooked the fact that what had nurtured the rapid rate of advance in use of electricity from 1920 to 1970 had been a series of important new electricity-intensive applications—air conditioning, electric space heating, large-scale production of aluminum and enriched uranium, and the like—and that, as of 1970, no other new uses of comparable importance were in view.

A further cardinal premise of the breeder program was that the nation's mounting electricity demands would be supplied to a rapidly increasing extent by nuclear power plants. This was a pardonable assumption in 1967, the year the AEC adopted the LMFBR as the centerpiece of its nuclear power efforts, because that was the year when power reactor orders reached their all-time peak. Contracts were awarded in 1967 for 31 nuclear plants, with an aggregate capacity of 25,780 MWe. This was more than half of all new generating capacity ordered that year by U.S. utilities and the first year nuclear orders had reached such a proportion. As noted earlier, the AEC was confidently predicting in 1969 that 150,000 MWe of nuclear capacity would be in operation by the end of 1980. The amount actually in place at that date turned out to be less than 52,000 MWe. After the record pace in 1967, nuclear orders slowed down markedly, amounting to 17 plants (11,462 MWe) in 1968 and only 4 plants (3,869 MWe) in 1969. As is well known, no new nuclear power plant of any description has been ordered in the United States since 1978, and all those ordered between 1974 and 1978 were canceled. The downturn, instigated at first by increasingly adverse economic comparisons with fossil-fuel plants, was exacerbated by regulatory and public acceptance problems born of environmental and safety concerns. After the Three Mile Island accident in 1979 it was apparent that for many years to come the number of nuclear power plants, and hence their need for the nuclear fuel that could be produced by breeders, would be far less than the AEC had projected.

Perhaps the most grievous error made in building the economic case for the breeder was the assumption that economically recoverable uranium would be in critically short supply. In the very early days of the AEC there did appear to be a great scarcity of uranium available for nuclear activities. But when the intensification of the Cold War led to a rapid expansion of facilities for the production of fissionable material in the 1950s, the AEC initiated a massive effort to discover and acquire uranium ore. As a result, domestic production of uranium concentrates increased from 80 tons in 1948 to 17,000 tons in 1959. By the 1970s vast reserves of economically recoverable uranium had been discovered around the world, such that the U.S. uranium industry began to have difficulty disposing of its product. In making its projections about uranium supply, the AEC might well have been derelict in not taking full account of what exploration might uncover based on the known geology.

Thus, one by one, the props on which had rested the argument for the breeder as a near-term economic necessity were cut away. At the same time that the Reagan White House was giving the program unprecedented political support, there was in reality very little economic justification for doing so. Without such justification, such a hugely expensive program could not be sustained for long.

OTHER COUNTRIES

At the briefing about the breeder in April 1971 (chapter 10) I told President Nixon and his cabinet that France, the United Kingdom, and the Soviet Union were further ahead with demonstration breeder plants than was the United States. In subsequent years, work also went forward on demonstration breeder plants in Germany and Japan. The economic lure of the breeder seemed greater for West European and Far Eastern countries than for the United States since, as compared with this country, they were more dependent on imported oil, appeared to have more limited access to uranium supplies, and in most cases had made greater relative commitments to nuclear power.*

But the intrinsic technical and economic problems of the LMFBR have caught up with the efforts of other countries as well as with our own. The French and British plants I mentioned to the president did indeed enter service, although somewhat behind schedule. The British one has since closed down. The French plant, Phénix, was succeeded by a larger one, Super-Phénix. The latter was beset by severe technical difficulties in 1987 and has since been shut down. Given the lack of economic justification, it is doubtful that an effort will be made to revive it. The Soviet plant, although completed before the others, never became operational because of a series of serious pipe ruptures. In Germany, general opposition to introduction of a plutonium economy led to a decision in 1989 not to operate a completed fast breeder prototype.

As of late 1992, the only nation that still seemed seriously interested in fast breeders was Japan, where a large prototype LMFBR, Monju, was scheduled to start up in 1993. Even there the program is subject to sharp controversy. There has been considerable international criticism of the program's requirement for repeated ocean transportation of large quantities of separated plutonium from French and British reprocessing plants, shipments that are thought to pose both a safety and a proliferation risk. When lack of economic justification and domestic antinuclear opposition are added to these international concerns, one has a situation that may in time lead Japan to follow the example of other nations and scale down, postpone, or even abandon its plans for fast breeder reactors.

---

* In 1991 France generated 72.7 percent of its electricity from nuclear power; Sweden 51.6 percent; South Korea 47.5 percent; Switzerland 40.0 percent; Taiwan 37.8 percent; Germany 27.6 percent; Japan 23.8 percent; United States 21.7 percent; and United Kingdom 20.6 percent (data from International Atomic Energy Agency).

NOTES

1. Nuclear Energy Policy Study Group, *Nuclear Power Issues and Choices,* p. 356.
2. Edward Cowan, "Reagan Delivers His Budget to Congress with a Warning to Remember 'Our Mandate,'" *New York Times,* March 11, 1981, p. 6.
3. Judith Miller, "Clinch River is Right at Home in Oak Ridge," *New York Times,* September 29, 1982, p. D27.
4. Data in this and the following paragraph are from the U.S. Energy Information Administration.

PART V

ADMINISTRATIVE MATTERS

13

A Matter of Justice

GROUNDS FOR SUSPICION

My diary for February 18, 1969, contained the following entry:

> *I discussed with members of my staff the growing concern that an officer of a certain industrial nuclear facility may have diverted appreciable amounts of enriched uranium-235 to Israel over the last several years. This possibility has apparently been brought to the attention of the president.*

What drew our attention to this matter on that date was a letter from FBI Director J. Edgar Hoover to AEC Director of Security William T. Riley strongly suggesting that the AEC might wish to revoke the individual's security clearance and cancel the facility's classified AEC contracts. Hoover made it clear that the suspected offenses included not only the diversion of material but also the divulging of classified information to representatives of Israel.

Neither in my diary entry nor in Hoover's letter were the facility or the individual identified by name. This was true of virtually all communications about the matter at the time, even telephone calls. The case seemed so sensitive that we wished to avoid all risk of public disclosure. There no longer is a need to be so circumspect since the story has by now been the subject of extensive public comment. As has been revealed, the company involved was the Nuclear Materials and Equipment Corporation (NUMEC) of Apollo, Pennsylvania, some 30 miles northeast of Pittsburgh. The individual whose security clearance Mr. Hoover wanted revoked was NUMEC's founder and president, Dr. Zalman Mordecai Shapiro.

A chemist with a 1948 Ph.D. from Johns Hopkins, and by all accounts a very brilliant scientist, Shapiro had worked for Westinghouse in the development of the reactor for the first nuclear submarine, Nautilus. He left Westinghouse in 1957 to establish his own nuclear materials processing company, NUMEC. Shapiro's original intent for the firm was that it would fabricate uranium oxide fuel for the burgeoning number of privately owned nuclear power plants. As it developed, however, much of NUMEC's early activity was on government contracts, one of the major ones involving the conversion of government-owned high-enriched uranium into fuel for a projected nuclear-powered rocket.

Contributing to the suspicion of Shapiro was his personal background. Son of an orthodox rabbi from Lithuania, he never made a secret of his sympathy for Zionist causes and, once it had been established, for the State of Israel. He had active and open relationships with the Israeli government, which he served as a technical consultant and for which he provided a training and procurement agency in the United States. He started a subsidiary of NUMEC in Israel, in partnership with the Israeli Atomic Energy Commission, to develop machinery for the preservation of fruits and vegetables by irradiation. He employed at least one Israeli, a metallurgist, in the Apollo plant, and he regularly received visits from Israeli officials, including the Israeli embassy's scientific attaché.

AEC's materials management staff conducted its first detailed surveys of NUMEC in November 1965.[1] It was estimated at that time that 93.2 kilograms of uranium-235 could not be accounted for. This estimate was known to be inexact, however, because of the inadequacy of NUMEC's records and measurements. Among the company's most glaring deficiencies had been a failure to develop methods for estimating the amounts of material lost in the processes of fabrication. For example, it was considered very possible that NUMEC had consistently underestimated the amounts lost in exhaust stacks, contaminated laundry, shoe covers, and sanitary sewers. Still, when a waste pit was dug up in 1965 at the behest of AEC investigators, the amount of fissionable material found was only a fraction of what Shapiro predicted would be found.

In keeping with its statutory obligation to keep the Joint Committee "fully and currently informed," the AEC duly reported its findings to the committee. John T. Conway, who was staff director of the Joint Committee in the mid-1960s, recalls being briefed on the matter by Howard Brown, AEC assistant general manager, in 1965. Conway thereupon sent two staff people to NUMEC where they talked to Shapiro and to several other professional employees. Neither the AEC nor JCAE investigators found any evidence leading to the conclusion that there had been a diversion to Israel.[2] The matter was also reported to the FBI, which at this time conducted only a brief inquiry to determine whether either Dr. Shapiro or NUMEC was a foreign agent. Concluding that they were not, the Bureau dropped the matter for the time being.

AEC'S SAFEGUARDS SYSTEM

I noted above that the AEC conducted its first detailed surveys of NUMEC in 1965. Considering that there had been evidence of material losses since 1960, it is a fair question why we delayed so long. The explanation may lie in some aspects of the historical development of AEC's safeguards system. (The word "safeguards," in this context, refers to measures designed to guard against the diversion to unauthorized uses of what the Atomic Energy Act calls "special nuclear material," namely, enriched uranium, plutonium, and uranium-233.) Under the original Atomic Energy Act (1946), all special nuclear material (SNM) was owned by the government with title remaining in the AEC or in contractors operating government-owned plants or laboratories. As a step toward greater participation by private enterprise in civilian nuclear power and other peaceful uses of atomic energy, a new, more permissive Atomic Energy Act was passed in 1954. The 1954 act still required that SNM be owned by the government. However, the legislation provided that SNM could be distributed under license to privately-owned enterprises such as NUMEC for their use in industrial operations.

Soon after passage of the 1954 act, the AEC made a basic policy decision as to its enforcement. The Commission determined that it would not impose on private enterprises requirements for safeguarding SNM as severe as those it applied to government-owned facilities. The AEC based this decision on the concept that it could rely on the companies' financial responsibility for the SNM, estimated to be worth fourteen times as much as gold, and on criminal penalties for unlawful use to insure that the material would be adequately safeguarded.

The decision not to employ a heavy hand in enforcing safeguards was consistent with the national priorities of the time. In the early 1960s the AEC had a plethora of nuclear material. There was a strong desire to use it to accelerate the development of peaceful uses of atomic energy both at home and abroad. Indeed, furtherance of the peaceful atom was considered an important, even vital, element of U.S. foreign policy. While the dangers of weapons proliferation were recognized—they had been a major reason advanced by President Kennedy in behalf of the 1963 Limited Test Ban Treaty, for example—such dangers did not have the prominent place in the national consciousness that they were later to acquire. To the extent that people worried at all about diversion, it was as something governments, but not private companies, might attempt. As noted safeguards scholars Mason Willrich and Theodore B. Taylor have written:

> In the early 1960s plant operations were not shut down or senior management alarmed if, after the closing of a formal material balance, substantial quantities of nuclear material were unaccounted for . . . The possibilities of diversion of nuclear material by non-governmental groups were not taken seriously by most persons.[3]

Largely in consequence of this relaxed attitude, the AEC's materials-accountability system as of 1960, the year when the discrepancies were first noted at NUMEC, left much to be desired. For example, it provided no means of ascertaining how much material a company might ship abroad other than by referring to the company's own records; there was no provision for AEC physical checks of shipments.* The system did not require that SNM be physically protected within, or when in transit to and from, private plants. Nor was every private employee who handled SNM required to have a security clearance or even to be a U.S. citizen. Furthermore, the AEC system failed to establish criteria for acceptable limits of materials unaccounted for, or to define what suspected transgressions would trigger an investigation. On the more technical side, there was a lack of adequate instrumentation and methods for detecting process losses and for determining SNM inventories. In addition, AEC staff did not seem to emphasize vigorous enforcement even of the existing requirements. There was an apparent misconception by staff that to the extent financial restitution was made in the event of loss all contractor responsibility for SNM was fulfilled.

Beginning in 1964, a number of events and circumstances led the AEC to change its approach. One was the detonation of a nuclear device by the People's Republic of China in October 1964—this led to a greater sense of alarm about the problem of nuclear weapons proliferation. The dangers of proliferation were also being underscored by the rapid increase in the number of nuclear power plants. Predictions were being made that by 1980 plutonium would be pro-

---

* With permission from the AEC, NUMEC was said to have shipped an estimated total of 1,000 pounds of high-enriched uranium to France, Italy, Germany, the Netherlands, and Japan (Weissman and Krooney, *The Islamic Bomb*, p.121).

duced throughout the world at a rate of more than 100 kilograms per day. A further cause for alarm was the spread throughout the world of politically oriented terrorism. The need for better safeguards enforcement were underscored by an August 1964 amendment to the Atomic Energy Act that, for the first time, permitted private ownership, as distinguished from mere custody, of SNM. Finally, in the Nonproliferation Treaty (NPT), which was signed in July 1968, the United States assumed obligations to prevent the spread of nuclear weapons to additional countries.

Giving heed to these developments, and following the recommendations of an ad hoc advisory committee convened after the revelations about NUMEC,[4] the AEC began to impose more severe safeguards requirements. At the same time, the AEC instituted a strong research and development program to develop improved safeguards equipment and methods. (Between 1967 and 1971, AEC's budget for safeguards research and development was increased from $500,000 to over $4 million.) To implement the changes, AEC's internal organization for safeguards was strengthened, and the safeguards staff augmented.

SUSPICION MOUNTS

The improvements in AEC's safeguards system came too late to remove suspicion from Zalman Shapiro, whose supposed offenses had predated the reforms. In 1968 the CIA received reports that the Israelis had somehow obtained a supply of enriched uranium. Although Israel was known to be capable of producing plutonium at a French-supplied test reactor at Dimona in the Negev desert,* it was not believed capable of producing U-235, and Israel's reported possession of a supply of that material directed attention once more toward NUMEC. Because the CIA is enjoined by law from conducting

---

* Seymour Hersh points out that the world outside Israel had little conception of the true capacity of the Dimona reactor and hence of the quantity of plutonium it could and did produce. It was capable of being operated at several times greater than the 24 megawatts acknowledged by the Israeli government (*The Samson Option,* pp. 119-20, 203-04). At a meeting of the Commission on July 11, 1969, we discussed plans for a team to visit and inspect Dimona "in order to make certain that it is being devoted to peaceful purposes." In due course application was made to the Government of Israel for permission to make such a visit, but it was refused.

domestic investigations, the agency called on the FBI for assistance. The Bureau thereupon conducted both physical and electronic surveillance of Shapiro for a period of more than a year. The surveillance disclosed that he had met on several occasions with Israeli citizens, including both the scientific attaché from the Israeli embassy and a suspected Israeli intelligence official. These meetings led to FBI suspicions that Shapiro was divulging classified information.* The CIA also was reported to have a "strong opinion" that NUMEC had diverted material to Israel.[5] It was in consequence of such views that J. Edgar Hoover wrote his letter to the AEC on February 18, 1969.

Whether the losses sustained at NUMEC were excessive for that industry at that time is open to question. Some years later Shapiro was quoted as saying that he had "been told by responsible officials that [NUMEC's] operations were pretty much in the ball park, in the range of similar facilities."[6] Although the AEC did not have much of a basis for comparison—there were only a handful of firms engaged in comparable activity—the staff tended to believe that the losses at NUMEC had indeed been excessive.

Still, based on all the available information AEC commissioners were unanimous in the belief that Shapiro and NUMEC had *not* diverted any nuclear material to Israel or to any other country for transshipment to Israel. We reached this conclusion in large part because there was no evidence to support a charge of diversion. It was hard to believe that such an effort could have occurred without leaving some trace of evidence for AEC, Joint Committee, and FBI investigators. We reached our conclusion also in consideration of the difficulties that any would-be diverter would have had to face. We did not believe it possible that diversion could have occurred without the knowledge of many of the employees in the plant. It seemed inconceivable that every one of these employees would have clandestinely agreed to suppress knowledge of a traitorous act. As to Shapiro himself, it was not reasonable to suppose that he would have undertaken such a hazardous course of action, whose penalty could have been a sentence of death. Nor was it consistent with his character, as we came to know it, to believe that he would have been motivated to commit an act of disloyalty to the United States. We had a simpler explanation for the losses. This was that NUMEC had subordinated other considerations to the pursuit of profit and, encouraged by AEC's lax enforcement, had adopted shortcuts in its processing that led to excessive and irretrievable losses of material. But solving the case to our satisfaction did not make it go away. We still had to confront

---

* Seymour Hersh has disclosed that many, if not most, of these meetings actually concerned ways of using scientific devices to protect Israel's water supply from terrorists (*The Samson Option*, pp. 249-50).

the fact that powerful individuals and organizations in the government had reached an opposite conclusion.

CONFRONTATION

Beginning about the time when J. Edgar Hoover wrote his letter to the AEC on February 18, 1969, news about the NUMEC case had spread widely in the upper echelons of the Nixon administration. Secretary of Defense Melvin Laird brought up the matter as I was concluding a meeting at the Pentagon with him and Deputy Secretary David L. Packard on February 25, 1969. After I explained the AEC's view that there had been no illegal diversion, Laird cautioned that we should make every effort to squelch the story, lest it result in a congressional report. What he no doubt had in mind was that the Joint Committee on Atomic Energy might choose to make a cause célèbre of the matter.*

I went directly from this Pentagon meeting to the Justice Department to discuss Hoover's letter to the AEC with Attorney General John M. Mitchell. Mitchell noted at once that President Nixon was personally interested in the case. I expressed the opinion that it would be a mistake to prosecute Shapiro on the assumption that an adequate case could be made against him.

On April 3, I wrote the attorney general a long letter. I noted that before we could revoke Shapiro's security clearance as the FBI director had suggested it would be necessary under AEC regulations to prepare a letter of notification to Shapiro setting forth any derogatory information and offering him a hearing before a personnel security board. Further, while cancellation of NUMEC's contracts did not require any formal procedure, the company could reasonably be expected to insist on a detailed explanation of the government's action. Since there was no incriminating evidence, the government's side of such proceedings would be difficult to sustain. I then offered for Mitchell's consideration an alternative suggestion, namely, that the AEC conduct an informal interview of Shapiro. Such a course, I wrote, might shed light on his contacts with Israelis and even diminish Israeli interest in him as a possible source of information. On the other hand, we "could not be sure that an interview would not evoke

---

* This was, in my opinion, a groundless fear. As indicated above, the committee had been fully informed on the matter in 1965 and, had they been so inclined, could have publicized it at that time. Nor had it ever been the practice of the committee to leak sensitive information.

public charges by the subject that he was being victimized by the AEC and FBI because of his support of the Israeli cause and had been subject to unlawful invasion of his privacy." I concluded by saying that we did not intend to conduct an interview before receiving the attorney general's advice and without knowing whether he planned to prosecute.

On the same day, April 3, I wrote to Joint Committee chairman Chet Holifield to inform him that the FBI investigation had been going on and that the AEC was seeking legal advice from the Department of Justice. The next day:

> *Ed Bauser of the JCAE staff called concerning my letter to Holifield and asked that someone go up to tell the committee more about it. I agreed, but cautioned that this case was very sensitive. He said that Holifield was still sweating out how to get this information out without hurting programs, individuals, etc., because this type of loss of materials could not stay hidden.*

On May 2 I learned that Mitchell had declined to give approval for the Joint Committee to see the FBI file on Shapiro. My initial reaction was that this was a mistake—that such a denial could not hold up if the committee decided to contest the issue. I called Mitchell to express this opinion. Without addressing my arguments, he merely repeated that he would prefer not to have anyone see the file.*

Mitchell also seemed to be having difficulty deciding whether to approve AEC's suggestion about conducting an informal interview with Shapiro. With Mitchell's assent, I therefore took the matter up with presidential assistant Peter Flanigan, who in turn discussed it with White House Counsel John Ehrlichman. The upshot of these conversations was a White House decision that the likely benefits of an interview outweighed the risks and that we should proceed. AEC staff members accordingly interviewed Dr. Shapiro on August 14 in AEC's downtown Washington office. On August 27, I summarized the results in letters to the Department of Justice, the FBI, and the Joint Committee. I indicated:

1. that what Shapiro reported of a particular meeting with an Israeli official was consistent with other reports the AEC had received of that meeting;

---

* Tom Wicker writes of Mitchell: "A forceful man, relentless in his advocacy, blunt to associates and in his public statements . . . he seemed to exemplify the kind of tough, no-nonsense attitude that Nixon most admired" (*One of Us,* p. 415).

2. that "he appeared to be less than completely candid" in the discussion of his relationship with some officials of the Government of Israel to the extent that he was vague and uncertain as to details that he should have been able to recall;* and

3. that "Dr. Shapiro did state that he had never been asked to furnish classified information, had never furnished, and would not, if asked to, furnish classified information to Israeli officials or to other unauthorized persons."

I concluded by stating that, on the basis of the information developed during the interview, the AEC "does not contemplate further action in this matter at this time."

Hoover replied a week later. He strongly implied that the AEC was making a mistake in not revoking Shapiro's security clearance. The FBI's "thorough and extended investigation of Shapiro for more than a year" had, he wrote, "developed information clearly pointing to Shapiro's pronounced pro-Israeli sympathies and close contacts with Israeli officials, including several Israeli intelligence officers. . . The basis of the security risk posed by the subject lies in his continued access to sensitive information and material . . . and the only effective way to counter this risk would be to preclude Shapiro from such access." But, since the AEC planned no further action, the FBI would also discontinue its active investigation, although they would pass along any information that came their way from other sources.

A NEW PHASE

There the matter could have rested were it not for the fact that Dr. Shapiro, in October 1970, accepted a position with a new employer, Kawecki Berylco Industries, Inc. (KBI), a metals-processing company also located in Pennsylvania. (He had previously sold his interest in NUMEC to the Atlantic Richfield

---

* As noted above, many of Shapiro's conversations with the Israelis probably dealt with efforts to protect Israel's water supply from diversion and contamination. Shapiro told Seymour Hersh that he "had decided not to discuss specifically all of his activities on behalf of Israel during the many government and congressional investigations into NUMEC . . . because of the continued threat to . . . the water supply: 'I didn't want to put any ideas into people's minds'" (Hersh, *The Samson Option*, p. 249).

Company, which, in turn, soon sold it to the Babcock and Wilcox Company. But Shapiro continued to manage the plant for the new owners.) The assignment that KBI had in mind for Shapiro required that he have access to weapons information, and he had accordingly applied to the AEC for the upgraded ("Sigma") security clearance that would permit such access. Looking back, it has seemed to me that Shapiro, knowing of the storm that had been swirling about his head, was somewhat injudicious in provoking a new security clearance confrontation. On the other hand, it seemed testimony to his innocence of any wrongdoing that he was willing to do so. For us in the AEC it was the beginning of a new round of headaches.

The question immediately arose whether Shapiro should not, under the circumstances, be subject to a formal security hearing before a decision was made on the Sigma clearance. But there was a major problem with that approach, as I told the attorney general in a phone call on November 3, 1970. The AEC people in charge believed they could not hold a meaningful hearing without the information contained in the FBI reports, and we already had been told that this information would not be made available to us. Thus, I wasn't at all sure we should hold a hearing. Alternatively, we could grant Shapiro the requested clearance and keep close surveillance over the weapons aspects of his activities. Mitchell said he would take a reading on the case and be back in touch with me.

In subsequent days word came from the Department of Justice reiterating that they could not make available in a hearing the information they had. The Commission thereupon decided on November 23 on a new preferred course of action. Instead of holding a hearing we proposed to grant Shapiro the Sigma clearance on condition that he sign an affidavit under oath that he had not passed sensitive information to any unauthorized person, that he would not do so in the future, and that he did not intend to move to another country.

The AEC's proposal did not sit at all well with the Justice Department. On December 8, AEC security chief William Riley and AEC attorney Sidney Kingsley met with Assistant Attorney General Robert Mardian.* After returning from the meeting, Riley and Kingsley briefed the members of the Commission. As noted in my diary:

> *Mardian had told them that it was the considered opinion of the Department of Justice, including John Mitchell, and of the*

---

* As head of Justice's internal security division, Mardian had authorized a number of wiretaps that were to become controversial during the Watergate proceedings.

White House, perhaps including Henry Kissinger and even the
president, that the Sigma clearance should be denied to Shapiro
without a hearing.
   This caused consternation among the Commissioners because
it would be the first instance of such a peremptory action in AEC's
history. It was agreed that I would talk to Mitchell, apprise him
of our views, and seek to determine whether some way might be
found to handle the situation through informal contacts with the
subject or his company.

Soon after, we learned that Shapiro had engaged as counsel one of the most
skillful and prominent attorneys in the country, Edward Bennett Williams, and
his associate, Harold Ungar. It was evident that Shapiro intended to fight to
clear his name.

My meeting with Mitchell took place on January 21, 1971. I was accompanied by security chief Riley and AEC general counsel Joseph Hennessey.
Mardian was present. It was quickly evident that the positions of the AEC and
the Justice Department were far apart.

   I said I thought the charges were essentially without substance
and that I strongly opposed denying a clearance without going
through the hearing process. I said this had never been done by
any government agency. Mitchell said he felt the charges were
serious enough that the man should not have access to sensitive
weapons information. He thought the case should be settled by
the courts. I emphasized that this could lead to a sensational
public relations problem since the man was being defended by
very prominent counsel and since they intended to put up a public
fight to defend his honor. I suggested that other executive depart-
ments be consulted for advice, in response to which Mitchell
suggested that I get in touch with Henry Kissinger and Secretary
of State Bill Rogers.

I saw both Rogers and Kissinger within the next few days, and also Science
Adviser Edward E. David. All three seemed to agree that it would be inappro-
priate to deny clearance without a hearing. David was particularly alive to the
danger that scientists, still smarting from the 1954 proceedings in which J.
Robert Oppenheimer's security clearance had been revoked, might rise up in
loud protest against another mistreatment of one of their number. He said he
would be ready to talk to Mitchell about it.

Meanwhile, KBI was becoming increasingly concerned about the delay in Shapiro's availability. While we could offer no encouragement about near-term resolution of the problem, the AEC urged the company to be patient and to take no action that would foreclose his employment. At a Commission meeting on January 28, AEC General Manager Bob Hollingsworth was instructed to investigate whether alternative contract work could be offered to KBI that would not require access to weapons information. Also becoming restive was attorney Edward Bennett Williams, who called me on February 3 urging haste in reaching our clearance decision lest his client lose the job with KBI.

The next day, Science Adviser David called. He and Flanigan had urged Mitchell not to deny clearance except in accordance with tradition and accepted procedures. We also learned that Kissinger had called Mitchell to the same effect. The result of all these interventions was communicated by Mardian on February 5: Mitchell, he said, was still of the opinion that Shapiro should be denied a clearance without a hearing.

It is hard to fathom why the administration was adopting such an obdurate and seemingly unwise attitude in this case. There was much to lose should Williams, for example, follow through on his announced intention to conduct a public fight for his client's reputation. In addition to the outraged uprising of scientists predicted by David, there was the danger of further perturbation in the administration's Middle East foreign policy, already in considerable disarray following the Israeli conquests in the Six-Day War of 1967.

RESOLUTION

The AEC now began to cast about for a compromise solution. At a Commission meeting on February 8, 1971, it was decided that Assistant General Manager John V. Vinciguerra, after checking with Mardian, should interview Shapiro with the object of trying to persuade him to withdraw his request for a Sigma clearance. Vinciguerra would offer to help him find another position. Vinciguerra, Riley, and Hennessey tried this idea on Mardian the next day. Mardian said he would not agree to this unless I made a prior commitment that, if Shapiro refused to go along, I would drop my opposition to denying clearance without a hearing. After rendering this judgment, Mardian dismissed his callers in summary fashion. I told Vinciguerra I would not accept the deal, and Mardian was so informed.

Science Adviser David seemed now to waver in his support of AEC's position. He agreed with my refusal to accept Mardian's terms, which he described as "just a power play." He asked, however, whether clearance could not be denied on the basis of previous falsification of materials accounting records. I told him that there had been no falsification—that NUMEC had merely delayed reporting losses of materials in the hope they would be found and that other firms did this also. He then asked whether the loss of material itself could not be a reason for denial. I pointed out that the AEC was on record as believing there was no evidence of illegal diversion. Based on the way David was talking, I expressed to him the guess that he must have run into the feeling around Washington that Shapiro actually did divert material. I said this was absolutely wrong, that no one in the AEC believed it. David said there were a lot of people involved by now and that he had been warned not to get into a head-on collision with Mitchell—hence his search for a compromise solution. Also, he felt he had to be very careful lest his involvement drag in the president. He alluded to a philosophy that, when in a tight spot where it seemed there was everything to lose and nothing to gain, the best thing to do was "to delay, and delay, and delay."

On February 12 David met with Mardian for one and one-half hours. Later in the day he described to me the gist of what had occurred. He emphasized to Mardian that Shapiro probably already had all the information necessary to make a simple nuclear weapon and that the additional information he might gain from the higher clearance would be of very little significance; accordingly, it would be a mistake to drive him out of the country by unfair treatment of his clearance application. David said that Mardian did not react.

Later the same day I had a call from Edward Bennett Williams. He said he was constantly being "bugged" by Shapiro and KBI as to when there would be a decision on the clearance. He added that it would be one thing if his client lost the position because of an adverse decision on his clearance; it would be quite another if he lost it because no decision was made. He asked whether his associate, Harold Ungar, might come to see me, and an appointment was made for February 17. Upon learning of this appointment Mardian said he would like to be present as well and, to make this possible, the appointment was rescheduled for February 25.

Because of persistent rumors that the CIA had information and was somehow involved in the case, Assistant General Manager Howard Brown and I sought out Director Richard Helms. Over lunch at CIA headquarters on February 18, we described to him the Justice-AEC impasse, emphasizing our view that Shapiro had not diverted any material. Helms assured us that he had no information that had not already been given to us.

Despite all the moves for a compromise, the Justice Department's position seemed only to harden. Vinciguerra, Hennessey, and Riley met with Mardian on February 24 to discuss the meeting among Williams, Mardian, and me scheduled for the following day. To their surprise, the AEC group learned that Mardian now wanted that meeting canceled and without indicating Justice Department involvement in the cancellation. He did, however, agree to Vinciguerra's suggestion that we inform Williams that Justice was advising the AEC to deny granting a clearance. Language, subsequently approved by Mitchell, was drafted for me to use in imparting this message. It was to have read:

> I have been advised by the Department of Justice that the granting of Sigma Access to Dr. Shapiro would be inconsistent with the Presidential Executive Order and the applicable AEC regulations issued pursuant thereto. I have been further advised to deny this access pursuant to Section 9 of Executive Order 10865 and the implementing regulations contained in 10 CFR 10.33 (c).

I and the AEC staff members involved agreed among ourselves that no such action should be taken by me without full consideration by the entire Commission.

The Commission assembled the next day and decided that the proposed notification to Williams was too bitter a pill for the AEC to swallow. After much discussion of a number of alternatives, none of which seemed very attractive, we decided on two courses of action. First, we would prepare a letter to Mitchell stating that we preferred not to deny clearance by the notification worked out with Mardian and would only follow this course if directed to do so. Second, we intended to have Commissioners Larson and Ramey meet with KBI officials in an effort to persuade them to transfer Shapiro to work not requiring a Sigma clearance.

That meeting took place on March 5. KBI was represented by its top three officials. They said that the proposed solution—offering Shapiro a different job—was next to impossible. Larson and Ramey then discussed with them a new idea, the possibility of finding him a job with another company.

In response to a request from KBI, the AEC agreed to extend Shapiro's existing security clearance. This was done by telegram within the week. Meanwhile we had received a phone call from Harold Ungar protesting the cancellation of the meeting that had been scheduled for him with Mardian and me and stating that the situation had become "virtually intolerable."

At a Commission meeting on March 17 we discussed whether Commissioners Ramey and Larson should meet with Shapiro. We decided instead to contact him through an intermediary, Frank (Francis P.) Cotter, a Westinghouse vice president and manager of its Washington office. It was also decided that AEC General Counsel Hennessey would call Ungar to suggest, without specifics, that the commissioners had problems in meeting directly with him or Williams.

The intermediary, Cotter, also shrank from meeting directly with Shapiro. He thought it would be better if someone else simply offered him a job. On March 23, 1971:

> *Ramey talked to John Simpson [president of Power Systems] of Westinghouse, who is willing to offer the subject a salary of $60,000 a year.* Ramey also talked to the subject himself, indicating to him that he should be patient. In this conversation no mention was made of the fact that we were helping to locate another job for him. For the first time we are seeing some light in this difficult case.*

On April 1 we learned that Simpson and another Westinghouse executive had themselves talked to Shapiro and offered him a position in a senior technical-advisory capacity. He promised an answer within 24 hours. Later that same day Cotter talked with Shapiro, a conversation in which the latter may have learned for the first time of the full scope of the difficulties involved in upgrading his security clearance. Cotter made it clear that the final decision on the clearance was beyond AEC control and that the prospects were not good. Following this conversation, Shapiro phoned Simpson and accepted the Westinghouse offer. About two weeks later Shapiro formally withdrew his request for the Sigma clearance.

Six months later, after I had left the AEC, I chanced to talk to Edward Bennett Williams on another matter.

> *He expressed satisfaction with the way I handled the case involving his client. I told Williams there was more to the case than he knew and that I would reveal more details to him some day. Knowing of my interest in the Washington Redskins, Williams, the team's owner, then expressed to me his opinion that quarterback Billy Kilmer was a better team leader than Sonny Jurgensen had been, even though he was not as good a passer.*

---

* As Cotter recalls it (note to John Conway, September 12, 1991), "Jim Ramey sought my help in Zal receiving a Westinghouse offer. Zal is so good that Simpson was delighted." A measure of how delighted is the fact that the $60,000 offer was equivalent to more than $200,000 in 1992 dollars.

SEQUELS

We in the AEC may have thought that the Shapiro-NUMEC matter had been laid to rest when he accepted the Westinghouse job offer in April 1971. It might have been but for a chain of events that culminated in the case being made a part of the public record.

As discussed at some length in chapter 14, the AEC was abolished by the Energy Reorganization Act of 1974, its regulatory functions, including nuclear materials management, being assumed by a newly established Nuclear Regulatory Commission (NRC). In December 1975 an NRC engineer, assigned to write a history of nuclear materials safeguards, discovered that the NUMEC file, which assumed importance in other documents, was missing. He persuaded his superiors to pursue the matter and the trail led to the CIA. The NRC thereupon requested a briefing by the CIA on the significance of the case and why the file could not be released.

The briefing, which took place in February 1976, was conducted by CIA's assistant director for science and technology, Carl Duckett. After discussing the historical record involving NUMEC and Shapiro, Duckett appended CIA's estimate that Israel already possessed a number of nuclear weapons. NRC chairman William A. Anders then brought the matter to the attention of President Gerald Ford, who promptly ordered a new FBI investigation of Shapiro. This investigation later culminated in an FBI finding that "there was no provable illegal act."[7]

A month after he briefed the NRC, Duckett injudiciously communicated the same estimate of Israel's nuclear capabilities and something about NUMEC to a group of business executives meeting at CIA headquarters. Word about Duckett's statement then leaked to the press. Proceeding through the Freedom of Information Act, two enterprising journalists, John J. Fialka of the *Washington Evening Star* and David Burnham of the *New York Times,* obtained release from the NRC of a voluminous amount of previously withheld AEC material. A spate of newspaper and magazine articles based on this material then appeared in 1977, 1978, and 1979. These accounts, as far as I have read them, revealed without gross inaccuracies much of what had occurred.* Several of the articles, however, left the reader with the strong, and erroneous, inference that Shapiro

---

* A notable exception was that none of the articles mentioned the confrontation between the AEC and the Department of Justice based on the latter's demand that Sigma clearance be denied to Shapiro without a hearing. Apparently no material on that aspect of the case, if any existed in the files, was released.

and NUMEC had indeed diverted enriched uranium to Israel. This impression has regrettably become part of the "conventional wisdom." Thus, even so highly respected a nonproliferation authority as Leonard S. Spector states in a recent book that "Israel is believed to have illegally diverted about 100 kilograms of highly- enriched uranium from a privately owned uranium fabrication plant, the Nuclear Materials and Equipment Corporation (NUMEC) facility, at Apollo, Pennsylvania."[8] I can only repeat here my conviction that if this is believed, the belief is erroneous.

In the years after his employment in 1971, Shapiro occupied positions of increasing responsibility with Westinghouse until his retirement in 1983, after which he has continued to work as a consultant. Distinguished as Shapiro's career has been, one cannot but wonder whether it might not have been even more illustrious had these unjust charges not been leveled against him.

NOTES

1. Much of the detailed information herein about the materials losses at NUMEC and the AEC's materials safeguards system is based on two documents: (1) Atomic Energy Commission, "Summary of Briefing on Safeguards and Domestic Material Accountability," presented on February 14, 1966, by Howard C. Brown, Jr., and (2) A. Altman, J. Hockert, and E. Quinn, "A Safeguards Study of the Nuclear Materials and Equipment Corporation Uranium Processing Plant, Apollo, Pennsylvania," NUREG 0627, Nuclear Regulatory Commission, December 1979.
2. Telephone conversation with Conway, November 6, 1991.
3. Willrich and Taylor, *Nuclear Theft: Risks and Safeguards*, p. 189.
4. The group's full name was Ad Hoc Advisory Panel on Safeguarding Special Nuclear Material. The report, dated March 10, 1967, became known as the Lumb report, after the panel's chairman, Ralph F. Lumb.
5. Weissman and Krooney, *The Islamic Bomb*, p. 121. Also Hersh, *The Samson Option*, pp. 241, 247.
6. David Burnham, "Nuclear Plant Got U.S. Contracts Despite Many Security Violations," *New York Times*, July 4, 1977, p. 15.
7. "Mystery of Israel's Bomb," *Newsweek*, January 9, 1978, p. 27.
8. Spector, *Going Nuclear*, p. 141.

14

Toward a Department
of Energy

> At this moment in our history, most Americans have con-
> cluded that government is not performing well. . . . The great
> danger, in my judgment, is that this momentary disillusion-
> ment with government will turn into a more profound
> and lasting loss of faith.
>
> —President Richard M. Nixon, March 25, 1971[1]

THE PROBLEM

The executive branch has tended to sprawl in haphazard fashion in modern times. This was particularly evident in the years after World War II. As Senator John McClellan, chairman of the Senate Committee on Government Operations, observed in May 1971: "The Executive Branch of the federal government is now the largest and most complicated enterprise in the world, with more than 1400 domestic programs distributed among 150 separate departments, agencies, bureaus, and boards."[2] Inevitably, in an establishment so cumbersome and complex, duplication and other inefficiencies have crept in, making the structure costly to operate and slow to respond when action is needed. In one of his messages on the problem, President Nixon gave some examples:

> . . . in 1972 it took 71 different signatures to buy one piece of construction equipment for certain federally funded urban renewal projects; five agencies and 56 signatures could be required in order to hire one person; nine federal departments and 20 agencies all had responsibility for educational programs; local water and sewer projects alone involved seven different agencies.[3]

A succession of presidents have attempted to deal with this problem by appointing groups to study it and to submit reorganization proposals. Richard Nixon fell naturally into this progression. It was one of the hallmarks of Nixon's approach to the presidency that he wanted very much to put his own stamp on things. In a memo to the budget director on June 1, 1969, for example, he wrote:

> I want it made clear to all departments and agencies that the budget going to Congress will be my budget and that it should reflect the goals and objectives of my administration.

Similarly, in a meeting on June 25, 1969, regarding SALT, I heard the president say:

> There is only one person responsible for the security of our nation, and I am that person. I shall listen carefully to all the viewpoints expressed, but in the end, when I lay it down, I expect it to be followed.

Despite these confident assertions, Nixon seemed to be haunted and frustrated by a feeling that the bureaucracy was out of his control. He recognized that many of the career people in middle and lower levels were unsympathetic to his policies. Indeed, he began to suspect that this was true as well of some of his own appointees to head executive departments and of their principal lieutenants. He recognized, moreover, as Richard P. Nathan has expressed it, "that in many areas of domestic affairs, *operations is policy*. Much of the day-to-day management of domestic programs—regulation writing, grant approval, and budget apportionment—actually involves policymaking."[4] Attempting to gain control over these processes was one of the main thrusts of Nixon's presidency, and it led to some very sweeping proposals to reorganize the structure of the government.

THE OFFICE OF THE PRESIDENT

In April 1969, Nixon appointed an Advisory Council on Executive Organization under the chairmanship of Roy L. Ash, a long-time supporter who had been president of Litton Industries, Incorporated, an industrial conglomerate.* The council was asked to make recommendations for "improving the functioning of the Executive Branch."

It was decided to start with the Office of the President itself, perhaps because congressional approval would not be required for any reorganization there.† After a study that lasted some eight months, the Ash council, as the group came to be known, brought forth a reorganization plan whose overall thrust was to bring greater control of the Cabinet departments into the White House. It did this by establishing two new organization units in the Office of the President: a Domestic Council and an Office of Management (later called the Office of Management and Budget). The Domestic Council's membership was to include the secretaries of all departments except State, Defense, and Post Office. It was to have a staff headed by an executive director; Nixon named John Ehrlichman to be the first occupant of this post. Like its counterpart on the international side, the National Security Council, the Domestic Council was expected to deal with specific program areas through interagency committees, advisory councils, task forces, and the like.‡ Besides carrying on the work of the Bureau of the Budget, the Office of Management, as its name implied, was to give increased emphasis to nonbudgetary processes of program implementation.

The plan was unveiled at a Cabinet meeting on March 4, 1970, that I was invited to attend along with many other non-Cabinet government officials. In his brief introduction before leaving the meeting, President Nixon indicated

---

* Other members of the group were Harvard Business School Dean George P. Baker; former Texas governor John B. Connally; Frederick R. Kappel, former chairman of the Executive Committee of AT&T; management consultant Richard M. Paget; and Walter N. Thayer, president of Whitney Communications Corporation. Murray Comarow was named staff director.

† The Reorganization Act of 1949 gave the president wide latitude to reorganize agencies of the executive branch provided neither House nor Senate disapproved within 60 days. It was amended in 1964, however, to exclude creation, abolition, or consolidation of Cabinet departments. Under the amended act, such actions would require legislation by Congress.

‡ It is noteworthy that Bill Clinton intends to establish a National Economic Council similar in concept to Nixon's proposed Domestic Council.

that the recommendations we were to hear had his complete endorsement. He acknowledged that they would affect the operations of many Cabinet officers and other government officials but he hoped for cooperation in making the reorganization successful. After the president departed Ash and fellow council member John Connally described the plan and recited its expected advantages. The reaction of Cabinet members lacked something in enthusiasm.

> *Secretary of Commerce Maurice H. Stans recalled that there had been a similar study under Eisenhower and that the Cabinet members who felt they would have been adversely affected managed to kill the plan.*
>
> *Secretary of Transportation John A. Volpe emphasized that some functions of his department had nothing to do with what other departments were doing, implying that for these functions a new coordinating mechanism like the Domestic Council was not needed. He also emphasized that recommendations made to the president by a Cabinet officer were staffed out, studied, revised, and generally "massaged" in the officer's department. It wasn't correct to assume that they came off the top of the Cabinet officer's head* [implying that they did not need further study in the White House]. *In response, Connally said that the reorganization would not interject a layer between any Cabinet officer and the president. What it would do, he said, was give the president a more powerful means for studying proposals that a Cabinet officer might bring to him.* [This statement by Connally was disingenuous if not deceptive, and the Cabinet officers obviously didn't buy it. What the plan did was exactly what Connally said it would not do: it inserted a new level of management between certain Cabinet members and the president.]
>
> *Secretary of State William P. Rogers noted that the new Office of Management would have the function of checking on how effective a Cabinet member was, and he wondered whether this didn't constitute a sort of built-in friction. Connally thought there needn't be any worry along these lines.*
>
> *Secretary of Housing and Urban Development George W. Romney asked if the manner in which a Cabinet officer was treated in the new setup, such as whether he was chosen for a task group that involved his interests, might not indicate whether the president had lost confidence in him. He said this had already*

been a problem in that the Cabinet seemed to have been left out in the determination of policy. Vice President Agnew jumped to his feet at this point and indicated by his manner that he thought the discussion was getting out of hand. He said that the meeting had not been intended as a forum to hear the views of Cabinet members on the reorganization—those could better be communicated to the president in writing. He insisted that the reorganization would improve the Cabinet which, as it existed, was not a working body. Agnew added very pointedly that the president had already indicated that the reorganization represented his wishes. The vice president then abruptly closed the meeting.

Of the secretaries who raised questions at this meeting, all but Rogers were soon to leave the Cabinet. This is not to say that their departures were directly related to their interventions at the meeting. Each had his own separate reason for wishing to depart or for falling from grace. Yet, their discontented grumbling at the meeting could not have escaped notice, as there were many members of the White House staff present, including both Messrs. Haldeman and Ehrlichman. The president was known not to take kindly to complaints from Cabinet members about lack of access to him. He referred to those who made such complaints as "crybabies."[5]

ZEROING IN ON THE AEC

While preparing its plan for the Office of the President, the Ash council and its fairly large staff had also been working on a sweeping proposal to reorganize the entire executive branch. It was inconceivable that the AEC would be spared in such an undertaking; there was too much controversy and criticism swirling about our heads for that. As summarized in the *Washington Post*, for example, we were charged with having an irresponsible and largely unnecessary weapons test program; an expensive, time-consuming, and often fruitless research program; and a power program that threatened to pollute the earth with radiation.[6] "After years of living in a balmy kind of political immunity," the *Post* article said, the AEC was "suddenly emerging as one of the most beleaguered branches of the federal government." Particularly threatening was a quote from Senator Allen Ellender. The AEC had been "a sacred cow," he said. "It's time somebody took a good look at their affairs." Ellender was in a key position to take the look himself. He was chairman of the Public Works Subcommittee of the Senate Appropriations Committee, which, under a 1969 reorganization of that committee, had assumed jurisdiction over AEC appropriations. In a similar vein the *New York Times* quoted Leo Goodman of the United Automobile Workers as saying: "Once they [the AEC] no longer have their halo—they're not God and king and country anymore—people begin to say out loud that the emperor has no clothes."[7] The AEC's main line of defense, the Joint Committee on Atomic Energy, was itself coming under increasing attack. The complaint that successive administrations had had against the Committee persisted—that because of its dominant jurisdiction over atomic energy matters in the Congress and the degree of its control over the AEC, it was encroaching to an unacceptable degree on the prerogatives of the executive branch. Epitomizing this attitude was Dwight Eisenhower's parting advice to newly inaugurated John F. Kennedy. "Frankly," he is reported to have said, "I see no need for the continuance of the JCAE."[8] There were undoubtedly some in the Nixon administration who thought that to get rid of the Joint Committee was by itself sufficient justification for dismembering the AEC.

The Joint Committee was also beginning to be challenged in other parts of the Congress, especially by members who felt strongly about the environment. The Committee had previously been recognized as having virtually exclusive jurisdiction over matters related to nuclear energy, but now other committees were beginning to assert themselves in this field. For example, Senator Mike Gravel of Alaska had steered legislation to restrict nuclear testing around the Joint Committee, managing to generate hearings before the Senate Foreign Relations Committee and Senator Edmund Muskie's subcommittee on air and water pollution. And hearings on AEC's construction budget before the Senate Appropriations Committee's Public Works Subcommittee, once relatively routine, were each year becoming more confrontational. The Joint Committee's power to initiate legislation—it was the only joint committee so empowered— also antagonized those who felt that this activity was undermining the bicameral nature of the Congress.

The AEC, for its part, did not have strong support among other government agencies. A common criticism was that the AEC's place in the overall structure of government was out of keeping with the general scheme of things and in need of correction. It was observed that whereas the traditional division among Cabinet departments was based on broad, purpose-oriented functions (for example, agriculture, labor, commerce, and defense), the AEC was organized around a single technology that cut across a number of functions. This oddity might have made good sense in 1946 when nuclear technology was known to very few and secrecy about it was believed to be essential; many thought the arrangement made less sense in 1969. This was especially so when, as increasingly was the case, the AEC's jurisdiction cut across the turf claimed by other agencies. The Interior Department, to give just one example, had a strong interest in the development of oil and gas resources and therefore did not look kindly on AEC's having exclusive jurisdiction, through its program for peaceful nuclear explosions (Plowshare), over the nuclear stimulation of natural gas production.

A loudly proclaimed criticism of the AEC had to do with its dual role as "both promoter and regulator" of the peaceful atom. This incongruity had been recognized by the Joint Committee when drafting the Atomic Energy Act of 1954, and consideration had briefly been given to establishing separate developmental and regulatory agencies. The reasons for not doing so at the time have been well summarized in George T. Mazuzan and J. Samuel Walker's definitive book, *Controlling the Atom*:

> Technical manpower was at a premium. Two separate agencies would of necessity have drawn from the same pool of human resources with the real possibility of shortchanging each other. The technology was in such an early stage that two organizations, one performing research and development, the other regulating, would have worked at cross-purposes, perhaps frustrating the overall goal of building a viable atomic industry. Consequently, the risk of a conflict of interest in making one agency perform two contradictory functions appeared a small price to pay for the anticipated benefits.[9]

As the years passed and as knowledge about atomic energy was imparted in many college courses and by experience gained in many industrial enterprises, the shortage-of-manpower argument became less persuasive, and the criticism of the apparent conflict of interest mounted. The Commission had itself made a concession to the criticism when early in 1961 it removed the regulatory activity from the supervision of its general manager, placing it instead under a coequal director of regulation and physically locating it in Bethesda, Maryland, some fifteen miles from the main AEC headquarters in Germantown, Maryland.* This satisfied few of the critics, however, since both wings of the agency continued to report to the same five commissioners. I personally recognized the

---

* It was the view of Commissioner Ramey and some others that the operating and regulatory sides of the agency had been separated to such an excessive degree that there was insufficient communication between them. (JCAE, *Hearings on Environmental Effects of Producing Nuclear Power*, 1969, Part 1, p. 112).

validity of the criticism, and occasionally suggested to my colleagues that the AEC voluntarily take steps to separate out its regulatory activity. I did not receive much support from other commissioners, top AEC staff, or the Joint Committee, and, perhaps regrettably, chose not to press the issue.

THE AEC'S FATE IN THE BALANCE

On January 29, 1970, I participated in the first of a series of meetings that were to take place with members of the Ash council or its staff dealing with reorganization schemes affecting the AEC. In these meetings a variety of proposals were advanced and decisions apparently made, only to be succeeded fairly soon by other proposals and other decisions as the tides of opinion and political influence shifted. Through it all, I and others representing the AEC attempted to ward off drastic changes as best we could. It was our view that while the AEC may have made mistakes, the important work that remained to be done in our field could best be done by keeping the organization, its personnel, and its laboratories together. We thought that the vendetta against the AEC and the Joint Committee was born largely of excessive environmental zeal and that it could possibly be overcome if the AEC tried harder and performed better.

The meeting on January 29 was a get-acquainted session between me and some members of the Ash council's staff. At this meeting the subject of placing the AEC's regulatory function in a separate agency for the environment was broached. As indicated above, I was prepared to give ground on the separation of our promotion and regulatory activities, but wanted to retain this concession as a bargaining chip for use in connection with more injurious suggestions I thought might lie ahead. So I gave what had become our stock answer to this suggestion—such separation would be "premature" pending the development of better regulatory standards and a larger resource of trained people to staff the regulatory arm. Next, the possibility was raised of separating out from the AEC's regulatory activity only the function of establishing regulatory standards. Here I pointed out that the AEC's standards for radioactive releases were based on the guidelines of the Federal Radiation Council (FRC) and the International Commission on Radiological Protection (ICRP)*, so that essentially, in this

---

* The ICRP, successor to the International Congress of Radiologists, was affiliated with the World Health Organization of the United Nations.

reliance on outside authority, there was already a degree of separation. There was next a broad discussion of government agencies that carried on activities in the field of energy and that could eventually be merged with the AEC to form an energy agency. The seeds of today's Department of Energy were being planted.

The first meeting between members of the Ash council staff and all five AEC commissioners occurred on April 8, 1970. Flanigan and Kriegsman from the White House were also present. It was evident, although there were as yet few specifics, that the Ash people were by now thinking of consolidating government agencies in related fields into a much smaller number of super-departments. They told us that they were considering moving the AEC's biology and medicine research into a new environmental entity; also that a new energy agency might be a likely resting place for several AEC programs, including civilian nuclear power, fusion research, Plowshare, uranium raw material, and uranium enrichment. I made the point that rather than break up the AEC it might be better to make it a focal point around which a new energy agency could be constructed. This idea was to become a central AEC suggestion throughout the reorganization discussions.

We also took the occasion to point out that there could be great political difficulties in effecting any drastic reorganization involving the AEC. In making this point we had principally in mind the likely opposition of Chet Holifield and his strategic placement not only as a ranking member of the Joint Committee on Atomic Energy but also as chairman of the House Committee on Government Operations, to which any reorganization legislation would have to be referred. Flanigan readily agreed with this point and, in bringing the meeting to a close, observed that the Ash panel and White House operatives present were starting at that moment to face the problem; they were on their way to a meeting with Holifield and the Joint Committee.

The following day I met with Roy Ash himself, along with several members of his council and some of its principal staff members. Ash asked if I would give my reactions to the changes they had under consideration regarding the AEC. I said that the projected move of biology and medicine research into an environmental agency would be difficult since the research took place either in our large multipurpose laboratories or under about five hundred university contracts and that much of the research applied also to other AEC work. I thought the projected energy agency made sense, hastening to point out that the AEC would make a logical focal point around which to build such an agency.

The Ash people then described their meeting with the JCAE the previous day. It had been "only moderately amicable." I said I hoped the problem of JCAE–executive branch relations could be solved and that it would not be a key factor in determining the future of the AEC. I had in mind that, although the AEC frequently benefited from its close relationship with the Joint Committee, there was also a possibility that the committee's increasing unpopularity might wash off on us, to our detriment.

On the way out of the Executive Office Building following this meeting, I ran into White House assistant Will Kriegsman, who gave me his impressions of how the Ash council was thinking in our field. He believed that the projected energy agency might include several functions from the Interior Department, even to the extent of dismembering that department. He doubted that they would adopt our idea of making AEC the focal point.

On April 16, the day after the deadline for the Ash council's staff to submit its recommendations to the president, Kriegsman briefed me on what they contained in our field. The AEC appeared to have lost the debate on every issue. The staff seemed to be recommending almost total dismemberment: power reactors, raw materials, uranium enrichment, Plowshare, and fusion research would go to a new energy entity; radiation standards and related biological research to a new environmental entity; and probably weapons development to Defense, and the national laboratories to the National Science Foundation. Kriegsman said that he was giving me more information than most Cabinet secretaries were getting at this stage; I was not to tell the other commissioners.

In due course the other commissioners were allowed to share in the bad news, and on May 7 we all had our opportunity to express ourselves on the energy aspects to Flanigan, Kriegsman, and members of the Ash council's staff. It was revealed at this meeting that the energy entity we had learned about previously was now slated to be part of a much larger Department of Natural Resources (DNR), which was to be drawn from a number of existing government agencies, as follows:

From the Department of the Interior

1. Bureau of Outdoor Recreation
2. National Park Service
3. Bureau of Sports Fisheries and Wildlife
4. Bureau of Land Management
5. Coastal Zone Management
6. Bureau of Reclamation
7. Office of Saline Water
8. Office of Water Resources Research
9. Geological Survey
10. Bureau of Mines
11. Oil Import Administration and Appeals Board

12. Power Marketing Agencies
13. Bureau of Indian Affairs

From the Department of Agriculture

1. Forest Service
2. Water resources planning functions of the Soil Conservation Service
3. Rural Electrification Service

From the Department of the Army

Water resources planning functions of the Corps of Engineers

From the Department of Commerce

National Oceanic and Atmospheric Administration

From the Atomic Energy Commission

Civilian power and related functions

It seemed clear that the Department of the Interior was to be the focal point around which DNR would be built. Commissioner Ramey asked why the alternative of building on the AEC as a focal point had been rejected. He observed that our industrial-contractor form of operation was very successful, whereas Interior used a government-employee form of operation that had little "get up and go." No clear answer was given to Ramey's question. Flanigan then observed, to our satisfaction, that gutting the AEC might result in two components (what was left of AEC and the new energy component of DNR) of such reduced effectiveness that the losses might exceed the gains. He invited the AEC and the Ash staff to prepare position papers that would evaluate this issue.

We sent in our paper to Flanigan on May 22. It contained a lengthy analysis that I summarized in a brief letter. The proposals seemed to stem, I wrote, "from an erroneous assumption that the [AEC] programs selected for transfer involve self-sufficient or self-contained units." On the contrary, I argued, they were part of a "unique governmental-industrial-university environment where the effective and economical accomplishment of any single major program objective involves the participation, and the interdependence and interdisciplinary capability, of numerous individual organizational entities." Consequently, we felt that the practical result of the changes "would be three new organizations that would be weaker, individually and in total, than the one strong organization that exists today." It was not by accident that this conclusion picked up on the language that Flanigan had himself used in propounding the question on May 7.

The notion that AEC's functions were interdependent and that they would suffer from being split apart was to become central to our argument from this time forward. It was probably the strongest argument we could make. There was of course an answer to it: The fact that two units are in separate organizations need not prevent them from interacting and cooperating with each other. This doubtless occurred to others and was one of the reasons why our argument did not carry everything before it.

There now ensued a period in which the whole reorganization effort in the administration seemed to be in such disarray that it was hard to follow from day to day just what was happening. On June 1 Flanigan phoned to say that the current plan was to proceed with the environmental agency and that it would incorporate AEC's division of radiation standards but that licensing authority would remain with the AEC. The idea of putting our biological research in the environmental agency had been dropped. As for the Department of Natural Resources, it was Flanigan's understanding that the president would shortly announce that this was "being studied." He complimented us on our "very persuasive" letter.

But on June 12 the *New York Times* (Anthony Ripley) quoted "administration sources" as saying that they were "seriously considering a plan to break up the Atomic Energy Commission." The plan discussed in the *Times* involved broadening the AEC into an overall energy agency. It also involved the transfer of all AEC weapons responsibilities to Defense and of "many research activities" to the National Science Foundation. Soon afterwards, however, I received a letter from former AEC chairman Lewis Strauss enclosing a letter to him from John McCone, my immediate predecessor as chairman. McCone wrote that he had spoken to Roy Ash by telephone about the report in the *Times* and was told that Ash's group had decided to make no recommendations whatever regarding any reallocation of AEC responsibilities. Ash said they had reached this conclusion after speaking with several people who were conversant with AEC matters. (Such "matters" might well have included the political influence and known sentiments of Chet Holifield.)

Such was the confused state of things as 1970 drew to a close.

THE GRAND DESIGN

Even though all the details obviously were not in place, President Nixon announced a broad reorganization proposal in his State of the Union message on January 22, 1971, in these words:

Based on a long and intensive study with the aid of the best advice obtainable, I have concluded that a sweeping reorganization of the executive branch is needed if the Government is to keep up with the times and the needs of the people. I propose, therefore, that we reduce the present twelve Cabinet Departments to eight. I propose that the Departments of State, Treasury, Defense, and Justice remain, but that all the other departments be consolidated into four: Human Resources, Community Development, Natural Resources, and Economic Development . . . Under this plan, rather than dividing up the departments by narrow subjects, we would organize them around the great purposes of government. Rather than scattering responsibility by adding new levels of bureaucracy, we would focus and concentrate the responsibility for getting problems solved.

Listening on television, I was struck by the stony silence with which Congress greeted this portion of the speech. Congressional comments after the speech seemed to reveal the reasons for the apathetic response. One "key Democrat" was quoted as saying: "Such a drastic change, affecting so many interests and people, will bring opposition out of the woodwork."[10] An "important Democratic insider" was more specific: "It won't happen. Can you see the Agriculture Committee chairman letting anybody abolish the Agriculture Department? Or do you think [AFL-CIO president] George Meany, with all his clout up there, will let anyone do away with the Labor Department? Not a chance."[11]

The cards being stacked so heavily against Nixon's drastic plan, there was speculation as to his motives in presenting it. Holifield offered an explanation. He thought the plan had a political motivation: to put the Democratically-controlled Congress on the defensive in the 1972 election for its predictable failure to approve the plan, the main thrust of which could be calculated to have some popular appeal.[12]

The fact that many were predicting the grand design would never be approved by Congress did not make us in the AEC feel that we were out of danger. There was a possibility that President Nixon could prevail over a reluctant Congress by going to the country, especially with a presidential election upcoming. Even if the larger scheme should fail, there was every prospect that attempts to do something about the AEC and the Joint Committee might still continue.

Certainly the chilly congressional reception of the reorganization plan did not stop administration forces from pressing forward with it. One of the most immediate tasks was to fill in some still missing details as to the exact makeup of the new superagencies.

THE DNR TASK FORCE

On January 26, 1971, within a week after the State of the Union address, I met with Will Kriegsman, Bud Krogh (a special assistant to Ehrlichman), and Andy Rouse (representing OMB director George Shultz). The purpose of the meeting was to ask me to serve on a task force that would provide technical guidance to aid in placing various functions and departments within the projected Department of Natural Resources (DNR). It was stated that no decisions had been made yet on removal of specific AEC functions but that they hoped to have all necessary decisions in hand within nine or ten weeks at the latest. I said that my working with the task group could place me in a very difficult position within the AEC, since I might seem to be collaborating in its dismemberment. I wanted it understood, therefore, that I would not endorse any reorganization that had a drastic effect on the AEC and that I was participating mainly to protect AEC's interests.

I also took the occasion to warn of the political and public reactions that might follow any move to transfer AEC's weapons functions to Defense. I emphasized the importance of getting Holifield's cooperation and said that it might be necessary to consider as a tradeoff releasing the $16 million needed to modernize the uranium-enrichment plants, one of his pet projects.* Krogh reported that the president was meeting with all of the affected Congressional committees to urge that his reorganization plan be granted a fair hearing. Holifield was thought to be among those on that day's schedule. I then cautioned about the dangers of making rapid, radical changes. Krogh answered that my presence on the task force was intended to flag just such problems.

The task force held its first meeting the following day, January 27. Its chairman, OMB Assistant Director Don Rice, gave us a tight time schedule: February 3-5: firm decisions as to what goes into DNR; February 20: first draft of the implementing legislation; March 1: first draft of the report to accompany the bill; March 15: final draft of the bill and report; March 25: presidential review completed; April 1: submission to Congress of a bill establishing the DNR. Comparable work was going forward with regard to each of the other

---

* In April 1971, after reorganization legislation had been introduced, the OMB held up action on the part of the AEC's 1972 budget that contained funds for this modernization program. Don Rice of OMB explained to me that this action was "tied up with what Holifield will do on the reorganization." This could have been the administration's way of showing that two could play at the game of quid pro quo.

three new superdepartments. Each member of the task group was asked to assign two people to work full time on the project until its completion. Rouse noted that the Ash council's proposal that there be a DNR paralleled the recommendations of prior groups that had worked on government reorganization, mentioning the Brownell Commission in 1939, the recommendations of the Hoover Commissions in 1949 and 1955,* the studies led by Governor Rockefeller during the Eisenhower administration, and those by Don Price and Ben Heineman during the Johnson administration. He implied that whether or not to establish such a department was not an issue before the task force. On the other hand, he listed a number of problem areas in the makeup of the DNR, one of which was to avoid the breaking of essential joints that held existing agencies together. He thought this might be a danger in taking some functions from the AEC. I picked up on this by citing Admiral Rickover's work on the light water breeder reactor for civilian plants, which was intertwined with his work on nuclear submarines. ("Intertwined" was to become one of my favorite words in coming weeks.)

Over the next weekend Chet Holifield called me to talk about the reorganization. It was clear from some of the things he said that he was thinking of the DNR in terms of what it might mean for the future of the Joint Committee.

> *Holifield said that, as he had suspected last year, the administration's idea was to abolish the AEC. He didn't concede yet that the reorganization would ever go into effect. It would receive a great deal of opposition, which he thought was what Nixon wanted. Holifield thought the president had brought up a big issue to create a lot of confusion that would take people's minds off other things, such as unemployment and inflation. It was a political ploy to get himself reelected. The DNR would be a conglomerate like the Litton Corporation [Roy Ash's old firm], and a step toward centralization of control of programs and policies in the executive branch and a weakening of the power of Congress. I said I thought some of the arguments being used to defend the reorganization made sense because there were many*

---

* The recommendations of the two Commissions on Organization of the Executive Branch of the Government headed by Herbert Hoover led, among other things, to the establishment of the Department of Defense and the Department of Health, Education, and Welfare. In these two instances they were similar to what Nixon was proposing in that they were consolidations of a number of previously separate agencies.

> *anomalies in the existing government structure. Holifield admitted there was some surface plausibility but insisted that the more I studied it the more I would see he was right.*

At about this time Holifield went public with his opposition to the administration's plans insofar as they affected the AEC. He announced that he was "completely opposed to any move to destroy the AEC," whether this was done by abolishing the agency or by transferring its functions to a larger department where they would be subordinated.[13] Considering Holifield's key position as chairman of the House committee that would consider all the reorganization proposals, his comments must have made grim reading for the administration.

The proposed transfers from the AEC to the DNR were discussed in some detail at the second meeting of the task force on February 4. I stated that although the AEC did not actively favor any of the proposals, we were not objecting to transfer of the raw materials, uranium enrichment, and civilian nuclear power programs if an executive decision was made to centralize all energy functions in the new department. The development of Plowshare devices, on the other hand, was so "intertwined" with weapons work that this activity could not very well be transferred. Fred Russell of the Interior Department took issue with this view,* but after some discussion, the group agreed that the development, fabrication, and emplacement of Plowshare explosive devices should remain with AEC, whereas DNR could handle the arrangements with industry for using the devices. I then took up the question of fusion (controlled thermonuclear) research. It was, I said, essentially a basic research program in plasma physics and so "intertwined" with weapons work in two of the laboratories that it would be premature to transfer it. The task force agreed with this, indicating that transfer of the fusion program might be deferred for a number of years until practical applications came into view.

On February 17 I met with George Shultz and Don Rice in Shultz's office at the White House. I told them that we had had second thoughts about transferring one aspect of the civilian nuclear power program, namely, the fast breeder. We thought that to transfer the breeder program might jeopardize its future in view of the extreme degree to which it was "intertwined" with other AEC operations, including almost day-to-day involvement of the

---

* This was in accord with Interior's interest in gaining some control over Plowshare's natural gas stimulation activities, as noted earlier.

commissioners, and of the intricacy of ongoing negotiations with utilities in connection with proposed demonstration plants. Shultz suggested that Rice and I get together to discuss this further. This subject was discussed at two subsequent meetings of the DNR task force, with some members opposing my notion that the breeder program should remain in AEC. The task force then decided that this was an issue that ought to be resolved at the Shultz-Ehrlichman level.

At the March 16 meeting of the task force I learned that Shultz and Ehrlichman had ruled that direction of the fast breeder program would go to DNR along with the rest of the civilian power program but that DNR would contract with AEC for technical support as needed. I said I didn't think this would work and, with Holifield very much in mind, predicted that it would be difficult to get through Congress. I also said that this approach might have a very negative effect on the willingness of U.S. utilities to help fund one or more fast breeder reactor prototypes. My comments proved so disturbing that one of the OMB staffers present left the room to fetch Don Rice. Rice then explained that Shultz and Ehrlichman thought it would be a cleaner operation if the direction and planning for all civilian nuclear power activities were gathered together in one place.

Within the next few days I had occasion to speak to Don Rice again. I told him that I thought a much better way of handling energy centralization in the government would be to place the AEC under a single administrator instead of a commission, transfer its regulatory functions to another agency, and then transfer to the AEC (of course renamed, since it would no longer be a commission) all of the energy functions of the government. This would make available to the combined operation the tremendous research and development capabilities of the AEC's national laboratories. It was the same idea we had been pushing since the Ash council was formed nearly two years earlier: an energy department built around the AEC as focal point.

A meeting with Rice on the civilian power program occurred on March 19. Attending with me from the AEC were General Manager Bob Hollingsworth and Assistant General Manager for Plans John J. Flaherty. Also present were William Rogers of Interior (not to be confused with Secretary of State William P. Rogers) and Dave Freeman of the Office of Science and Technology. After a good deal of discussion, it was decided to recommend: (1) that DNR should carry on the budgeting and program management for all the energy functions of the federal government; but (2) that DNR should contract with the AEC for civilian nuclear power research and development.

LEGISLATION

By March 22, a draft bill ("To promote more effective management of certain related functions of the Executive Branch by reorganizing and consolidating those functions in a new Department of Natural Resources, and for other purposes") was in hand, and the AEC submitted its comments in a letter to Shultz. They were generally a statement, in quite precise terms, of our understanding of what the bill would do, or not do, insofar as AEC programs were concerned. In broadest terms, we noted that the bill would:

1. transfer to DNR AEC's civilian power program, except for research and development;
2. transfer to DNR AEC's raw materials and uranium enrichment programs;
3. transfer to DNR the budgeting and utilization arrangements for, but not the research, development, testing, and execution aspects of, AEC's Plowshare program; and
4. leave untouched in the AEC all its weapons, licensing, and international cooperation activities.

Our letter did not contain any statement of approval or disapproval of the bill except for this final sentence: "Commissioner Ramey requests that you be informed that he does not believe the draft bill is desirable or workable as it affects the programs and organization of the Commission." It could easily have been surmised that Ramey's views corresponded to those of Holifield.

Even though some details, as in the AEC's case, had not yet been worked out, the president submitted the full package to Congress in a special message on March 25, 1971, well ahead of the schedule that had been presented to the DNR task force. It comprised a set of four bills to establish the four new superdepartments: Natural Resources, Community Development, Human Resources, and Economic Affairs. Explaining the administration's reasoning about the Department of Natural Resources, Nixon said that "intragovernmental conflicts in the environmental area" were preventing effective coordination of federal land, water, mineral, forestry, recreation and energy policies.[14]

Initial reactions from Congress mirrored those that had greeted the proposals when they were first announced in the State of the Union message. Holifield termed the proposals a "mammoth technical job of legislation, the biggest I have ever seen that has been sent to Congress." He noted that it would be difficult to consider the individual bills one at a time, and yet the reorganization was "too big a bite to swallow all at once." He estimated that it would take at least four years for his committee to process the legislation. Other members of Congress were clearly upset by the prospect of widespread shifting of jurisdiction among congressional committees. Several observers noted that business and labor groups that had developed comfortable relationships with the bureaucracy as it existed would see no benefit in changing and that such groups could be the most entrenched obstacles to reform.

Notwithstanding the dubious prospects, both House and Senate government operations committees held hearings on the legislation. The merit in the president's proposals was recognized by several prominent witnesses, including John W. Gardner, chairman of Common Cause, and Joseph A. Califano, chief counsel of the Democratic National Committee. Gardner's testimony was particularly trenchant, and also prophetic. The president's recommendations, he said,

> . . . distill some of the best thinking of a generation of thoughtful students of government. The reorganization is long overdue. Structurally speaking, most organizations, public and private, are designed to solve problems that no longer exist. There is no better example than our federal government . . . It is a fact, unknown to the general public, that some elements in Congress and some special interest lobbies have never really wanted the departmental secretaries to be strong. Questions of public policy nominally lodged with the Secretary are often decided far beyond the Secretary's reach by a trinity consisting of 1) representatives of an outside lobby, 2) middle-level bureaucrats, and 3) selected members of Congress, particularly those concerned with appropriations . . . When a reorganization plan comes up, the special interests move in like hornets . . . And the reorganization plan fails to come off.[15]

On June 7 I wrote to Holifield conveying the AEC's formal comments on the merits of the DNR bill. We gave it a lukewarm endorsement, saying, in stodgy bureaucratese: "From the standpoint of AEC's programs and activities..., we have concluded, after very careful consideration, that the separation of functions in . . . the bill is feasible and that the cooperative interplay between the new department and AEC envisioned in the concept can well be depended on to produce intended effects in an effective manner." Once again Ramey appended his objection, using the same words as in the March 22 letter to Shultz.

The fact that Ramey alone spoke up in opposition did not mean that the other AEC commissioners favored the loss of AEC functions that the legislation would have produced. In varying degree, and with different shades of emphasis, I think the rest of us felt that we had dodged a bullet in the form of the once-threatened virtually complete dismemberment of the AEC and that the functions left to us were sufficient to permit the AEC's survival as a viable agency. Under the circumstances, we concluded that there was nothing to be gained by going on record as opposing the recommendations of the president. I personally felt some sense of accomplishment based on the belief that my participation in interagency discussions in the DNR task force and elsewhere had helped prevent a more drastic proposal.

We also were aware that there was much doubt that Congress would pass the reorganization legislation. I discussed this with Holifield while we were flying to Austin, Texas, for the dedication of the LBJ Library on May 22, 1971. He mentioned that in a recent conversation OMB director George Shultz had asked his help in steering the reorganization legislation through Congress. Holifield said that he had emphasized the difficulties involved. These included the reluctance of many committee chairmen and committee members with jurisdiction over particular departments to lose their committee assignments if the departments were abolished as separate entities. In general, he said that he hadn't made a strong commitment to help but had offered some encouragement.

Indications that the Joint Committee might actively oppose the DNR bill continued to concern the administration. At lunch on June 3 Interior Secretary Rogers C. B. Morton suggested to me that transfer of planning and budgeting for the civilian power program might be dropped from the bill, leaving civilian nuclear power entirely with the AEC, "at least for a while." I suggested the possibility of setting up a council composed of representatives of all the interested agencies to coordinate the development of energy sources. Morton seemed to like this idea.

The Senate Government Operations Committee held a hearing specifically on the DNR bill on August 5. Although I was in Europe at the time, my support of the bill, along with that of AEC chairman-designate James Schlesinger, was announced at the hearing. AEC Commissioner Larson testified for the bill, saying, in part: "Considering the substantial changes that will be taking place in the energy field, it is logical and important that one government agency have the total picture and be able to establish policy and to allocate funds for development of appropriate and necessary energy resources." Commissioner Ramey, consistent to the end, continued to object to putting AEC functions in the new department.

SEQUELS

When the congressional government operations committees failed in 1971 to clear Nixon's bills for consideration by the full Congress, the president reaffirmed them in his 1972 State of the Union message. He then sent a special message on March 29, 1972, urging Congress to act. But none of the four bills ever emerged from committee.

The president did not resubmit the reorganization bills to the 93rd Congress, which assumed office in January 1973, at the beginning of his second term. What he did instead is described in his memoirs:

> Congress had smothered my attempt in 1971 to streamline the government, so I . . . asked Ehrlichman and Roy Ash, the incoming Budget Director, to set up task forces and consult with constitutional lawyers to determine how much reorganizing I could legally do on my own. They advised that I could in fact create by executive authority a system closely resembling the one I had requested in the 1971 reform proposal.
>
> We decided to organize six of the eleven Cabinet departments and some of the hundreds of federal agencies under four general management groups: Human Resources, Natural Resources, Community Development, and Economic Affairs. George Shultz would head Economic Affairs and one of the current Cabinet secretaries would be named Counsellor to the President for each of the remaining three areas. [The three named were Earl Butz of Agriculture for Natural Resources, Caspar Weinberger of HEW for Human Resources, and James T. Lynn of HUD for Community Development.] These men would then be directly responsible to me for all the programs under their supervision. Under my reorganization plan, the Counsellor in charge would be responsible for eliminating duplication and inefficiency.[16]

What Nixon failed to mention in this account was that the new supersecretaries actually were to report to him through four White House assistants whose job was "to integrate and unify policies and operations throughout the executive branch . . . and to oversee the activities for which the President is responsible."[17] These four trusted lieutenants were Haldeman, Ehrlichman, Ash, and Kissinger. What seemed to be sought was what Nixon had always wanted, maximum personal and White House control over the bureaucracy.

The reorganization was announced on January 5, 1973. Before the new arrangements could take effect, however, the White House was engulfed by the Watergate scandal. Haldeman and Ehrlichman resigned on April 30. For the remainder of Nixon's term, the White House's control, particularly over domestic programs, was weakened. Soon after he became president in August 1974, Gerald Ford quietly discontinued the concept of having some Cabinet secretaries be more equal than others.

In his final reorganization plans, Nixon gave separate consideration to the AEC problem. On April 19, 1973, he proposed legislation to establish an Energy and Natural Resources Administration. This legislation provided the basis for the Energy Reorganization Act of 1974 that was ultimately signed by President Ford on October 11, 1974. It abolished the AEC and created in its stead two agencies, the Energy Research and Development Administration (ERDA) and the Nuclear Regulatory Commission (NRC), both of which began operation on January 19, 1975. In introducing the legislation on the floor of the Senate, Senator Abraham Ribicoff (D-CT) said that it was "a response to the growing criticism that there is a basic conflict between the AEC's regulation of the nuclear power industry and its development and promotion of new technology for the industry."[18] While AEC's staff and programs provided the nucleus for ERDA, the new agency was mandated to give increased emphasis to nonnuclear energy sources, conservation, and environmental protection.

During President Ford's term, mounting shortages of natural gas and petroleum products plagued the economy. In their 1976 election campaigns both Ford and Jimmy Carter emphasized the need for a comprehensive national energy policy and program to be centered in a single department. After his election, Carter introduced legislation to this effect. The bill established a cabinet-level Department of Energy (DOE), which began operation on October 1, 1977. Besides absorbing ERDA in its entirety, DOE also embraced the policy-making functions of the National Energy Agency, the regulatory activities of the Federal Power Commission, the production and marketing functions—mainly involving hydroelectric installations—of the Department of Interior, several regional power commissions, and a number of specialized functions from other agencies.

Thus, as matters ultimately came to rest, there seemed to be in existence substantially what the AEC had argued for in 1971 and what I continued to argue for after I left the Commission,* namely, an energy agency built around former AEC programs, including its national laboratories, as a focal point. One major respect in which the new agency differed from the AEC was that it did not have the constant protection and supervision of the Joint Committee on Atomic Energy. Once ERDA was established in January 1975, the leaders of

Congress began to circumvent and generally to ignore the Joint Committee. This change in attitude coincided, incidentally, with the departure of both Chet Holifield and Craig Hosmer from Congress. In 1977 the Atomic Energy Act was amended to bring formally to an end the existence of the once proud and powerful committee.

---

* In June 1972 *Science* (p. 1189) contained an editorial written by me entitled "For a U.S. Energy Agency." In this I summarized the alternative sources of energy and the problems each had to overcome to become economic and environmentally acceptable. I concluded by noting that the AEC had, more than any other federal agency, the scientific expertise, technical capability, and organizational strength to "launch a unified program for meeting the energy needs of the American people."

NOTES

1. "Special Message to the Congress on Executive Branch Reorganization," in *Public Papers of Presidents of the United States, Richard Nixon 1971*, p. 473.
2. Quoted in *1971 Congressional Quarterly Almanac*, p. 765.
3. Richard Nixon, *RN, The Memoirs of Richard Nixon*, p. 767.
4. Nathan, *The Plot That Failed*, pp. 62-3. Emphasis in original.
5. Ehrlichman, *Witness to Power*, p. 111.
6. Thomas O'Toole, "Once-Immune AEC Drawing Heavy Fire," *Washington Post*, June 5, 1970.
7. Anthony Ripley, "Atomic Power: A Bitter Controversy," *New York Times*, July 16, 1970, p. 1.
8. Quoted in Green and Rosenthal, *Government of the Atom*, p. 231.
9. Mazuzan and Walker, *Controlling the Atom*, p. 60.
10. "Washington Whispers," *U.S. News and World Report*, February 8, 1971, p. 8.
11. "The President vs. the 92nd Congress," *Newsweek*, January 25, 1971, p.16.
12. *Facts on File*, 1971, p. 47.
13. *Nucleonics Week*, February 25, 1971.
14. *1971 Congressional Quarterly Almanac*, p. 765.
15. *Ibid.*, pp. 765-66.
16. Nixon, *RN, The Memoirs of Richard Nixon*, pp. 766-67.
17. Quoted in Nathan, *The Plot that Failed*, p. 69.
18. *Facts on File, 1974*, p. 745.

Greeting guests at a U.S. reception during the Fourth UN Conference on Peaceful Uses of Atomic Energy, Geneva, September 5, 1971, with my successor, the new AEC chairman, James R. Schlesinger, left. I stood in the line for over an hour, receiving more than 1,000 guests.

This was the Atomic Energy Commission for most of the period covered in this book. From left, Theos J. Thompson, Wilfrid E. Johnson, Seaborg, Clarence E. Larson, and James T. Ramey. The occasion was the swearing-in ceremony for Larson, September 2, 1969.

With two distinguished predecessors: David E. Lilienthal, the AEC's first chairman
(November 1, 1946 to February 15, 1950); and Lewis L. Strauss, one of the first five
AEC commissioners and chairman from July 2, 1953, until June 30, 1958.

I made four trips to the Soviet Union as AEC chairman. Here, on the final trip in August 1971, an opportunity to do a little sightseeing with my wife. We are at the ruins of the fifteenth-century Bibi-Khanym Mosque in Samarkand, Uzbek SSR.

The author was formally presented with a foreign membership in the USSR Academy of Sciences, a rare and cherished honor, in a ceremony at the Soviet embassy in Washington, July 13, 1971. Ambassador Anatoly Dobrynin made the presentation. At right is Professor Igor Morokhov, deputy chairman of the State Committee for the Utilization of Atomic Energy.

On February 27, 1970, President Nixon presented Atomic Pioneer Awards to three pillars of the World War II atomic bomb project, General Leslie R. Groves, Dr. Vannevar Bush, and Dr. James B. Conant. It was the first and only presentation of this award.

With President Nixon at the White House, February 27, 1970.

Recognizing some of those who made the wheels turn: the author officiating at an AEC Distinguished Service Awards ceremony, February 18, 1971. From left: General Manager Robert E. Hollingsworth; Assistant General Manager for Administration John V. Vinciguerra; Kenneth A. Dunbar, Manager of the Chicago Operations Office; Assistant General Manager Howard C. Brown, Jr.; Commissioners Ramey, Johnson, and Larson; and Director of Regulation Harold L. Price. Awards were presented to Vinciguerra, Brown, and Dunbar.

Three distinguished members of the atomic energy community at the 25th anniversary observance of the signing of the Atomic Energy Act, August 1, 1971. From left, Dr. Alvin M. Weinberg, a pioneer nuclear physicist, who served as director of the Oak Ridge National Laboratory from 1955 to 1973; Dr. Gerald F. Tape, an AEC commissioner from 1963 to 1969 and then president of Associated Universities, Inc., which managed Brookhaven National Laboratory; and New Mexico senator Clinton P. Anderson, a member of the Joint Committee on Atomic Energy from 1951 to 1972 and twice its chairman during the 1950s.

Epilogue

A RECORD OF ACHIEVEMENT

In its 28 years of existence (January 1, 1947–December 31, 1974), the Atomic Energy Commission could take credit for some outstanding accomplishments.[1] In the military sphere, the agency's main preoccupation in its early years, an array of sophisticated nuclear weapons was developed, tested, and produced. The AEC also supported the development of propulsion reactors that made possible the creation of a fleet of reliable nuclear submarines and surface ships. Together, these achievements provided a cornerstone of the nation's military and foreign policy during the years of the Cold War and were instrumental in preventing an outbreak of hostilities between the superpowers. The knowledge of military realities obtained in this work also enabled the AEC to provide expert advice to American diplomats as they negotiated arms control treaties that helped to curb the nuclear arms race.

Through its development of reactor technology, its construction and operation of demonstration plants, and its fostering of a private nuclear power industry, the AEC helped bring civilian nuclear power to a point where it was able to produce a significant fraction of this nation's electric power output (21.7 percent in 1991) and significantly higher fractions in some other countries. While nuclear power has suffered recent reverses in the United States, its fortunes may yet be revived, as discussed below.

The AEC sponsored pioneering research in the physical sciences that covered a wide spectrum of knowledge and applications, including the search for new knowledge about nuclear structure and behavior, the discovery of new elements, and the expansion of nuclear technology. Much of this work required very large, specialized machines, and several major research facilities were constructed and operated by the AEC, including the Fermi National Accelerator Laboratory at Batavia, Illinois, which contained the world's most powerful proton synchroton. The AEC also sponsored research at hundreds of universities and other institutions. In 1970 alone, for example, the physical research program gave rise to more than 5,400 scientific publications.

A comparable effort was undertaken in the biomedical sciences, from which came a fund of knowledge about radiation and its effects on man and his environment. Largely as a result of the AEC's work, radiation has been called the most studied and best understood of the many hazards to which man is exposed. From the biomedical research have also come important nuclear medicine accomplishments, both in diagnosis and therapy.

By underwriting the development of nuclear technology, the AEC helped to make the specific advantages of nuclear science available for practical applications in science, medicine, and industry. When I left the agency in 1971, for example, there were about 5,000 doctors in about 2,000 hospitals in the United States administering about 6,000,000 applications of radioisotopes each year for a variety of diagnostic and therapeutic purposes.

During the 1960s the AEC produced a series of radioisotope-powered and reactor-powered electric generating units for space applications. Newly discovered heavy isotopes, such as californium-252, were found to be useful both in research and in industry.

The AEC was instrumental in fostering international cooperation in the nuclear field. It took a leading part in establishing the International Atomic Energy Agency; in negotiating some 35 bilateral agreements to provide research reactors, power reactor fuel, and technical information to friendly nations; and in planning and organizing four United Nations Conferences on Peaceful Uses of Atomic Energy. There were also several agreements for cooperation with the Soviet Union that involved joint projects and exchanges of information, visits, and personnel. The AEC played an energetic role in fostering U.S. advocacy of the Nonproliferation Treaty, in its negotiation, and in getting it implemented.*

---

* During my chairmanship I traveled to some sixty countries, often accompanied by other AEC personnel and other American scientists and engineers, to visit nuclear facilities and to confer with the scientists, engineers, and officials (including heads of state) of other nations. I also hosted return visits by foreign delegations. I am convinced that these exchanges contributed significantly to the constructive use of the peaceful atom and to better international relations

A FAVORED BEGINNING

That the AEC was able to accomplish so much in a relatively brief time owes much to the circumstances attending its birth. The agency came into existence on the wings of a wartime triumph that many people credited to atomic energy and thus to the scientists and engineers who formed the nucleus of the new agency. There was also at this time a popular enthusiasm for science and much deference to scientists. Such sentiments persisted in the years after Sputniks I and II, the Soviet Union's 1957 space triumphs, which seemed to presage ballistic missiles that might threaten this nation's very existence if we did not keep pace in science with the seemingly onrushing Soviets.

Impressed by the urgency of the moment, Congress gave the new agency at its outset in 1947 extraordinary powers and independence. It was entrusted with development, production, and control of both military and peaceful applications of the atom. Its employees were exempted from the Civil Service System. Because of the felt need for great security and secrecy,* all nuclear material production facilities and nuclear reactors were to be government-owned, and all technical information and research results were to be under Commission control, excluded from the normal application of the patent system.

The legislation establishing the AEC also gave the new agency a congressional ally. The Joint Committee on Atomic Energy (JCAE) was established as

---

generally. There is a fellowship among scientists that bridges international boundaries and that can be a continuing force for peace and progress in the world. It was gratifying to know that President Johnson, for one, in repeatedly encouraging me to take trips abroad, appeared to share my belief in their value. A particularly important visit was one that I and other American scientists made to the Soviet Union in May 1963. The progress of our visit was communicated to the highest levels in the Kremlin, and an interview was arranged for me with a still relatively unknown but rising politician named Leonid Brezhnev, who held the largely ceremonial position of president. I am persuaded that this visit played an important role in building a favorable atmosphere for the Moscow test ban negotiations that commenced about six weeks later.

* Many of the early decisions about the organization of the AEC were based on the notions that there was a "secret" about the atomic bomb, that the United States was in sole possession of this "secret," and that it was possible by rigid security measures to keep things that way for an extended period of time. Scientists attempted from time to time to disabuse government officials and the public of such notions, but without much success.

a watchdog to assure that the new agency did not transgress legislative prerogatives or otherwise misuse its extraordinary grant of powers. From the outset, a majority of those selected to serve on the JCAE were able and enthusiastic advocates of proceeding vigorously with both military and civilian nuclear programs. While often quite critical of the AEC, the JCAE also acted as a protector of the agency and a facilitator of its programs. The committee was given virtually exclusive jurisdiction over all legislation in the atomic energy field. Largely to shield the AEC from unfavorable actions by the House Appropriations Committee, the JCAE sought and obtained authorizing power over each year's AEC budget. The JCAE's control became so strong that other committees and members of Congress tended to defer to it in matters relating to the AEC, which accordingly enjoyed for a while what the *Washington Post* described as "a balmy kind of political immunity."[2] The dominant role of the Joint Committee also made it difficult for successive administrations to exercise full executive-branch sway over the AEC. This difficulty was compounded by the staggered terms of the commissioners, who were appointed to overlapping terms of five years. Such factors led noted legal scholar Harold P. Green, with some exaggeration, to conclude in a 1970 interview that the "Executive Branch in atomic energy affairs is virtually powerless."[3]

The Joint Committee's role was far more than one of oversight of AEC programs and activities. It acted as a partner of the AEC in developing the direction of policy, and from time to time it assumed a vigorous role in pushing favorite projects of its own. An example was the ill-advised program to build a nuclear-powered airplane, an effort on which over a billion dollars were spent over a fifteen-year period before the program was terminated by President Kennedy in March 1961. The committee's energetic role undoubtedly enlarged the amount of activity and money devoted to nuclear endeavors over the years. It also simplified life for the AEC to have to report in the main to only one committee. By contrast, today's Department of Energy must report in one way or another to about 30 committees. This is, of course, enormously time-consuming and can subject the agency to conflicting pressures.

The AEC's relative independence from congressional and administration pressures helped to make it a superior organization for getting things accomplished, particularly in its beginning years. It was less political. It had a minimum of red tape. It made decisions rapidly. Added to these organizational factors were superior facilities and a talented staff. Initially many of these facilities and staff members were acquired from the lavishly funded wartime atomic bomb project. In subsequent years the AEC continued to be able to attract very talented and dedicated people and to build or obtain the use of superb additional facilities.

By the end of 1971 AEC's total plant and equipment (completed or under construction) was valued at some $10 billion, and its annual budget was about $2.3 billion, of which some 37 percent was devoted to weapons-related activity. The AEC's inheritance of a large network of facilities from the wartime effort argued for the adoption from the outset of a decentralized plan of operations rather than for any attempt to micromanage endeavors from Washington.* Thus, at the end of 1971, there were about 7,000 employees on the AEC payroll, mostly in field offices, supervising some 125,000 contractor employees scattered around the country.

HASTE AND WASTE

In addition to its outstanding accomplishments, the AEC also left behind one very unfortunate legacy. This was the massive residue of contaminated wastes at Hanford and other nuclear materials production sites, the full extent of which did not come to light until the late 1980s. The General Accounting Office has estimated that Hanford's waste tanks alone leaked 800,000 gallons of contaminated water into the soil. In addition, a large amount of liquid waste there was discharged directly into the soil. Department of Energy officials have estimated that cleaning up the entire weapons complex will take 30 years and cost $100 billion.[4]

At least a partial explanation for this debacle was the frantic haste that animated the atomic bomb effort in the United States during World War II, when many of the waste disposal practices that caused the present situation were put in place. The thinking that underlay this sense of urgency has been well described by AEC historians Richard E. Hewlett and Oscar Anderson:

> Since Germany, Britain, and the United States had started from the same point in 1939, was it not possible that the Germans had proceeded at least as far as the Western powers? In view of known German interest in nuclear research and the slow start of the United States program, was it not even possible that the Germans were in the lead? If all these questions could be answered in the affirmative, then every minute counted.[5]

---

* A notable exception to this mode of operation, of course, was the breeder reactor program discussed in chapters 10 through 12.

It was with such considerations in mind that James B. Conant, newly selected as chairman of the National Defense Research Committee planning the U.S. effort, concluded in the summer of 1941 "that only efforts which were likely to yield results within a matter of months or, at most, a year or two were worthy of serious consideration."[6]

Impelled by the extreme time pressures, DuPont, the first contractor at Hanford, elected to employ standard industrial practices of the time for waste disposal and storage. As experience began to indicate that improvements were needed, the AEC sought during the 1960s to get better waste tanks built, but the Bureau of the Budget repeatedly denied funds, saying that this was something that could be deferred "until next year." I regret that we did not attach sufficient importance to the matter to make it a subject for appeal at the presidential level. An indication of what we had in mind can be found in the waste tanks at the Savannah River plant. They were built ten years after the first Hanford tanks and are in much better condition, although even there serious problems have become evident.

FALL FROM GRACE

The relative insulation that helped the AEC to get off to such a fast start in its early years gradually wore away over time. It is beyond the scope of this book to describe in detail how this came about, but some of the factors responsible included the following:

- political wrangling in the early 1950s over whether nuclear power should be predominantly a government or a private industry endeavor
- entry of private industry into civilian nuclear power activity, made possible after the 1954 Atomic Energy Act permitted private ownership of nuclear facilities and private access to civilian nuclear technology
- the appearance of reactors and other nuclear facilities in many communities throughout the nation
- revelations about the harmful effects of radioactive fallout from nuclear weapons tests, causing concern not only about continuing the tests but about other sources of radiation as well

Although the erosion of AEC's favored status continued during the Kennedy and Johnson administrations, it did not seriously hamper significant activities until the Nixon years when, as recounted herein, the AEC was subject to severe challenges. Some of these came from the public. Questions raised about the safety of reactors, and then about their environmental effects, had given rise to antinuclear sentiments and then to organized antinuclear movements. Widespread opposition to the Vietnam War stimulated a hostility to and a loss of faith in government endeavors. This was correlated with the flowering of the environmental movement and some loss of confidence in science and technology.

At the same time that they were being attacked by elements of the public, AEC programs were subject to increasing pressure from within government. AEC's budget proposals were cut with unprecedented severity. During the Kennedy and Johnson administrations appeals directly to the president had succeeded in restoring the most serious cuts advocated by the Bureau of the Budget. As chairman I was privileged to present these appeals personally in give-and-take sessions with very attentive presidents. I recall with special satisfaction trips I took to President Johnson's ranch in four successive Decembers, from 1964 to 1967, where I was almost 100 percent successful in winning the president's support for contested items. This experience was not repeated in the Nixon years. Although the budget cuts made under Nixon were severe, I was permitted only one budget appeal audience with the president, in December 1969. This was strictly a pro-forma performance on his part. He listened, nodded his head periodically, said nothing, and in the end turned us down on virtually every item. Subsequently I was required to present appeals to the director or other officials of the Office of Management and Budget, a generally fruitless endeavor since this was the organization that had turned us down in the first place. Nor did the Joint Committee, itself under attack by some members of Congress who resented its efforts to maintain exclusive jurisdiction in the nuclear field, retain its former ability to shield us. Other less friendly members and committees began to play increasing roles in our affairs. Within the executive branch as well, there were agencies that newly challenged AEC's exclusive domain over all things nuclear when the matter at issue also involved their primary missions. Examples included the interest of the Interior Department in natural gas resources affected by our Plowshare program and in the discharge of reactor effluents into bodies of water. These conflicts called into question the whole concept of organizing an agency around a single technology. While this had seemed appropriate in 1946, when nuclear matters were little understood and highly secret, it seemed less so in the late 1960s.

The largest single factor weakening the credibility of the AEC may have been its dual role in both regulating and promoting the development of nuclear power plants. This apparent conflict of interest made the AEC a target of attack by both supporters and opponents of nuclear power. Because of its relative political immunity in the early years, and also because most of its activities remained secret for so long, the AEC was unskilled in explaining itself to the public. I doubt, however, that with all the skill in the world it would have been possible to stave off for long the logical resolution of this situation. On the whole, I think the ultimate decisions to split off the AEC's regulatory activity and to merge its operating functions into a comprehensive Department of Energy were sensible ones.

NUCLEAR POWER: A NEEDED OPTION

I cited earlier (chapter 10) the optimistic predictions of the late 1960s about the future of nuclear power, culminating in the forecast that after the year 2000 virtually all central station electric power plants built in the United States would be nuclear. Shortly after these forecasts were made, as we know, nuclear power ran into a series of stunning reverses. New regulatory requirements and long regulatory delays caused such steep escalations in cost that nuclear power seemed no longer able to compete economically with fossil fuel plants. After the accidents at Three Mile Island and at Chernobyl, moreover, public acceptance diminished markedly, such that utilities hesitated to subject themselves to the community relations headaches a nuclear plant would involve. Waste disposal, although apparently amenable to technical solutions, remained a problem for lack of a politically acceptable site. Consequently, we have now a situation where no construction has started on a U.S. nuclear plant ordered after 1973, nor are there indications that any U.S. utility is planning to order a nuclear plant any time soon.

I believe that the current situation of nuclear power in the United States has not been due to any intrinsic deficiency in nuclear power technology—the experience of France, where nuclear power accounted in 1991 for 72.7 percent of total generation, is testimony to that—but rather to mismanagement on a national scale. Because of an impatience to achieve economic benefits quickly, U.S. nuclear plants were prematurely escalated in size to proportions that strained the technology and magnified the potential consequences of an accident, no matter how unlikely. For reasons having to do with economic competition and local idiosyncrasy, there was a failure to standardize the design of the facilities. There are a large number of plants called pressurized-water reactors and another large group called boiling-water reactors, but within these groups the plants may not be the same in important ways. This caused each new plant to present individual design, construction, and regulatory problems. In order to satisfy changing regulatory requirements, nuclear plant designs grew increasingly complex. One estimate has it that "a 1,000 megawatt plant today may have as many as 40,000 valves."[7] In France the plants have been standardized, with the result that there have been fewer regulatory problems. As Ivan Selin, chairman of the Nuclear Regulatory Commission, said in 1991, in France "there are 365 kinds of cheese and one kind of reactor. In the United States it's the opposite."[8] One consequence has been that the French have been able to build their nuclear plants in five years, as have the Japanese, as opposed to a U.S. average nearly twice as long.

I submit that there still is a need for nuclear power in America's future in order to reap the technology's environmental benefits. The demand for electric power, while no longer bounding forward at the pace of the period from 1920 to 1970, continues to increase. The Department of Energy, taking full account of efforts at conservation that it is energetically sponsoring, predicts that U.S. electricity consumption will rise 50 percent in the next twenty years. To meet this near-term demand and also to replace older plants that must be retired, new power plants will be needed. The question is: What sort of power plants will they be? Great technical progress has been made in advancing the technology of renewable sources such as solar and wind power, but it is doubtful that these technologies can meet more than a small fraction of the need for the next 50 years. Hydroelectric sites are virtually exhausted. The only quantitatively significant options now available are therefore fossil-fueled and nuclear plants. Faced with this choice, the American people have a powerful reason for selecting nuclear plants. The reason is that fossil-fueled plants discharge greenhouse gases and noxious chemicals into the atmosphere, whereas nuclear plants do not do so.

Fortunately, the kind of nuclear power plant that can be made available today is much superior to those that were being offered when the long hiatus in nuclear power plant orders began. During this period, much constructive thought and planning has been taking place. Several new types of reactors are being proposed. Particular promise is attached to the advanced light water reactor (ALWR) being developed jointly by government and industry. Mid-sized reactors in the 600 megawatt range, they would be standardized. Large portions of the plants would be prefabricated at the factory, where quality control is easier and labor productivity higher than it is in the field. They would be "passively safe" in that they would rely primarily on natural forces, such as gravity and convection, to shut themselves down in emergencies, with a minimum of human intervention. They would be simpler in design, having many fewer pumps, valves, and other appurtenances than existing plants. It is expected that when a standardized design is completed, the Nuclear Regulatory Commission would be able to give it an advance certification, eliminating the uncertainties that were associated with the regulation of today's custom-built plants. There is every prospect that the new plants would be economically competitive, or nearly so.

Whether even this very rational approach will be able to gain public acceptance, and whether the political resistance to underground waste repositories can be overcome remain, of course, very open questions. I submit that it would be in the national interest, and that of the planet, to at least have this new nuclear option available.

NOTES

1. A part of this account borrows from Alice L. Buck, "A History of the Atomic Energy Commission," Department of Energy, July 1983 (DOE/ES-0003/1); from Richard E. Hewlett, "AEC in Retrospect," unpublished manuscript, U.S. Energy Research and Development Administration, 1976; and from Allardice and Trapnell, *The Atomic Energy Commission*.

2. Thomas O'Toole, "Once Immune AEC Drawing Heavy Fire," *Washington Post*, June 15, 1970.

3. Anthony Ripley, "Atomic Power: A Bitter Controversy," *New York Times*, July 16, 1970, p. 2.

4. *Arms Control Today*, October 1991, p. 35.

5. Hewlett and Anderson, *The New World*, p. 69.

6. Rhodes, *The Making of the Atomic Bomb*, p. 367.

7. Robert Livingston, "The Next Generation," *Nuclear Industry*, July-August 1988, p. 3.

8. Thomas W. Lippman, "NRC Chief Seeks to Restore Nuclear Power's Image and Fortunes," *Washington Post*, December 2, 1991, p. A15.

APPENDIX

AEC Commissioners During Chairmanship
of Glenn T. Seaborg

	From	*To*	*Remarks*
John S. Graham	Sept. 12, 1957	June 30, 1962	Resigned
Robert E. Wilson	Mar. 22, 1960	Jan. 31, 1964	Resigned
Loren K. Olson	June 23, 1960	June 30, 1962	Term expired
Leland J. Haworth	Apr. 17, 1961	June 30, 1963	Resigned
John G. Palfrey	Aug. 31, 1962	June 30, 1966	Resigned
James T. Ramey	Aug. 31, 1962	June 30, 1973	Term expired
Gerald F. Tape	July 15, 1963	Apr. 30, 1969	Resigned
Mary I. Bunting	June 29, 1964	June 30, 1965	Term expired
Wilfrid E. Johnson	Aug. 1, 1966	June 30, 1972	Term expired
Samuel M. Nabrit	Aug. 1, 1966	Aug. 1, 1967	Resigned
Francesco Castagliola	Oct. 1, 1968	June 30, 1969	Term expired
Theos J. Thompson	June 12, 1969	Nov. 25, 1970	Deceased
Clarence E. Larson	Sept. 2, 1969	June 30, 1974	Term expired

SELECTED BIBLIOGRAPHY

Books

Allardice, Corbin, and Edward R. Trapnell. *The Atomic Energy Commission.* New York, Praeger Publishers, 1974.

Ambrose, Stephen E. *Nixon, The Triumph of a Politician, 1962-1972.* New York: Simon and Schuster, 1989.

Carson, Rachel. *Silent Spring.* Boston: Houghton Mifflin Company, 1962.

Cohen, Bernard L. *Nuclear Science and Society.* Garden City, NY: Anchor Books, 1974.

Commoner, Barry. *The Poverty of Power: Energy and the Economic Crisis.* New York: Alfred A. Knopf, 1976.

Curtis, Richard, and Elizabeth Hogan. *Perils of the Peaceful Atom.* London: V. Gollancz, 1970.

Duncan, Francis. *Rickover and the Nuclear Navy.* Annapolis, MD: Naval Institute Press, 1990.

Ehrlichman, John. *Witness to Power: The Nixon Years.* New York: Simon and Schuster, 1982.

Foreman, Harry, M.D., ed. *Nuclear Power and the Public.* Minneapolis: University of Minnesota Press, 1970; republished in paperback, Garden City, NY: Anchor Books, 1972.

Galbraith, John Kenneth. *Ambassador's Journal: A Personal Account of the Kennedy Years.* London: Hamilton Publishers, 1969.

Gofman, John W. and Arthur R. Tamplin. *Poisoned Power: The Case Against Nuclear Power.* Emmaus, PA: Rosedale Press, 1971.

Golden, William T., ed. *Science Advice to the President.* New York: Pergamon Press, 1980.

Graham, Frank, Jr. *Since Silent Spring*. Boston: Houghton Mifflin Company, 1970.

Green, Harold P., and Alan Rosenthal. *Government of the Atom: The Integration of Powers*. New York: Atherton Press, 1963.

Hersh, Seymour M. *The Price of Power: Kissinger in the Nixon White House*. New York: Summit Books, 1983.

Hersh, Seymour M. *The Samson Option: Israel's Nuclear Arsenal and American Foreign Policy*. New York: Random House, 1991.

Hewlett, Richard E., and Oscar E. Anderson, Jr. *The New World, 1939-1946*, vol. 1 of *A History of the United States Atomic Energy Commission*. University Park: Pennsylvania State University Press, 1962.

Hewlett, Richard G., and Francis Duncan. *Atomic Shield, 1947-1952*, vol. 2 of *A History of the United States Atomic Energy Commission*. University Park: Pennsylvania State University Press, 1969.

Hewlett, Richard G., and Jack M. Holl. *Atoms for Peace and War, 1953-1961: Eisenhower and the Atomic Energy Commission*, vol. 3 of *A History of the United States Atomic Energy Commission*. Berkeley, University of California Press, 1989.

Johnson, Lyndon Baines. *The Vantage Point: Perspectives of the Presidency, 1963-1969*. New York, Holt, Rinehart and Winston, 1971.

Kaku, Michio, and Jennifer Trainer. *Nuclear Power: Both Sides*. New York: W. W. Norton & Company, 1982.

Kissinger, Henry. *White House Years*. Boston: Little, Brown and Company, 1979.

Mazuzan, George T., and J. Samuel Walker. *Controlling the Atom: The Beginnings of Nuclear Regulation 1946-1962*. Berkeley: University of California Press, 1984.

Nathan, Richard P. *The Plot That Failed: Nixon and the Administrative Presidency*. New York: John Wiley & Sons, Inc., 1975.

Newhouse, John. *Cold Dawn, The Story of SALT*. New York: Holt, Rinehart and Winston, 1973.

Nixon, Richard. *RN: The Memoirs of Richard Nixon*. New York: Grosset and Dunlap, 1978.

Novick, Sheldon. *The Careless Atom*. Boston: Houghton Mifflin Company, 1969.

Nuclear Energy Policy Study Group (sponsored by the Ford Foundation). *Nuclear Power Issues and Choices*. Cambridge, MA: Ballinger Publishing Company, 1977.

Oudes, Bruce, ed. *From: The President: Richard Nixon's Secret Files.* New York: Harper & Row, 1989.

Rhodes, Richard. *The Making of the Atomic Bomb.* New York: Simon and Schuster, 1986.

Seaborg, Glenn T. *Journal of Glenn T. Seaborg,* 28 volumes. Berkeley, CA: Lawrence Berkeley Laboratory, 1989.

Seaborg, Glenn T., with the assistance of Benjamin S. Loeb. *Kennedy, Khrushchev and the Test Ban.* Berkeley, CA: University of California Press, 1981.

Seaborg, Glenn T., with Benjamin S. Loeb. *Stemming the Tide: Arms Control in the Johnson Years.* Lexington, MA: Lexington Books, 1987.

Seaborg, Glenn T., and William R. Corliss. *Man and Atom: Building a New World Through Nuclear Technology.* New York: E. P. Dutton & Company, 1971.

Smith, Gerard. *Doubletalk: The Story of the First Strategic Arms Limitation Talks.* New York: Doubleday & Co., Inc. 1980.

Spector, Leonard S. *Going Nuclear.* Cambridge, MA: Ballinger Publishing Company, 1987.

Tamplin, Arthur R., and John W. Gofman. *"Population Control" Through Nuclear Pollution.* Chicago: Nelson Hall Co., 1970.

Walker, J. Samuel. *Containing the Atom: Nuclear Regulation in a Changing Environment, 1963-1971.* Berkeley: University of California Press, 1992.

Weart, Spencer R. *Nuclear Fear, A History of Images.* Cambridge, MA: Harvard University Press, 1988.

Weinberg, Alvin M. *Reflections on Big Science.* Cambridge, MA: The MIT Press, 1967.

Weissman, Steve and Herbert Krooney. *The Islamic Bomb.* New York: New York Times Books, 1981.

Wicker, Tom. *One of Us: Richard Nixon and the American Dream.* New York: Random House, 1991.

Willrich, Mason and Theodore B. Taylor. *Nuclear Theft: Risks and Safeguards.* Cambridge, MA: Ballinger Publishing Company, 1974.

Government Documents

Public Papers of the Presidents of the United States: Richard Nixon. Washington, U.S. Government Printing Office, 1971.

U.S. Atomic Energy Commission, *Annual Report to Congress of the Atomic Energy Commission.* Washington, D.C., 1968-1974.

U.S. Congress, Congressional Research Service, 96th Cong., 2d Session. *Nuclear Proliferation Factbook.* Washington, D.C., September 1980.

U.S.Congress, Joint Committee on Atomic Energy, 91st Cong., 1st Sess. *Hearings on Environmental Effects of Producing Electric Power,* Part 1. Washington, D.C., October 28-November 7, 1969.

U.S. Congress, Senate Committee on Foreign Relations, 88th Cong., 1st Sess. *Nuclear Test Ban Treaty, Hearings.* Washington, D.C., August 12-27, 1963.

U.S. Congress, Senate Committee on Foreign Relations, 90th Congress, 2d Sess. *Hearings on Nonproliferation Treaty.* Washington, D.C., July 1968.

U.S. Congress, Senate Committee on Foreign Relations, 90th Congress, 2d Sess. *Hearings on Nonproliferation Treaty,* Part 2. Washington, D.C., February 1969.

INDEX

president, 3-6; trip to Soviet Union while vice president, 4-5; and President's Science Advisory Committee, 5-6, 96; partiality toward Plowshare, 11, 16, 17, 95; press relations of, 17; on need for ABM deployment, 33-34; lukewarm support of Nonproliferation Treaty, 53-54; and beginnings of SALT, 75; on SALT options, 76-77, 78; on use of intelligence, 77; on strategic sufficiency, 78-79; on need to consult with allies, 80-81; on SALT negotiating tactics, 81; approach to arms control, 84, 89; opposes MIRV ban, 84; low opinion of Agnew, 89n; uneasy relations with scientists, 95-96; support of breeder reactor program, 162-66; on need for executive branch reorganization, 212; wish to control bureaucracy, 212, 231; relations with his appointees, 215; proposes executive branch reorganization, 222-23; submits superdepartment legislation, 228-29; establishes White House supersecretaries, 231-32

Nonproliferation: as principal arms control challenge, 68-69; steps to strengthen regime, 69; heightened concern after Chinese test, 196-97

Nonproliferation Treaty: negotiation under Johnson, 51; provisions, 52; review conferences, 52-53; approved (1968) by Foreign Relations Committee, 53; resubmitted to Senate by Nixon, 53; Senator Aiken's concerns about PNE costs, 54-55; second (1969) Senate review, 55-56; ratification by U.S., 56-58; entrance into force, 58-59; recent accessions to, 68; principal holdouts, 68; apparent failure in Iraq, 69; renewal prospects, 90-91. *See also* IAEA safeguards agreements.

Northern States Power Company: decides on nuclear plant, 101; legal challenge to state, 105. *See also* Monticello Nuclear Generating Station

North Korea, and Nonproliferation Treaty, 68

Novick, Sheldon (*The Careless Atom*), 116

Nuclear Materials and Equipment Corp.: establishment and early activity, 194; materials discrepancies at, 194, 198. *See also* Shapiro, Zalman M.

Nuclear power: in France, 250, 251; need for in U.S. future, 251. *See also* Nuclear power program, U.S.

Nuclear power program, U.S.: Seaborg arguments for, 118-19; optimism following 1964 Jersey Central order, 153; downturn in new orders, 187, 250; proposed transfer out of AEC, 227; mismanagement of, 250-51

Nuclear Regulatory Commission, U.S.: and Clinch River project, 184; and Shapiro case, 208; established, 232; possible advance certification of standardized plants, 252

Nucleonics Week, 120

Office of Management and Budget, initial proposal for, 213-14

Office of President reorganization proposal: Ash Council's plan presented, 213-15; cool reception by Cabinet, 214-15

One of Us (Wicker), 114

Pacific Northwest Laboratory, 172-74

Pakistan, as proliferation threat, 68

Panama Canal Plowshare project: origin, 12; arguments for, 12-13; discussed by Under Secretaries, 22; rejection of, 23-24

Pastore, John O., 145, 162n, 164-65

Paxton, Hugh, 170

Peaceful nuclear explosions: projects studied worldwide, 12; technical talks with Soviets, 24-25. *See also* Plowshare program, U.S.

Perils of the Peaceful Atom (Curtis and Hogan), 116

Pitzer, Kenneth S., 315. *See also* Pitzer Panel on safety of tests

DATE DUE

DEC 30 1997			
			Printed in USA